# Keynote

## PRE-INTERMEDIATE
### Teacher's Book

NGL.Cengage.com/Keynote
PASSWORD  keynoteTchr#

**Claire Hart and Colleen Sheils**
Communicative Activities by
**Eunice Yeates**

Australia • Brazil • Mexico • Singapore • United Kingdom • United States

**Keynote Pre-intermediate Teacher's Book**
Claire Hart and Colleen Sheils with Eunice Yeates

Vice President, Editorial Director: John McHugh
Executive Editor: Sian Mavor
Publishing Consultant: Karen Spiller
Editor: Ruth Goodman
Head of Strategic Marketing ELT: Charlotte Ellis
IP Analyst: Kyle Cooper
IP Project Manager: Carissa Poweleit
Media Researcher: Leila Hishmeh
Senior Content Project Manager: Nick Ventullo
Manufacturing Manager: Eyvett Davis
Compositor: MPS North America LLC
Cover/Text Design: Brenda Carmichael
Audio: Tom Dick and Debbie Productions Ltd
Cover Photo: Siyanda Mohutsiwa speaks at TED2016 - Dream, February 15–19, 2016, Vancouver Convention Center, Vancouver, Canada. © Bret Hartman/TED.

© 2018 National Geographic Learning, a Cengage Learning Company

ALL RIGHTS RESERVED. No part of this work covered by the copyright herein may be reproduced or distributed in any form or by any means, except as permitted by U.S. copyright law, without the prior written permission of the copyright owner.

"National Geographic", "National Geographic Society" and the Yellow Border Design are registered trademarks of the National Geographic Society ® Marcas Registradas

For product information and technology assistance, contact us at
**Cengage Learning Customer & Sales Support, cengage.com/contact**
For permission to use material from this text or product,
submit all requests online at **cengage.com/permissions**
Further permissions questions can be emailed to
**permissionrequest@cengage.com**

ISBN: 978-1-337-27402-9

**National Geographic Learning**
Cheriton House, North Way, Andover,
Hampshire, SP10 5BE
United Kingdom

National Geographic Learning, a Cengage Learning Company, has a mission to bring the world to the classroom and the classroom to life. With our English language programs, students learn about their world by experiencing it. Through our partnerships with National Geographic and TED Talks, they develop the language and skills they need to be successful global citizens and leaders.

Locate your local office at **international.cengage.com/region**

Visit National Geographic Learning online at **NGL.Cengage.com/ELT**
Visit our corporate website at **www.cengage.com**

**Credits**

**Photos:** 163 (3) © DigitalStock/Corbis; 163 (7, 10) © Creatas/Jupiterimages; 163 (11) © Hung Chung Chih/Shutterstock.com; 163 (14) © Shane Gross/Shutterstock.com; 163 (15) © tratong/Shutterstock.com; 163 (18) © Corel Images; 170 (t) © Photodisc/Getty Images; 170 (mt) © Simon Krzic/Shutterstock.com; 170 (mmtl) © SeanPavonePhoto/Shutterstock.com; 170 (mmtm, mmbr) © Artville; 170 (mmtr) © Stockbyte/Getty Images; 170 (m) © Tatiana Popova/Shutterstock.com; 170 (mmbl) © Ollyy/Shutterstock.com; 170 (mmbm) © Narcis Parfenti/Shutterstock.com; 170 (b) © SUE ASHE/Shutterstock.com; 183 (tl) © Tetra Images - Shawn O'Connor/Getty Images; 183 (tr, br) © PhotoDisc/Getty Images; 183 (ml) © alexkotlov/Getty Images; 183 (mr) © Creatas/Jupiterimages; 183 (bl) © Jo Ann Snover/iStockphoto.

**Illustrations:** MPS North America LLC.

**Cover:** © Bret Hartman/TED.

Printed in Greece by Bakis SA
Print Number: 01   Print Year: 2017

# Contents

| | |
|---|---|
| Introduction | 4 |
| **1** Conservation | 11 |
| **2** Family connections | 21 |
| **3** Global stories | 30 |
| **4** Music | 42 |
| **5** Good design | 52 |
| **6** Inspiring people | 62 |
| **7** Ethical choices | 74 |
| **8** Better cities | 84 |
| **9** Giving | 94 |
| **10** Mind and machine | 106 |
| **11** Nature | 117 |
| **12** Discovery | 127 |
| Photocopiable tests | 139 |
| Tests answer key | 158 |
| Photocopiable communicative activities | 163 |
| Communicative activities teacher's notes | 187 |

# Introduction – Pre-intermediate

## 1 What is *Keynote*?

*Keynote* is a six-level, multi-syllabus English course that takes learners from Elementary level (A1) to Proficient (C2). It is suitable for all adults or young adults in higher education or in work who need English in their professional or personal lives. It is suitable for all teachers, however experienced – extensive teaching notes will help the inexperienced teacher plan lessons, while valuable background information, teaching tips and extension activities will be of great use to even the most experienced teacher.

The units in *Keynote* Pre-intermediate culminate in a TED Talk. These talks are given by speakers from all walks of life, countries and fields of work and provide a rich and varied basis for the teaching and learning of authentic English. See section 2 for more about TED.

Each level contains enough material for between 90 and 120 hours' classroom work. Teachers can reduce this time by giving some preparation tasks to students to do at home (such as watching the TED Talks) or extend it with the extra activities in the teaching notes and the photocopiable communicative activities at the back of this book.

### What are the components of *Keynote* Pre-intermediate?

**Student's Book**

- twelve units of five lessons each (See section 3 below for details.)
- four Presentation lessons, one after every three units
- a grammar summary and extra exercises to accompany each unit
- audioscripts and TED Talk transcripts
- DVD-Rom with all TED Talks, Vocabulary in context exercises, Presentation skills montages, Check your answers videos and recordings for listening and pronunciation exercises

**Workbook**

- consolidation and extension of all the learning objectives in the Student's Book
- additional TED input via playlists related to the featured talks
- a pronunciation focus in every unit provides additional help with the sounds of English

**Teacher's Book**

- full teaching notes for all the units and Presentation lessons, containing answers, TED Talk and audio transcripts, teaching tips, optional and alternative ways of dealing with the Student's Book exercises, extension activities and background information
- four photocopiable progress tests, with sections looking at the grammar, vocabulary, reading, speaking, writing and often listening presented in the previous three units, with answer key
- twenty-four photocopiable communicative activities, two for each unit, with full teaching notes, containing a variety of activities such as information gap, interactive crosswords and mingling. While most of the worksheets are copied and given to the students, some are to be cut into cards and given to the students. In these cases, it may be best to copy the page onto card (and possibly laminate it), so that the cards are sturdier and can be used several times if necessary.

**Website**

- video streaming of the TED Talks from the Student's Book, Vocabulary in context, Presentation skill montages and Check your answers videos.
- worksheets for *Keynote* Intermediate–Proficient levels organized by industry (e.g. manufacturing, tourism, education) and business function (e.g. human resources, marketing, research and development) that provide highly targeted practice of the language specific to the learners' field of work. They can be used in class or for self study.
- mid- and end-of-year tests
- two bonus grammar lessons (with infographics) to extend the grammar coverage of the Intermediate level
- Word versions of all the audio/video scripts and reading texts that can be 're-packaged' by teachers to create additional practice material or tests

## 2 What is TED?

TED is a non-profit organization based on the idea that many people from all areas of life have 'ideas worth spreading', and should be given a platform to spread those ideas. There are currently more than 2,000 TED Talks on the TED website, and new talks by leading thinkers and doers across a wide range of fields are constantly being added. TED originated at a conference in 1984 centred on Technology, Entertainment and Design, but the talks now cover far more than those three areas. The talks are given by speakers from across the world, ranging from highly respected business leaders to school students, all of whom have an idea worth spreading. The talks can last as long as eighteen minutes, but are generally much shorter. By providing this platform, TED aims to 'make great ideas accessible and spark conversation'. For more on TED, see www.TED.com.

### Why are TED Talks great for learning English?

TED Talks feature remarkable people communicating passionately and persuasively, and are a unique source of engaging and often amusing real language. The talks are intrinsically interesting, and are watched by millions of people around the world. In the ELT classroom they provide:

- motivating content that learners choose to watch in their leisure time for entertainment and edification
- educational content, i.e. students learn about the world as well as learning English
- authentic listening input
- exposure to different language varieties: *Keynote* has a mix of talks given by British English, American English and Australian speakers and includes a glossary in each TED Talk lesson to compare and contrast language
- exposure to different accents (native, such as British and US, as well as non-native)
- up-to-date language
- ideal material for developing critical thinking skills
- probably the best models in existence for presentation skills

## 3 How do I teach with *Keynote* Pre-intermediate?

### Unit structure

Each unit in the Student's Book contains a warm-up page which introduces students to the overarching unit theme, and five lessons around the unit topic:

- the first provides key vocabulary that students will need to engage with the topic; a listening exercise that reinforces the vocabulary and exposes students to a variety of authentic speakers; a model speaking exercise which gives students the chance to practise the new language
- the second is the grammar lesson, with real input in the form of an infographic that provides a context for the presentation of the grammar and practice, and ends in a spoken output using the new language
- the third is on a reading text featuring the TED Talk speaker or topic, with a variety of comprehension, reading skills and vocabulary exercises, further preparing students for the TED Talk
- the fourth lesson is the TED Talk lesson where students watch the talk in short sections and do further vocabulary work (mining the talk for interesting vocabulary and collocations), as well as work on critical thinking and presentation skills
- the last lesson in each unit focuses on functional language, and comprises communication skills with a focus on speaking, as well as a writing exercise

The grammar, reading and functional lessons in each unit have 21st century outcomes, i.e. the lessons provide and practise the skills and knowledge needed by students to succeed in their professional and personal lives in the 21st century.

The grammar, vocabulary and skills presented in each unit are practised further in the Presentation lessons after every three units. These give students the opportunity to perform their own presentations on a familiar topic.

### Grammar

Grammar is presented in a natural and clear context using an infographic, which means that there is not a huge amount of reading for the students to do in order to find the examples of the grammar. Students are led to understanding of the grammatical points through guided discovery, focusing on language from the infographic picked out in one or two grammar boxes, and studied through the use of concept check questions. Students are then directed to the Grammar summary at the back of the book to read about the grammar in more detail. The exercises accompanying the Grammar summaries focus mainly on form and can be done at this point before students tackle the exercises in the unit, which focus more on meaning and use, or they can be done for homework.

### Vocabulary

**Vocabulary and Understanding vocabulary**

Key vocabulary is always introduced in the first lesson and in the reading lesson. This build up of vocabulary is designed to equip students with the language they'll need to understand the key message of the TED Talk when they watch it in the fourth lesson. Further relevant vocabulary is also introduced at the beginning of the TED Talk lesson.

**Vocabulary in context**

The Vocabulary in context section always appears in the fourth lesson, after students have watched the TED Talk. Here, short excerpts which contain useful words, phrases or collocations are repeated and the lexical items are matched with synonyms and then practised in a personalization activity.

### Skills

**Reading**

Each unit has a reading lesson based on a contemporary, real-world text that focuses on the TED Talk speaker or the topic of the TED Talk. The accompanying exercises cover reading comprehension, reading skills and vocabulary work, but also elicit a personal response to the content of the text.

**Writing**

There is a focus on writing in each final lesson, covering a functional writing skill, such as introducing yourself by email or making a recommendation. There are on-page models for students to analyse and follow in their own writing.

**Listening**

Listening is a key component of the course and is dealt with in various ways. To help students deal with the authentic, native speaker-level language of the TED Talks, *Keynote* has a comprehensive listening skills syllabus that allows students to understand listening material which is usually well above their productive level. (See Teaching tip 3 below.) There is always listening in the grammar lessons, consolidating the new language.

There are a large number of audio/video tracks in *Keynote* Pre-intermediate which give students the opportunity to hear how new vocabulary is pronounced. In the first lesson, students can listen to a variety of real-life speakers and watch an animated model of the speaking conversation. In the second lesson, the infographic and Language focus box are recorded. The reading text in the third lesson is recorded in its entirety, and of course in the TED Talk lesson students have multiple opportunities to watch the TED speaker.

### Speaking

Each unit has a lesson that focuses specifically on functional and situational language that is relevant to students. This is supported by a Communication skill box containing a number of expressions relevant to the function or situation. There are also speaking activities throughout the units.

### Pronunciation

There is a pronunciation syllabus, integrated with the grammar and speaking lessons where there is a relevant pronunciation area.

## 4 Teaching tips

The following teaching tips apply throughout the course. There are lesson-specific teaching tips through the units.

### Teaching tip 1  Developing presentation skills

After students have watched a TED Talk in each unit, they focus on a particular aspect of presentation skills such as 'using questions to signpost' or 'personalizing the presentation'. Before embarking on the Presentation skills sections, it's probably worth finding out from your students the kinds of situations when they might have to present (in their first language or in English). Many of your students will need to present information at work and students in academic situations will have to present their research. Even students who don't often give presentations will benefit from presenting in your class because it's an opportunity to build confidence in speaking in English and to develop a key communication skill.

The four Presentation lessons give students further opportunity to review the Presentation skills they have learned about in the previous units. A video is provided for students to watch, showing a model presentation delivered by a student. They are then invited to plan and deliver their own presentations and give each other feedback.

At first, some of your students might not feel comfortable with giving presentations in English. That's why many of the presentations tasks in *Keynote* can be done in pairs, with students taking turns to present to each other. As the course progresses, you could ask students to present to larger groups and once they are more confident, to the whole class.

Remember to allow plenty of preparation time for the presentations. Often it's a good idea to set a presentation task and ask students to work on it for homework before they give their presentation in the next lesson. It's also useful to provide students with preparation strategies such as making notes on pieces of card to refer to, rehearsing in front of a mirror, or presenting to family and friends at home. You will find more tips on setting up and delivering classroom presentations in the relevant part of each unit of this Teacher's Book.

### Teaching tip 2  Vocabulary

One way of dealing with the Vocabulary activity in the first lesson of each unit is to write the key words on the board. Read out the first definition and nominate a student to say the correct word. If they guess correctly, read out the second definition and nominate another student to guess that word. Continue until they have matched all the words and their definitions in this way. However, whenever a student guesses incorrectly, start from the very beginning again and read out the first definition, nominating a different student each time. The activity ends once the class has correctly matched all the words and definitions in a row without any mistakes.

### Teaching tip 3  Dealing with difficult listening activities

The TED Talks are authentic English and may be challenging for some students, which can be a cause of frustration. Here are some ideas to increase your students' ability to deal with authentic language:

- Students need time before and after listening to prepare and compare: before, to read the task, ask questions and to predict possible answers, and after, to write their answers and to compare them with a partner.
- Time for writing answers is particularly important when watching clips rather than listening because it is hard to watch the video and write at the same time. This is one reason the TED Talks are broken into short parts.
- Let students read the transcript while they listen or watch.
- Watch the Check your answers video once students have completed the task. This isolates the few seconds of the video where the answer lies and reveals the correct answer.
- It's hard in long clips to keep concentrating all the time, so pause just before an answer comes up in order to warn students that they should refocus.
- There are ways of changing the speed that video is played back. You may want to investigate how to slow down talks slightly for your students using certain media players.
- If a task is difficult, make it easier. For example, if students have to listen for a word to fill gaps, you could supply the missing words on the board, mixed up, for them to choose.
- Celebrate the successes, however small. If a student hears only one thing, praise them for that. Don't supply extra information which you heard, but they did not, unless you have a good reason.
- Remind them now and again that they aren't expected to understand every word, to stay relaxed and to keep listening. Reassure them that listening improves with repeated practice and that the best thing they can do for their listening skills is to persevere.

# Unit walk through

## Warm up

Introduces students to the unit theme

## Vocabulary

Key vocabulary that students will need to engage with the topic is presented

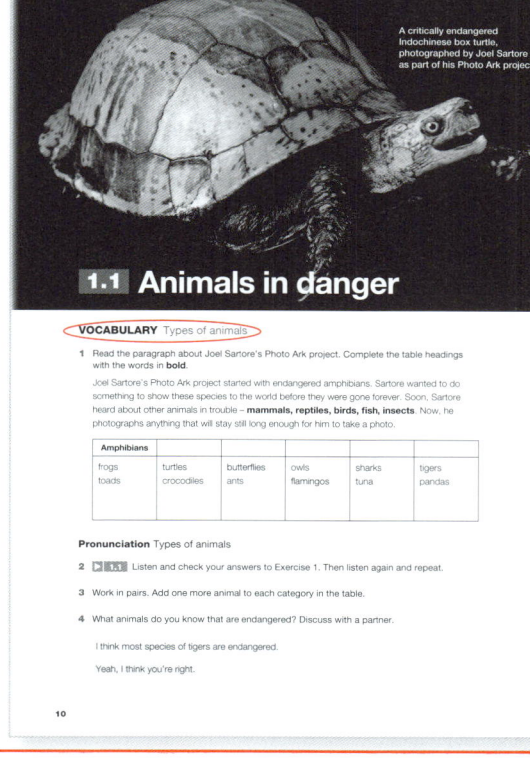
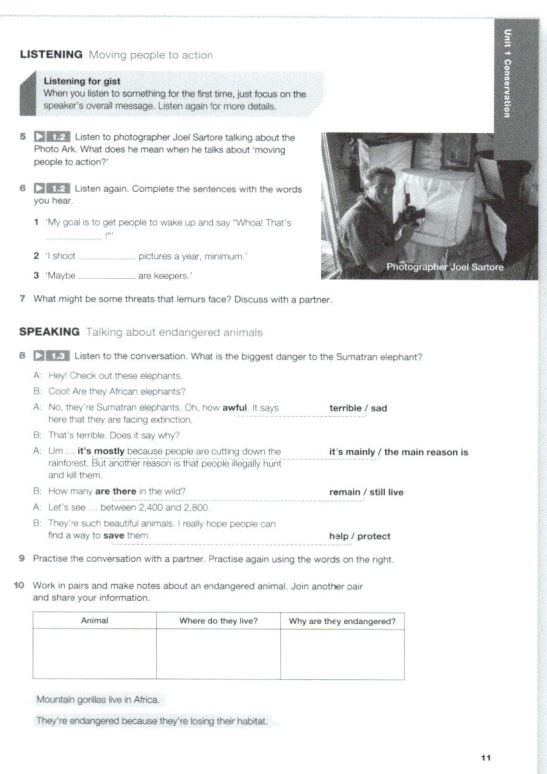

Introduction 7

# Grammar

Grammar is presented in real-world contexts and practised for real-world outcomes

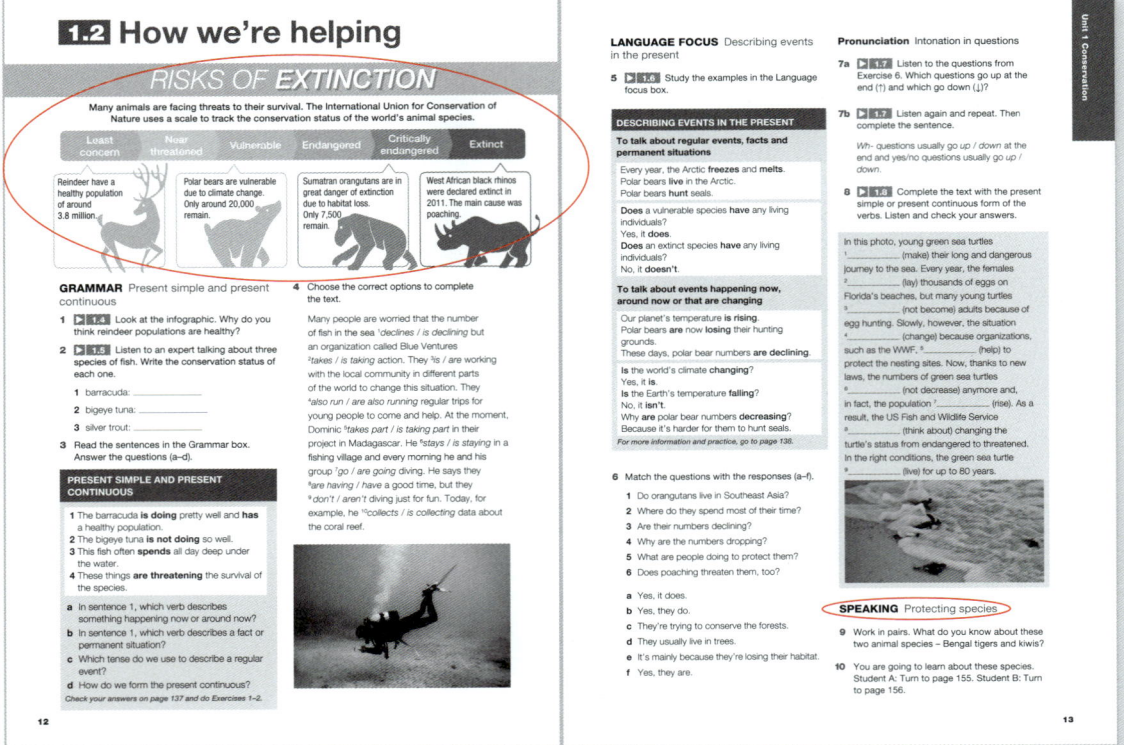

# Reading

Texts featuring the TED Talk speaker or topic are exploited for reading skills, vocabulary and interest

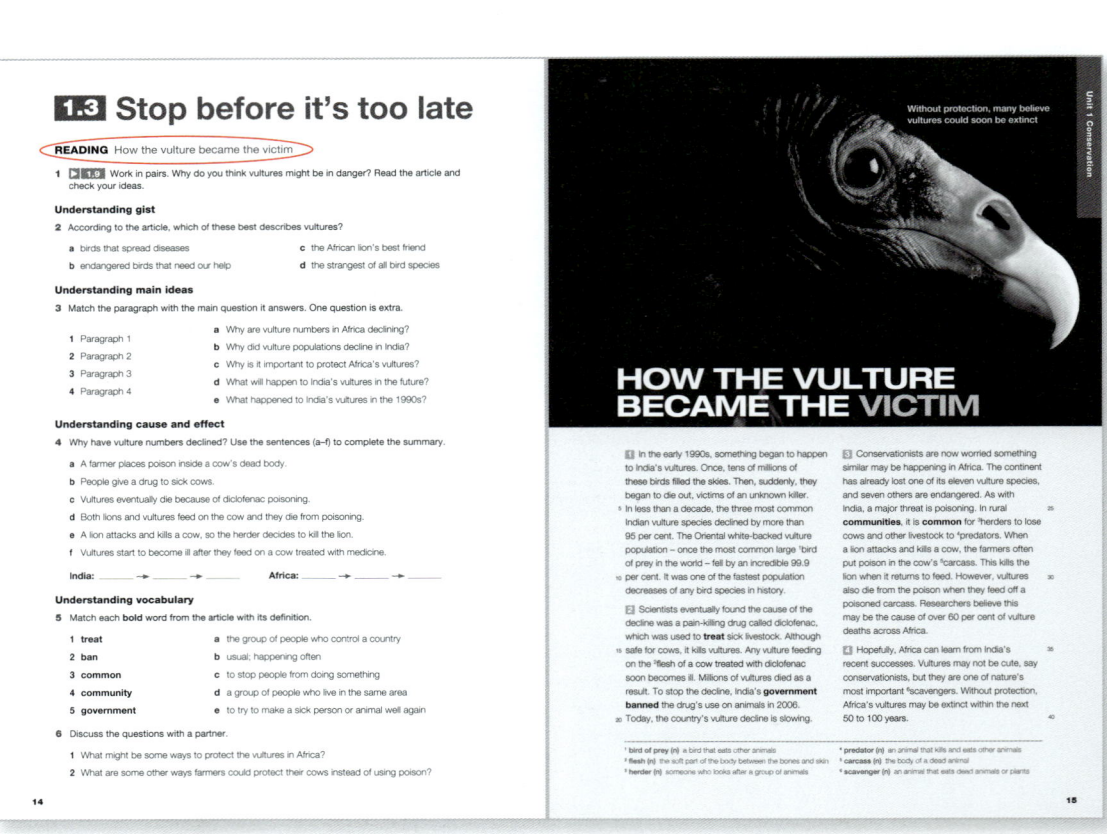

# TED Talk lesson

TED Talks are great for discussion, vocabulary, critical thinking and presentation skills

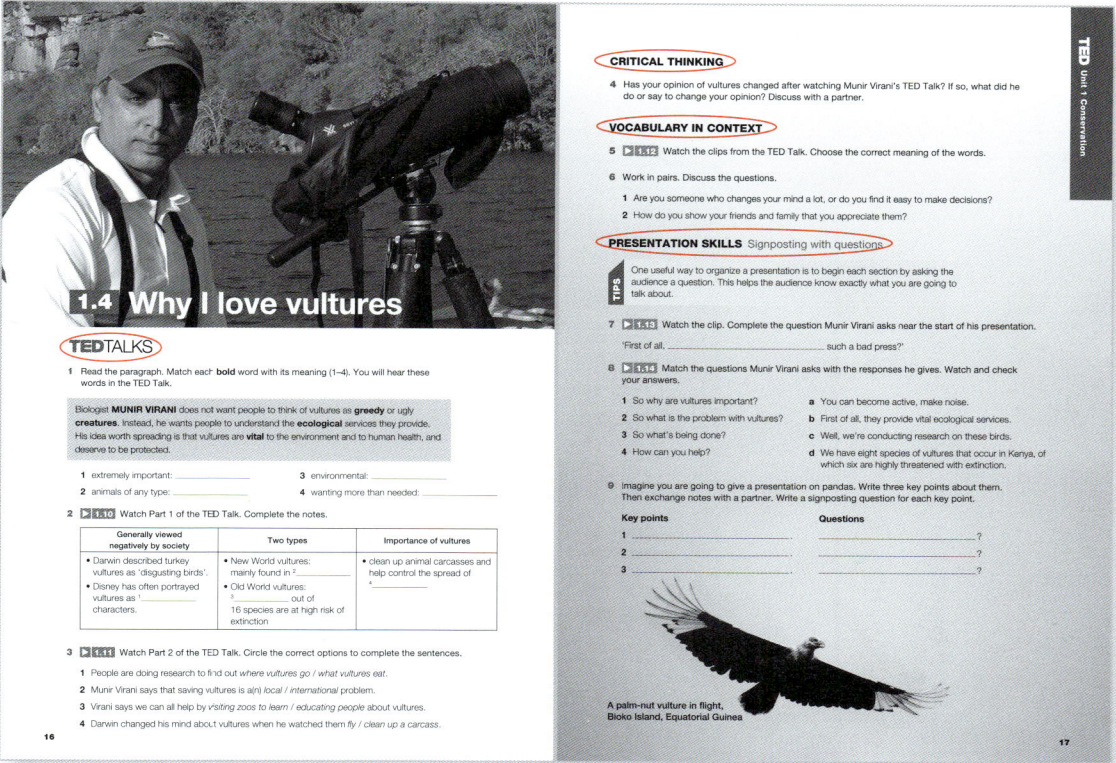

# Communication and writing

Functional language is presented via common, everyday situations where students need to interact in English

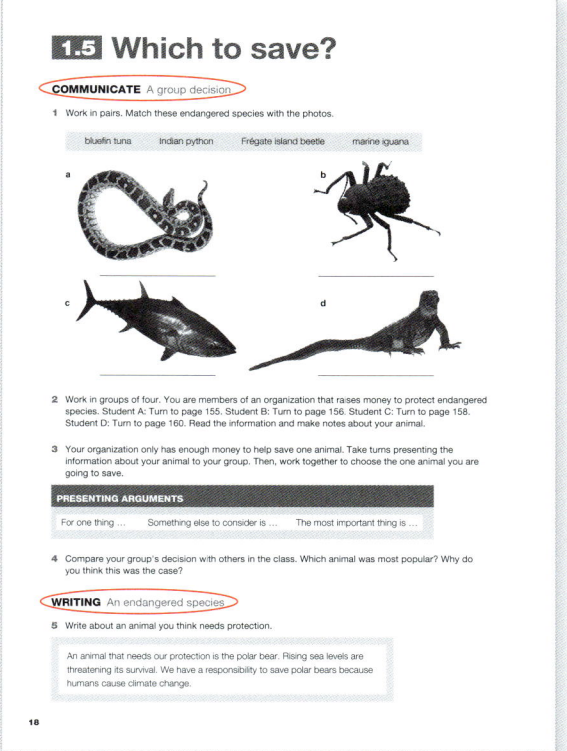

Introduction 9

# Presentation lessons

Presentation lessons review the presentation skills, grammar and vocabulary from the previous units

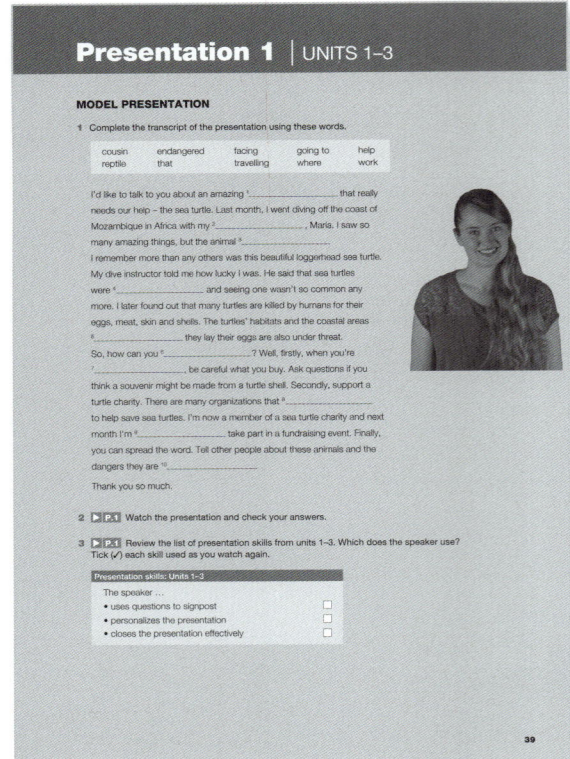
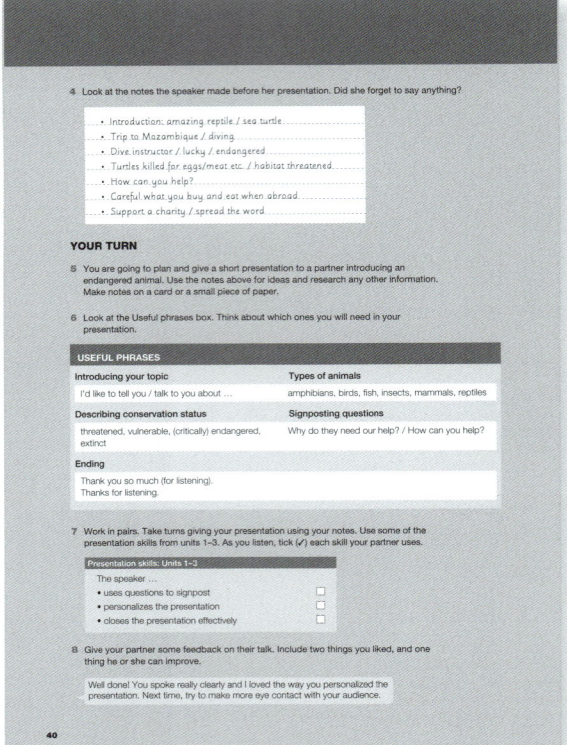

# 1 Conservation

**UNIT AT A GLANCE**

**THEME:** Conservation
**VOCABULARY:** Types of animals
**LISTENING:** Moving people to action
**SPEAKING:** Talking about endangered animals, Protecting species
**GRAMMAR:** Present simple and present continuous
**PRONUNCIATION:** Types of animals, Intonation in questions
**READING:** *How the vulture became the victim*
**TED TALK:** *Why I love vultures*. In this TED Talk, Munir Virani talks about why vultures are worth saving and what we can do to help them.
**PRESENTATION SKILLS:** Signposting with questions
**WRITING:** An endangered species

## WARM UP

- Books open. Draw students' attention to the unit title and check the meaning of *conservation* (efforts to protect natural resources, especially plants and animals). Then, draw their attention to the photo on page 9 and ask them to guess which country the photo was taken in, without looking at the caption. They can then read the caption to find out if they were right.

- Put students into pairs or small groups (three to four students) to discuss the questions.

- **Question 1**. Direct students to the photo. Elicit that the trees need the posts to help them stay standing because they're very old. Have students consider and discuss whether they think it's important to conserve old trees, giving reasons. If students think that it is important, they can also consider how important it is and compare its importance with that of conserving other types of plant or animal life.

- **Question 2**. Ask students to think about other plants, animals or natural features which people can conserve. Then, have them discuss which ones we should be working hard to preserve and why.

- **Optional step**. If students have access to the Internet, they can find images online of the things they think we should work hard to conserve and show them to their partner as they talk about them.

- **Question 3**. Bring in students' own experiences and ask them to talk about any examples of problems in the natural world that they've seen first-hand, e.g. flooding, glaciers melting, trees being cut down, animals or birds moving away from an area or dying out.

## 1.1 Animals in danger

### VOCABULARY Types of animals

**1**

- Direct students to the title of this section, the photo and caption and elicit or explain that animals that are in danger, like this turtle, are called *endangered animals* or *endangered species*.

- Students are now going to categorize some animals. Ask them to read the text about the Photo Ark project. Then, have them read the names of animals in the table and re-read the types of animals in bold in the text. Draw students' attention to the fact that although the plural forms of most words for animals and types of animals end in -*s*, they have irregular plural forms, e.g. *fish* and *tuna*. Clarify that *fish* is the usual plural form of *fish*, but *fishes* is also used by biologists.

- Have students complete the headings with the names for types of animals in bold. Check the meaning of: *amphibian* (an animal that lives on both the land and in the water, but must lay its eggs in the water), *mammal* (a warm-blooded animal with hair or fur that produces milk for its young), *reptile* (a cold-blooded animal that has scaly skin and lays eggs) and *insect* (a very small animal with six legs) with students before they start, or leave them to deduce their meanings from the examples in the table.

- **Optional step**. If students find it difficult to categorize the animals and they have access to the Internet, they could look for photos of the animals online to help them.

- Ask students to compare their answers in pairs, but don't confirm answers at this stage.

**Answers**

| Reptiles | Insects | Birds | Fish | Mammals |
|---|---|---|---|---|
| turtles | butterflies | owls | sharks | tigers |
| crocodiles | ants | flamingos | tuna | pandas |

### Pronunciation Types of animals

**2**

- ▶1.1 Play the recording and ask students to listen and check their answers to Exercise 1.

- Then, play the recording so that students can listen and repeat the words. You may need to model and drill the pronunciation of some words, e.g. *amphibians* /æmˈfɪbiənz/.

> **Transcript**
>
> 1 *Amphibians: frogs, toads*
> 2 *Reptiles: turtles, crocodiles*
> 3 *Insects: butterflies, ants*
> 4 *Birds: owls, flamingos*
> 5 *Fish: sharks, tuna*
> 6 *Mammals: tigers, pandas*

**3**

- Put students into pairs. Ask them to think of one more animal for each category and write these in the table.

- Conduct whole-class feedback on the animals that students have chosen and check that they're able to pronounce them correctly.

**Extra activity**

**The photo ark**

Ask students to go online and browse through some of the other photos of animals on Joel Sartore's website: http://www.joelsartore.com/galleries/the-photo-ark/2/. There are a lot of photos, so don't expect students to look at all of them. Have students test their knowledge of vocabulary for animals in English by asking them to say the English name of the animal in each photo, without looking at the captions underneath. Then, ask them to write the names of the animals they looked at in the correct columns in the table in Exercise 1.

> **TEACHING TIP**
>
> **Recording and organizing vocabulary**
>
> It's important that students find a way of organizing and recording new and known vocabulary that they want to remember. In order to help them, you could elicit methods that students have used in the past and any other ideas students have in class. They can then choose one that they think would work for them. Possibilities include: using word webs or mind maps, listing words that are connected to each other in groups, drawing pictures, writing definitions of or example sentences with the target vocabulary or simply organizing the vocabulary in a list alphabetically.
>
> After a few weeks, get feedback from students on what method(s) they're using to record and organize their vocabulary and how effective they find it/them to be.

**4**

- Put students into pairs and check the meaning of *endangered* (at risk of or close to dying out completely).

- Ask students to think of some animals that they think are endangered. In pairs, they can then tell each other what animals they've thought of and give their reactions to their partners' ideas, as in the model conversation.

- **Optional step**. If time allows and students have access to the Internet, they can do a web search to find out whether the animals they think are endangered actually are. Draw their attention to the fact that animals' status may change from time to time, for example giant pandas had been classified as an endangered species for many years before they were taken off the list in 2016.

- Conduct whole-class feedback on the animals which students think are endangered.

## LISTENING  Moving people to action

> **TEACHING TIP**
>
> **Strategies for listening for gist**
>
> You can help students with listening for gist by going through some strategies with them. Possible strategies include: relaxing, focusing on what they do understand rather than on what they don't, not worrying if they don't understand every word they hear, listening out for the words that the speaker says more loudly than others, listening for words that the speaker repeats. After students have done a listening for gist activity, ask them to reflect on what strategies helped them to understand the gist of what they were listening to. They could share their reflections in pairs.

**5**

- ▶ 1.2  Direct students to the Listening for gist box and check the meaning of *gist* (the general or overall message). Tell students they're going to listen to Joel Sartore, who they can see in the photo, talking about the Photo Ark project they read about in Exercise 1. Their task is to listen for gist.

- Ask students to read the question. Then, play the recording and ask students to make notes on the key words Joel says.

- Have students compare their answers in pairs and then check answers in class. Elicit or explain that, in this context, a *keeper* is a good photo, i.e. one that's good enough to keep.

## Transcript

*My job, my passion, or what I'm trying to explore and share is the fact that we are throwing away the ark, which is my attempt to document as many of the world's captive species as I can before I die. I think photography has tremendous potential in terms of moving people to action. These are pictures that go to work. These are pictures that work every day. Long after I'm dead, these things are going to go to work to save species. My goal is to get people to wake up and say, 'Whoa that's amazing! What do I gotta do to save that!?' And then they actually do save it. To create a picture that outlasts us – that's really tough. I shoot 30,000 pictures a year, minimum. Maybe three or four are keepers. Three or four! I got more fingers on this hand than the number of keepers I get in a year, and all I do is shoot pictures, and that's all I've done since I was eighteen years old, is take pictures. But boy, those three or four are pretty good!*

> **Answer**
>
> Sartore is referring to the way his photos can motivate people to help to save the animals.

## 6

- ▶ 1.2 Tell students that they're going to listen to the recording again and focus on some of the specific information that Joel gives.

- Ask students to read the sentences they have to complete and predict what the missing words are, based on what they can remember from their first listening and what they think. Then, play the recording and ask students to listen and complete the sentences.

- Students can compare their answers in pairs before you check answers in class.

> **Answers**
>
> 1 amazing   2 30,000   3 three or four

## 7  21st CENTURY OUTCOMES

***Demonstrate knowledge and understanding of society's impact on the natural world***

- Put students into pairs to discuss the question. Check students know what a *lemur* is (it's a small primate with a long tail that lives in Madagascar).

- Then, ask students to think of possible threats to the lemur and discuss their ideas in pairs. In order to fulfil the 21st CENTURY OUTCOMES, students should be able to show awareness of the impact that people are having on the lives of lemurs. Conduct whole-class feedback on students' ideas.

> **Answers**
>
> Students' own answers.

## SPEAKING  Talking about endangered animals

## 8

- ▶ 1.3 Ask students to read the conversation about an animal that faces extinction before they listen to it. Check the meaning of *extinction* (dying out completely) and draw students' attention to the verb-noun collocation *to face extinction* (to be in danger of becoming extinct). Tell students to ignore the word choices on the right for the moment as they will focus on those in Exercise 9.

- Play the recording and ask students to read and listen to the conversation at the same time. Tell them to identify the biggest danger to the Sumatran elephant.

- Check answers and elicit that another danger to the Sumatran elephant is people illegally hunting and killing them.

> **Answer**
>
> People are cutting down the rainforest.

## 9

- Model the conversation that students have just listened to aloud with a student. Then, have students work in pairs to practise the conversation together. Make sure they alternate between A and B roles.

- Have students practise the conversation again using the words on the right instead of the words in bold in the conversation.

## 10

- Put students into pairs and ask them to choose an endangered animal: one of the animals they talked about in Exercise 4 or another one. Then, have students make notes on the animal they've chosen in the columns of the table. If students don't know the answers to the questions for their animal and they have access to the Internet, they could go online and search for this information.

- When students have finished making notes, put each pair together with another pair. They then use their notes to tell each other about their animals. Direct them to the example sentences and ask them to use these as model sentences when they're speaking.

- Circulate and monitor students while they're talking to each other and give them feedback when they've finished.

▶ Set Workbook pages 4 and 5 and for homework.
▶ Photocopiable communicative activity 1.1. Go to page 163 for further practice of types of animals vocabulary. The teaching notes are on page 187.

**1  Conservation**

## 1.2 How we're helping

**GRAMMAR** Present simple and present continuous

**1**

- ▶ 1.4 Direct students to the infographic and ask them to read the text and look at the pictures. Check the meaning of a *concern* (worry) and *vulnerable* (here: possibly in danger).
- Ask students to think of possible reasons why reindeer populations are healthy and then put them into pairs to discuss these.
- Conduct whole-class feedback on students' ideas. Possible reasons are: reindeer are usually safe from other animals that want to eat them (predators), humans don't often hunt them either and they usually live in isolated areas where humans haven't had a negative impact on the environment.

**2**

- ▶ 1.5 Tell students that they're now going to listen to an expert talking about the conservation status of three different species of fish. Ask them to read the names of the fish and find out if they know what each one is. The words in their names should help them to get some idea of what the species of fish look like.
- **Optional step.** If students have access to the Internet, they could find images of each of the fish online so they can see what it looks like.
- Play the recording and ask students to listen for and write the conservation status of each fish. Referring to the infographic and the words for different types of conservation status in it should help them to do this. Check answers in class.

### Transcript

*The barracuda is a species of fish that is doing pretty well and has a healthy population. The barracuda is classified as a species of least concern. The bigeye tuna, however, is not doing so well. Right now, there are certain things threatening the survival of the species – such as overfishing. As such, the bigeye tuna is classified as vulnerable. For vulnerable species like the bigeye tuna, it's important that we work to protect them now, before they become endangered or even extinct. The silver trout is just one example of a species of fish that is now extinct.*

### Answers
1 least concern
2 vulnerable
3 extinct

**3**

- Ask students to read the example sentences. It's important they understand that the present continuous can be used to describe activities that are happening right at this moment, but it can also be used for activities happening 'around now', which aren't. Clarify that activities that happen 'around now' are activities that started in the past and will finish in the future, but aren't happening right at this moment.
- Students can check their answers and overall understanding of the contrast between the present simple and present continuous by turning to the Grammar summary on page 137.
- If you feel that students need more controlled practice before continuing, they could do the exercises in the Grammar summary. Otherwise, you could continue on to Exercise 4 in the unit and set the Grammar summary exercises for homework

### Answers
a is doing
b has
c present simple
d be + verb + -ing

### Answers to Grammar summary exercises
1
1 carry   2 don't drink   3 needs   4 become
5 tastes   6 stays
2
1 's/is studying   2 are learning   3 are getting
4 's/is also writing   5 's/is hoping   6 isn't thinking

**4**

- Tell students that they're now going to practise using the present simple and present continuous in context. The exercise aims to test whether students know how to form the present continuous and whether they know when to use the present simple and when to use the present continuous. Ask students to read the text and then choose the correct options.
- Have students compare their answers in pairs before checking answers in class.

### Answers
1 is declining   2 is taking   3 are   4 are also running
5 is taking part   6 is staying   7 go   8 are having
9 aren't   10 is collecting

## LANGUAGE FOCUS Describing events in the present

### 5

- ▶ 1.6 Tell students that they're now going to look at some more examples of present simple and present continuous sentences so they can see how to use each tense. Ask students to read the Language focus box and pay attention to the form of the two types of sentences and the types of events that they refer to.

- Students can check overall understanding of the language focus by turning to the Grammar summary on page 138.

- If you feel that students need more controlled practice before continuing, they could do the exercises in the Grammar summary. Otherwise, you could continue on to Exercise 6 in the unit and set the Grammar summary exercises for homework.

> **Answers to Grammar summary exercises**
>
> **1**
> 1 What is happening in the Sahara? Is climate change making it hotter?
> 2 The temperatures are rising every year.
> 3 Is it getting drier?
> 4 No, it isn't getting drier. It's getting greener!
> 5 So are more plants growing there now?
> 6 People think the Sahara is slowly becoming like it was 12,000 years ago!
>
> **2**
> 1 'm phoning
> 2 do you have
> 3 work
> 4 do you like
> 5 love
> 6 like
> 7 are you doing
> 8 'm studying

### 6

- Ask students to read the questions and responses. Check the meaning of *poaching* (the illegal killing of animals). Have students match the questions with the responses. Tell students to refer back to the examples in the Language focus box to help them if they need to.

- **Optional step**. Give weaker students some tips to help them match the questions with the responses, e.g. if a question starts with *do/does*, the short answer to it will also contain *do/does*; if a question starts with *are*, the short answer to it will also contain *are*; If a question starts with *why*, the answer will contain a reason.

- Ask students to compare their answers in pairs before checking answers in class.

> **Answers**
> 1 b   2 d   3 f   4 e   5 c   6 a

## Pronunciation Intonation in questions

### 7a

- ▶ 1.7 Check the meaning of *intonation* (the rise and fall of your voice when you speak). Tell students that it's important to use the right intonation when you speak English and, if you don't, this can make it difficult for other people to understand what you want to say.

- Play the recording and ask students to listen to and read the questions from Exercise 6 and focus on whether the intonation goes up or down. Students use the up or down arrows to mark their answers next to the questions. Play the recording more than once if necessary and then have students compare their answers in pairs.

- Check that students have correctly identified the intonation in the questions.

> **Answers**
> 1 Do orangutans live in Southeast Asia? ↑
> 2 Where do they spend most of their time? ↓
> 3 Are their numbers declining? ↑
> 4 Why are the numbers dropping? ↓
> 5 What are people doing to protect them? ↓
> 6 Does poaching threaten them, too? ↑

### 7b

- ▶ 1.7 Play the recording so that students can listen to the questions again and repeat them with the correct intonation. Model and drill the intonation with weaker students.

- Ask students to use what they've noticed about the intonation we use with the two different types of questions to complete the rule. Check answers in class.

> **Answers**
> down, up

1   Conservation   **15**

**8**

• ▶1.8 Tell students that they're now going to do some more practice with the present simple and present continuous in the context of a text about green sea turtles. Encourage them to read the text all the way through for gist first and then focus on the type of event that is being described in each sentence to help them complete the text. Students can refer back to the Language focus box or the Grammar summary on pages 137–138 if they need to.

• Ask students to compare their answers in pairs before checking answers in class.

> **Answers**
> 1 are making   2 lay   3 don't become   4 is changing
> 5 are helping   6 aren't decreasing   7 is rising
> 8 is thinking about   9 lives

## SPEAKING Protecting species

**9**

• Put students into AB pairs and ask them to read the names of the two animals in the question. Students should already be familiar with at least one of the two, so ask them to say what they know about them: what type of animal they are, what they look like, where they live, what their conservation status could be.

**10**

• In the same pairs, ask students to turn to their partner files and read the information about their species and the information they have to complete about the other species. Students then take it in turns to ask and answer questions about the two species and complete their file with the information their partner gives them. They will need to use the present simple to ask questions about the facts and the present continuous to ask questions about how people are helping.

• Give students feedback on how successfully they've used present simple and present continuous questions and responses and the correct intonation for them.

▶ Set Workbook pages 6 and 7 for homework.

# 1.3 Stop before it's too late

## READING How the vulture became the victim

**1**

• ▶1.9 Check students know what a *vulture* is – they can see a photo of one on page 15.

• Put students into pairs to discuss possible reasons why vultures might be in danger. Encourage them to draw on what they've already read and heard about reasons why animals are at risk. Don't confirm the correct answer at this stage as students are now going to quickly read the article to find it.

> **Answer**
> Scientists found the cause of the decline of vultures was a pain-killing drug called diclofenac, which was used to treat sick livestock.

## Understanding gist

**2**

• Review the meaning of *gist*, which students encountered in the Listening for gist box on page 11. Students will already know how to read for gist in their first language, so encourage them to approach this task in the same way they would approach a text in that language. Give students 20 or 30 seconds to scan the text for words and phrases used to describe vultures and then have them choose the correct option.

• Ask students to compare their answers in pairs before you check answers in class.

> **Answer**
> b

## Understanding main ideas

**3**

• Tell students they're now going to read the text again more slowly and focus on understanding the main idea in each paragraph. Ask students to read the questions. They can then go through the text one paragraph at a time and match the questions with the paragraphs that give an answer to them. There's one extra question.

• Point out the glossary at the bottom of the text and tell students to refer to it as they read or to look at the words and definitions before they start reading.

• Ask students to compare their answers in pairs before you check answers in class.

- **Optional step**. Ask students to write a one-sentence summary of each of the paragraphs in the article that answers the questions from Exercise 3. Weaker students can do this in pairs. Conduct whole-class feedback on students' sentences.

> **Answers**
> 1 e   2 b   3 a   4 c

## Understanding cause and effect

**4**

- Make sure students are aware of the fact that three of the sentences refer to what has happened in India and the other three refer to what has happened in Africa. Students will have to decide which sentences refer to which country.

- Ask students to write the letters for the sentences in the right places in the flow chart. Stronger students can do this without referring to the article, whereas weaker students will probably need to refer to it.

- Check answers in class.

> **Answers**
> India: b → f → c
> Africa: e → a → d

> **TEACHING TIP**
>
> **Cause and effect**
>
> Draw students' attention to how cause and effect is expressed in the second paragraph of the article, e.g. *the cause of* ... *was* ...; *Millions of vultures died as a result*.; *Any vulture feeding on the flesh of a cow treated with diclofenac soon becomes ill*.; *To stop the decline, India's government* ... Elicit any other similar words and phrases for cause and effect that students know and write these up on the board, e.g. *this causes* ...; *this makes* ...; *consequently* ...; *this leads to* ..., etc. Then, ask students to use these words and expressions to say or write an explanation of what has happened to vultures in India and Africa using the events students ordered in Exercise 4.

## Understanding vocabulary

**5**

- Ask students to read the words and match them with their definitions. If students are unsure about which words and definitions go together, they may find it helpful to look back at the text, where these words are highlighted in bold, and see how the words are used in context.

- Check answers in class.

> **Answers**
> 1 e   2 c   3 b   4 d   5 a

**6**  **21st CENTURY OUTCOMES**

*Investigate and analyse environmental issues, and make accurate conclusions about effective solutions*

- Put students into pairs and have them think about and brainstorm possible ways of protecting vultures and of protecting cows without using poison. They can use what they've learned so far about vultures and their general knowledge of what we can do to protect animals. In order to fulfil the 21st CENTURY OUTCOMES, students should be able to use what they've learned about the issues affecting vultures and cows to propose effective solutions to these problems.

- Conduct whole-class feedback on students' ideas.

- **Optional step**. Have them reach a consensus as a class on what they think is the best way to protect the vultures and the cows.

### Extra activity

#### Another solution for vultures?

Richard Turere, a young man from Kenya, gave a TED Talk when he was just thirteen years old in which he shared his idea of using lights to scare away lions and keep his family's cattle alive. Have students watch his TED Talk, 'My invention that made peace with lions' to learn more about this solution and then have them consider whether this solution could also be used to help the vultures.

▶ Set Workbook pages 8 and 9 for homework.

▶ Photocopiable communicative activity 1.2. Go to page 164 for further practice of the present continuous and animals vocabulary. The teaching notes are on page 187.

## 1.4 Why I love vultures

### TEDTALKS

**1**

- Tell students that they're now going to watch a TED Talk by biologist Munir Virani. Direct them to the title of Virani's talk and elicit or explain that vultures usually have a negative image. Ask students to speculate about possible reasons why someone would love vultures.

- Have students read the summary of the talk and match the words in bold with their synonyms or definitions.

- Students can compare their answers in pairs before you check answers in class. Model and drill the pronunciation of *ecological* /ˌiːkəˈlɒdʒɪk(ə)l/ and *vital* /ˈvaɪt(ə)l/.

> **Answers**
> 1 vital   2 creatures   3 ecological   4 greedy

1   Conservation   **17**

## 2

- ▶ 1.10 Tell students that they're now going to watch the first part of Virani's talk in which he introduces the vulture and the problem it's facing to the audience. Ask them to read the notes and check the meaning of *disgusting* (very unpleasant or causing extreme dislike), *portray* (to present something in a specific way) and *carcass* (the dead body of an animal).

- Then, play Part 1 of the talk. Ask students to listen out for the specific pieces of information in the notes and complete them by writing one or two words in each gap. Check answers in class.

### Transcript

*I would like to talk to you about a very special group of animals. There are 10,000 species of birds in the world. Vultures are amongst the most threatened group of birds. When you see a vulture like this, the first thing that comes to your mind is, these are disgusting, ugly, greedy creatures that are just after your flesh, associated with politicians. I want to change that perception. I want to change those feelings you have for these birds, because they need our sympathy. They really do. And I'll tell you why.*

*First of all, why do they have such a bad press? When Charles Darwin went across the Atlantic in 1832 on The Beagle, he saw the turkey vulture, and he said, 'These are disgusting birds with bald scarlet heads that are formed to revel in putridity.' You could not get a worse insult, and that from Charles Darwin. You know, he changed his mind when he came back, and I'll tell you why. They've also been associated with Disney – personified as goofy, dumb, stupid characters.*

*[…] So there's two types of vultures in this planet. There are the New World vultures that are mainly found in the Americas, like the condors and the caracaras, and then the Old World vultures, where we have sixteen species. From these sixteen, eleven of them are facing a high risk of extinction.*

*So why are vultures important? First of all, they provide vital ecological services. They clean up. They're our natural garbage collectors. They clean up carcasses right to the bone. They help to kill all the bacteria. They help absorb anthrax that would otherwise spread and cause huge livestock losses and diseases in other animals.*

*Recent studies have shown that in areas where there are no vultures, carcasses take up to three to four times to decompose, and this has huge ramifications for the spread of diseases.*

### Answers

1 goofy/dumb/stupid   2 the Americas
3 11   4 diseases

## 3

- ▶ 1.11 Tell students that they're now going to listen to Part 2 of Virani's talk in which he talks about what people are doing and what the audience can do to help to save vultures.

- Ask students to read the sentences summarizing this part of the talk and speculate about what the correct options could be, based on what they've already learned about vultures. Then, play Part 2 of Virani's TED Talk and ask students to focus on listening out for the information in the sentences and identifying the correct options. Check answers in class.

### Transcript

*So what is the problem with vultures? We have eight species of vultures that occur in Kenya, of which six are highly threatened with extinction. […] In South Asia, in countries like India and Pakistan, four species of vultures are listed as critically endangered, which means they have less than ten or fifteen years to go extinct.*

*[…] So what's being done? Well, we're conducting research on these birds. We're putting transmitters on them. We're trying to determine their basic ecology, and see where they go. We can see that they travel different countries, so if you focus on a problem locally, it's not going to help you. We need to work with governments in regional levels. We're working with local communities. We're talking to them about appreciating vultures, about the need from within to appreciate these wonderful creatures and the services that they provide.*

*How can you help? You can become active, make noise. You can write a letter to your government and tell them that we need to focus on these very misunderstood creatures. Volunteer your time to spread the word. Spread the word. When you walk out of this room, you will be informed about vultures, but speak to your families, to your children, to your neighbours about vultures.*

*They are very graceful. Charles Darwin said he changed his mind because he watched them fly effortlessly without energy in the skies. Kenya, this world, will be much poorer without these wonderful species. Thank you very much.*

### Answers

1 where vultures go   2 international
3 educating people   4 fly

## CRITICAL THINKING

### 4  21st CENTURY OUTCOMES

**Respond open-mindedly to different ideas and values**

- Tell students that the critical thinking skill they'll be using is the ability to reflect on the effect that finding out new information about a subject has on their opinion of it.

- Put students into pairs and have them discuss the questions. In order to fulfil the 21st CENTURY OUTCOMES, students should be able to show that they respect Virani's ideas and opinions and they're prepared to take them into account.

- Conduct whole-class feedback on how and why students' opinions of vultures have changed.

## VOCABULARY IN CONTEXT

### 5

• ▶ 1.12 Play the clips from the TED Talk. When each multiple-choice question appears, pause the clip so that students can choose the correct definition. Discourage the more confident students from always giving the answer by asking students to raise their hand if they think they know.

#### Transcript and subtitles

*1 When you see a vulture like this, the first thing that comes to your mind is, these are **disgusting**, ugly, greedy creatures that are just after your flesh …*
What does **disgusting** mean?
   a horrible
   b funny
   c attractive

*2 I want to change those feelings you have for these birds, because they need our **sympathy**.*
You might feel **sympathy** for an animal if it is _____.
   a suffering
   b living in a wild place
   c eating a meal

*3 'These are disgusting birds with bald scarlet heads that are formed to revel in putridity.' You could not get a worse **insult**, and that from Charles Darwin.*
What does **insult** mean?
   a idea
   b rude comment
   c description

*4 You know, he **changed his mind** when he came back, and I'll tell you why.*
If you **change your mind**, you start to _____.
   a have a different opinion
   b make someone else think differently

*5 We're talking to them about appreciating vultures, about the need from within to **appreciate** these wonderful creatures and the services that they provide.*
If you **appreciate** something, you realize how _____ it is.
   a interesting
   b useless
   c valuable and important

#### Answers
1 a   2 a   3 b   4 a   5 c

### 6

• Students are now going to discuss their personal experiences of two of the ideas dealt with in the talk: changing your mind and showing appreciation. Check the meaning of *appreciate* (here: to show how thankful you are for something or someone).

• Put students into pairs and ask them to say their own answers to the questions, giving as much detail as they can. Monitor students' discussions and give them feedback when they've finished.

## PRESENTATION SKILLS Signposting with questions

### 7

• ▶ 1.13 Direct students to the Presentation skills box. Then, ask them to read the question and elicit that Virani uses this question to let the audience know what is coming in the next part of his presentation, i.e. the answer to the question. Using questions in this way also helps to get the audience's attention. Then, play the clip and ask students to notice and write in the missing words.

• Check answers and elicit or explain that when something *gets/has a bad press*, a lot of people have a negative image of it.

#### Answer
why do they have

### 8

• ▶ 1.14 Ask students to read the questions and decide what the matching response for each one is. Then, play the clips and ask students to listen out for the questions and answers and check that they've matched them correctly.

• Confirm students' answers in class.

• **Optional step**. Draw students' attention to the words at the start of responses b (*First of all*) and c (*Well*) and elicit or explain that *first of all* is used by presenters to order their ideas, whereas *well* is used here to focus the audience's attention on what the presenter is going to say next.

#### Answers
1 b   2 d   3 c   4 a

### 9

• Ask students to brainstorm things they know about pandas. Encourage them to think about pandas in a conservation context, i.e. What is their conservation status? What threats are there to their survival? What can people do to protect them?

• Have students select what three key points they would include in a presentation about pandas and make notes on them. They can then think of a question they would answer when talking about each of the three key points in a presentation.

### Extra activity

### Panda presentations

Put students into pairs. Give them some time to prepare to give the presentation about pandas which they prepared in Exercise 9. Weaker students can make notes on what they want to say in their presentations and use them when they're speaking. Stronger students could just write a few key words for each point on a prompt card as a memory aid rather than writing full sentences. Students take it in turns to give their presentations and then give each other feedback on how effective they think each other's presentations were. Monitor students' presentations and add your global feedback when they've finished.

▶ Set Workbook page 10 for homework.

## 1.5 Which to save?

### COMMUNICATE A group decision

**1**

- Have students read the names of animals in the box and look at the photos of them. They then match the names of the animals with their photos.
- Check answers in class and model and drill the pronunciation of *python* /ˈpaɪθ(ə)n/ and *iguana* /ɪˈɡwɑːnə/.

> **Answers**
>
> a Indian python   b Frégate island beetle
> c bluefin tuna   d marine iguana

**2**

- Put students into groups of four and ask them to decide who will be Student A, B, C and D. Direct students to their file and have them read and make notes on the information given about one of the animals from Exercise 1. They can check the meaning of any vocabulary that they're not familiar with in a dictionary.

**3**

- Give students some time to prepare three arguments for preserving the animal in their file. Direct students to the Presenting arguments box and ask them to use a phrase from it to introduce each of their three points.
- Students take it in turns to present the arguments they've prepared in their groups. After listening to all of the arguments, they choose an animal to save. They may find it helpful to make brief notes on the arguments as they listen.

**4**

- Ask the person who made notes on the animal that their group chose to tell the rest of the class which animal they chose and why.
- When every group has presented their choice, establish which animal is the most popular and have students to discuss why they think this animal is the most popular in class.

### WRITING An endangered species

**5**

- Ask students to read the example text about the polar bear and notice its structure: 1) what animal, 2) why it needs protection, 3) why you should protect it. Tell students to use this structure as a model for their texts.
- Students then choose an animal that needs protecting (not the polar bear) and write their own texts about it. Circulate and monitor while they're writing, offering assistance and feedback where appropriate.

> **Answers**
>
> Students' own answers.

▶ Set Workbook page 11 for homework.

# 2 Family connections

## UNIT AT A GLANCE

**THEME:** Families
**VOCABULARY:** Extended family
**LISTENING:** My family history
**SPEAKING:** Talking about family, My family
**GRAMMAR:** Future plans
**PRONUNCIATION:** Pausing with lists, Weak forms (1): *be going to*

**READING:** *A passion for genealogy*
**TED TALK:** *The world's largest family reunion*. In this talk, A. J. Jacobs talks about the relevance of genealogy today and how it can be used to bring people together.
**PRESENTATION SKILLS:** Personalizing a presentation
**WRITING:** Inviting people to a family reunion

## WARM UP

- Books open. Draw students' attention to the unit title, the photo and the caption on page 19.
- Put students into pairs or small groups (three to four students) to discuss the questions.
- **Question 1**. Direct students to the photo and ask them to spend a minute looking closely at it. Then, put students into pairs and have them tell each other what type of relationship they think the grandfather and grandson have.
- **Question 2**. Ask students to consider and discuss the importance of the grandparent-grandchild relationship. If students feel comfortable, encourage them to bring in their own experiences and talk about what relationships they have/had with their own grandparents and how important these relationships are/were to them. They could share examples of things they do/did with their grandparents.
- **Question 3**. Elicit or explain that your extended family includes family members that aren't your parents or brothers and sisters. Ask students to choose at least one family member that they have a good connection with and describe that person/people and what type of connection they have with them.

> **TEACHING TIP**
>
> **Sensitivity when talking about family**
>
> Our family is usually one of the most personal aspects of our lives and your students will doubtless have many different family backgrounds. Some will have a large extended family that they get on very well with and some may have little or no contact with their families for a range of different reasons. There may also have been a recent death in students' families. As a result, it is important to keep this mind when students are doing activities where they have to talk about their own families. Don't push students to offer information about their family or ask them questions about it as this may provoke a negative reaction from them. In extreme cases, it may even result in them deciding not to attend the English course anymore.

## 2.1 Family ties

### VOCABULARY Extended family

**1**

- ▶ 2.1 Ask students to look closely at the family tree and look at the words in the box. Then, ask them to use the words in the box to complete the sentences.
- Check answers in class. Elicit or explain that we use the term *in-law* to show that two people are connected through marriage.

> **Answers**
>
> 1 mother-in-law   2 cousin   3 grandfather
> 4 son-in-law   5 grandchild   6 brother-in-law
> 7 niece   8 nephew

**2**

- Put students into pairs. Ask them to think of some members of their extended family. They then take it in turns to describe their connection to them. Students have to guess their partner's connection with the person he/she describes. Direct students to the model conversation and tell them to use the same structure for their conversations.
- **Optional step**. If students don't have an extended family, they can just make up some possible family members.
- Monitor students' conversations and give them feedback on their use of vocabulary for member of your extended family.

### Extra activity

### Family trees

Ask students to work alone to draw a family tree of their extended families going back as far as they can. Then, put them into pairs. Have them show their trees to their partner and explain how the people in it are connected to them, using the vocabulary from this section. Students may need some assistance with additional vocabulary, e.g. *second cousin*, *great-grandmother*, in which case, they can consult a dictionary or ask you for help.

2 Family connections 21

## LISTENING  My family history

### 3

- ▶2.2  Direct students to the Listening for contractions and possessives box and check the meaning of *contraction* (a short form, e.g. *it's*) and *possessive* (the form of a noun which shows that something or someone belongs to someone or something). Ask students to look at the examples and notice the difference in what the apostrophe + -s is used for.

- Tell students that they're going to listen to Ken Lejtenyi, who they can see in the photo, talking about his family history. Ask them to look at his photo, read the countries in the box and predict which countries he mentions.

- Play the recording and ask students to listen out for the names of the countries in the box and circle the correct options. They can then compare their answers in pairs before you check answers in class.

### Transcript

My family history is pretty interesting. I'm from Canada, but my ancestors all come from different places.

My grandparents on my mother's side of the family moved from Scotland to Canada in the nineteenth century. In the 1930s though, my grandfather was working in England. So my mother, aunts and uncle were born in London and lived through World War Two. In the 1950s, my grandfather was offered a job in Canada, and so the family moved back there.

My grandfather on my father's side was from Transylvania, which is now part of Romania. In the 1920s, he went to university in Scotland. While he was there, he met, fell in love with and eventually married a local girl – my grandmother. They moved back to Transylvania, which is where my father was born. Shortly after though, they moved to neighbouring Hungary.

My father grew up in Hungary, but in 1956, there was a revolution and my father, who was nineteen at that time, was forced to leave. He eventually settled in Canada, which is where he met my mother. My father passed away in 2010, but our family is doing great. My mother and two brothers are still in Canada, my sister lives in Germany and I've been in Singapore since 2001. I'm still Canadian, but I'm proud of my Scottish and Hungarian background. And my wife is Singaporean, so that's made my family tree even more international.

> **Answers**
>
> Canada, England, Romania, Scotland, Hungary, Singapore

### 4

- ▶2.2  Tell students that they're going to listen to the recording again and focus on some specific information about Ken's parents. Before they listen, ask them to read the sentences and speculate about what the missing words are.

- Play the recording and ask students to complete the sentences. They then compare their answers in pairs before you check answers in class.

> **Answers**
>
> 1 Scotland   2 London, England   3 Scotland   4 Hungary

## Pronunciation  Pausing with lists

### 5

- ▶2.3  Play the recording and ask students to listen to the sentences while reading them and notice where the speaker pauses. Elicit or explain that the speaker pauses after each item on the list and this is because it makes these items easier to understand.

- Put students into pairs. Have them take it in turns to practise saying the sentences with pauses between the items on the list.

## SPEAKING  Talking about family

### 6

- ▶2.4  **Optional step**. Check the meaning of *family reunion* (a time when members of an extended family come together to spend time with each other) and draw their attention to the collocation: *to hold a family reunion*. Ask students if they've ever been to a family reunion. If so, you can ask: *How many members of your family were there? Did some of them come from a long way away? What did you and your family do together? Did you enjoy the experience?*

- Ask students to read the conversation through once before they listen to it. Tell them to ignore the word choices on the right for the moment as they will focus on those in Exercise 7.

- Play the recording and ask students to read and listen to the conversation at the same time. Ask students to compare their answers in pairs before checking answers in class. Elicit or explain that a *sibling* is a brother or sister.

> **Answer**
>
> At a restaurant. It's a big family and the house is too small.

### 7

- Model the conversation that students have just listened to aloud with a student. Then have them work in pairs to practise the conversation together. Make sure they alternate between A and B roles.

- Have students practise the conversation again using the words on the right instead of the words in bold in the conversation.

## 8

• Put students into pairs. Check the meaning of *immediate family* (parents, spouses, children and siblings). Then, have students read the example sentence and use it as a model to say how many people are in their immediate family, and who they are, and how many are in their extended family.

• Monitor students while they're talking to each other and give them feedback when they've finished.

▶ Set Workbook pages 12 and 13 for homework.

▶ Photocopiable communicative activity 2.1. Go to page 165 for further practice of extended family vocabulary. The teaching notes are on page 188.

## 2.2 Generations

### GRAMMAR Future plans

### 1

• ▶2.5 Direct students to the infographic about family records and ask them to look at the pictures and read the information about unusual families.

• Put students into pairs. Ask them to decide which record they find the most amazing and why and then tell their partner.

• Conduct whole-class feedback on which record students chose and why.

### 2

• ▶2.6 Ask students to read the sentences and check the meaning of *first cousin* (someone with whom you share a set of grandparents) and *second cousin* (someone with whom you share a set of great-grandparents).

• Play the recording. Ask students to listen out for what the speaker says about who Chris and Emily are and circle the correct options. Check answers in class.

### Transcript

**A:** Are you doing anything interesting this weekend?

**B:** Yes. I'm going to meet my second cousin, Chris.

**A:** Your second cousin?

**B:** Yeah, I'm researching my family tree. Chris is my grandfather's sister's grandchild. And he's bringing his daughter Emily, too. She's my second cousin once removed.

**A:** That's cool. How did you get in touch?

**B:** Through my grandfather. I'm going to ask Chris to help me find out more about the family. He seems really interested.

**A:** Where are you meeting them?

**B:** At my place. They can meet the rest of the family, too.

**A:** That's great.

| Answers |  |
|---|---|
| a second | b daughter |

### 3

• Ask students to read the example sentences and notice the difference in form and meaning between these two ways of talking about future plans. Check the meaning of *intend to do something* (to want and plan to do something).

• Students can check their answers and overall understanding of using *be* + *going* + infinitive and the present continuous to talk about future plans by turning to the Grammar summary on page 138. Draw students' attention to the fact that, although it would be grammatically correct, we don't usually use *be* + *going* + infinitive with the verb *to go*.

• If you feel that students need more controlled practice before continuing, they could do the exercises in the Grammar summary. Otherwise, you could continue on to Exercise 4 in the unit and set the Grammar summary exercises for homework.

### Answers
a 1    b 2    c 1    d 2

### Answers to Grammar summary exercises

**1**

2 're going to stay with my brother and family for three nights from 2nd July

3 'm going to meet a client called Mr Rose on 5th July

4 's going to visit MOMA and the Empire State Building on 5th July

5 's going to travel to Washington DC for an interview on 6th July.

6 'm going to take the train to Chicago to see my cousin Judith on 6th July

7 're going to spend one night in a hotel in NYC on 7th July

8 're going to return home on 8th July

**2**

2 I'm meeting Uncle Bernard

3 Ben's arriving at 4pm

4 Mike and I are / We're visiting Jo's new school

5 Mike, the children and I are / We're going to a school concert

6 I'm taking Simon swimming

7 Mum and Dad are coming for dinner

**4**

- ▶2.6 Have students complete the sentences from the conversation they listened to in Exercise 2.
- Students can compare answers in pairs, then play the recording again so students can listen and check their answers.

> **Answers**
> 1 doing  2 meet  3 bringing  4 ask  5 meeting

**5**

- ▶2.7 Ask students to read the text, identify the four mistakes and correct them. You could make this slightly easier for students by telling them that the mistakes have been made with the form of either *be + going to* + infinitive or the present continuous. Students can refer back to the examples in the Grammar summary if they need to.
- Students can compare answers in pairs, then play the recording again so they can check their answers.

> **Answers**
> After I finish university, ~~I~~ **I'm** going to take a year out. I think I need a break before I start working. I'm going to travel around South America with my best friend, Maki. We're ~~meet~~ **meeting** this weekend to work out our plans. We're definitely going to start in Argentina, but we don't know where we're ~~go~~ **going** after that yet. We don't have very much money so we're mainly going **to** stay in hostels. I can't wait. It's going to be a great adventure.

## LANGUAGE FOCUS Talking about future plans and arrangements

**6**

- ▶2.8 Ask students to read the Language focus box and focus on the types of events or situations that the two verb forms refer to.
- Students can check overall understanding of the language focus by turning to the Grammar summary on page 139.
- If you feel that students need more controlled practice before continuing, they could do the exercises in the Grammar summary. Otherwise, you could continue on to Exercise 7 in the unit and set the Grammar summary exercises for homework.

> **Answers to Grammar summary exercises**
> 1
> 2 When / What time are you arriving?
> 3 Are you going with Paolo?
> 4 Why is he/Paolo coming later?
> 5 What are you doing after dinner?
> 6 Am I staying at the hotel?

**2**

| | | |
|---|---|---|
| 1 When are you going to get married? | | c |
| 2 How many children are you going to have? | | f |
| 3 What are you going to call them? | | a |
| 4 Where are you going to live? | | b |
| 5 How are you going to pay for your beautiful house? | | e |
| 6 Are you going to remember me when you're famous? | | d |

**7**

- Students are now going to practise forming questions with either *be + going* + infinitive or present continuous for future plans. Tell students to refer back to the examples of questions in the Language focus box to help them if they need to.
- Have students compare their answers in pairs before checking answers in class.

> **Answers**
> 1 Are you seeing your grandparents this weekend
> 2 Which family member is going to visit you next
> 3 Are you spending your next holiday with your family
> 4 Are you speaking to anyone in your family this evening

## Pronunciation Weak forms (1): *be going to*

> **TEACHING TIP**
>
> **Weak forms**
>
> Check the meaning of *weak* (not strong). Elicit or explain that weak forms are words we shorten that come in between the key content words. Doing this helps the listener to focus on the key content words. When we shorten weak forms, this results in them having a different sound, e.g. with the word *are*, /ɑː/ becomes /ə/ and with the word *to*, /tuː/ becomes /tə/. One-syllable grammar words, like *are*, and prepositions like *of* and *to*, are typical examples of words that are usually weak. Ask students to think about which words are likely to be weak forms as they're saying or reading sentences out loud during the subsequent activities in this unit and to say them appropriately.

**8a**

- ▶2.9 Ask students to read the questions. Then, play the recording and ask them to focus on the pronunciation of the words *are* and *to*. Elicit or explain that the speakers have shortened the sounds of the words *are* and *to* because they're the weak forms in these questions.

**8b**

- Put students into pairs and ask them to practise asking the questions, with the appropriate sounds for the weak forms, and giving answers which are true for them. Monitor students to make sure they're saying the weak forms correctly.

## 9

- ▶ 2.10 Ask students to read the conversation and focus on understanding its gist. Then have them read it again, identify which type of event each gapped sentence describes and complete the sentences accordingly.

- Ask students to compare their answers in pairs before checking answers in class.

> **Answers**
> 1 're celebrating   2 are you having
> 3 're all meeting   4 Are your sister and brother-in-law coming   5 're not arriving   6 Are you going to see
> 7 'm not going to visit   8 your parents are going to do
> 9 're going to have

## SPEAKING My family

## 10

- Ask students to read the list and formulate questions for each item on it. With weaker students, you may want to go through the list and elicit the question for each one in class. Students can also use the model conversation to help them.

- Then, ask students to circulate and ask their questions. Give students a time limit for this activity, e.g. 15–20 minutes, and ask them to try to get as many *yes* answers as they can in that time.

- Remind students to ask a follow-up question when they get a *yes* answer. However, make sure that students' answers aren't too detailed, otherwise they won't be able to talk to many students.

- Monitor students and give them feedback when they've finished. Stop the activity once the time limit you set has been reached and find out which student(s) got the most *yes* answers.

### Extra activity

#### Future plans with family

Put students into pairs. Ask them to take two statements from the survey that are true for them and have an even more detailed discussion about each of them. Tell students to use either *be* + *going* + infinitive or the present continuous, as appropriate, and give as many specifics as they can. If none of the statements in the survey are relevant, have students talk about two other plans that they've made with family members recently.

### TEACHING TIP

**Mumble drill**

A 'mumble drill' involves saying phrases or sentences under your breath – in other words, mumbling them. Doing a 'mumble drill' can help students to prepare for saying phrases or sentences out loud with other students. You could ask students to do mumble drills with the questions they need to ask in Exercise 10 so they can practise using the appropriate rising intonation and differentiating between weak and non-weak forms before they circulate and ask the questions.

## 11

- Ask students to look at the notes they made in Exercise 10 and decide which pieces of information they think are the most interesting. In class, ask students to take it in turns to summarize the most interesting things for the rest of the group. Remind them to use the appropriate future forms as they do so.

▶ Set Workbook pages 14 and 15 for homework.

## 2.3 One big happy family

### READING A passion for genealogy

## 1

- Check the meaning of *genealogy* (the study of family history) and model and drill its pronunciation /ˌdʒiːniˈælədʒi/.

- Put students into pairs to brainstorm possible reasons. If they or someone they know has searched for information on their family history, ask them to bring in their own experiences and say why they or the people they know did this.

- Ask students to scan the article for reasons why people want to search for this information and discuss what they find in pairs. Conduct whole-class feedback.

> **Answers**
> Students' own answers.

### Extra activity

#### Questions about your ancestors

Have students work individually to make a list of questions about their own ancestry. Tell them to write five questions about people in their family tree that they'd like to know more about. Put students into pairs to share their questions with each other. Students then discuss what they think the best way to find answers to each of the questions would be, e.g. look for a birth certificate or census online, etc.

## Understanding purpose

**2**

- ▶ **2.11** Check the meaning of *purpose* (the reason why we do something). Elicit or explain that when someone writes a text, they usually have a specific reason in mind for writing it.
- Ask students to read the two options and check that they understand the difference between them. Then, have them read the article all the way through and focus on what the person who wrote it wanted to communicate to the reader.
- Students can compare their answers in pairs before you check answers in class.

**Answer**
b

## Understanding main ideas

**3**

- Have students read the list of main ideas and predict which paragraph they should match. Then, have them to go through the article again with the objective of identifying the main message in each paragraph. They can compare their ideas with the options given and choose the correct option for each paragraph.
- Point out the glossary at the bottom of the text and tell students to refer to it as they read or to look at the words and definitions before they start reading.
- Students can compare their answers in pairs before you check answers in class.

**Answers**
1 d   2 c   3 a   4 b

## Understanding details

**4**

- Check the meaning of *proof* (something which confirms that something you think is true) and *quotation* (something – usually a sentence – that someone said or wrote which is repeated and re-used).
- Ask students to read the questions and answer options and then read the article all the way through and focus on finding information about the things the questions refer to. They can then circle the correct options.
- Check answers in class.

**Answers**
1 b   2 b   3 a   4 b

## Understanding vocabulary

**5**

- Ask students to read the words and match them with their definitions. If students are unsure about which words and definitions go together, they may find it helpful to look back at the text, where these words are highlighted in bold, and see how the words are used in context.
- Check answers in class. Model and drill the pronunciation of *wealth* /wɛlθ/, *ancestor* /ˈænsestə(r)/ and *curiosity* /ˌkjʊəriˈɒsəti/.

**Answers**
1 e   2 d   3 a   4 b   5 c

**6**

- Put students into pairs and ask them to read the two questions. Draw their attention to the use of *would* in the questions, which shows they're asking about a hypothetical situation that could become a reality in the future.
- Ask students to discuss their answers to the questions, using the hypothetical *would* and drawing on the ideas in the article they've just read as well as their own ideas.
- Conduct whole-class feedback on students' ideas.

▶ Set Workbook pages 16 and 17 for homework.

## 2.4 The world's largest family reunion

### TEDTALKS

**1**

- Tell students that they're now going to watch a TED Talk by A. J. Jacobs, whose interest in genealogy they read about in **2.3**.
- Have students read the summary of the talk and then choose the correct options in the definitions of the words in bold. If students are unsure about which words to match with which items, encourage them to use deduction or simply have a guess.
- Students can compare their answers in pairs before you check answers in class. Model and drill the pronunciation of *fascinating* /ˈfæsɪneɪtɪŋ/.

**Answers**
1 interesting   2 kinder to them   3 biologically related

## 2

- ▶ 2.12 Tell students that they're now going to watch the first part of Jacobs' talk, in which he talks about the state of genealogy today. Ask them to read the sentences and speculate about which of the points Jacobs will make.

- Then, play Part 1 of the talk and ask students to listen out for information that's relevant to the opinions in the statements and tick the points Jacobs makes. Students can then check answers in pairs before you check answers in class.

### Transcript

*Six months ago, I got an email from a man in Israel who had read one of my books, and the email said, 'You don't know me, but I'm your twelfth cousin.' And it said, 'I have a family tree with 80,000 people on it, including you, Karl Marx, and several European aristocrats.'*

*[…] So this email inspired me to dive into genealogy, which I always thought was a very staid and proper field, but it turns out it's going through a fascinating revolution, and a controversial one. Partly, this is because of DNA and genetic testing, but partly, it's because of the Internet. There are sites that now take the Wikipedia approach to family trees, collaboration and crowdsourcing, and what you do is, you load your family tree on, and then these sites search to see if the A. J. Jacobs in your tree is the same as the A. J. Jacobs in another tree, and if it is, then you can combine, and then you combine and combine and combine until you get these massive, mega-family trees with thousands of people on them, or even millions. I'm on something on Geni called the world family tree, which has no less than a jaw-dropping 75 million people. So that's 75 million people connected by blood or marriage, sometimes both. It's in all seven continents, including Antarctica. I'm on it. Many of you are on it, whether you know it or not, and you can see the links. Here's my cousin Gwyneth Paltrow. She has no idea I exist, but we are officially cousins. We have just seventeen links between us. And there's my cousin Barack Obama. And he is my aunt's fifth great-aunt's husband's father's wife's seventh great nephew, so practically my older brother.*

*[…] Now, I'm not boasting, because all of you have famous people and historical figures in your tree, because we are all connected, and 75 million may seem like a lot, but in a few years, it's quite likely we will have a family tree with all, almost all, seven billion people on Earth. But does it really matter? What's the importance?*

### Answers
a, b, d

## 3

- ▶ 2.13 Elicit or explain that supporting details are pieces of information or examples that a presenter can give to show that the things they say are true or correct. Then, play Part 2 of Jacobs' talk and ask students to identify which supporting details he uses for each idea he talks about.

- Check and answers in class.

### Transcript

*First, it's got scientific value. This is an unprecedented history of the human race, and it's giving us valuable data about how diseases are inherited, how people migrate, and there's a team of scientists at MIT right now studying the world family tree. Number two, it brings history alive. I found out I'm connected to Albert Einstein, so I told my seven-year-old son that, and he was totally engaged. Now Albert Einstein is not some dead white guy with weird hair. He's Uncle Albert.*

*[…] Number three, interconnectedness. We all come from the same ancestor, […] so that means we literally all are biological cousins as well, and estimates vary, but probably the farthest cousin you have on Earth is about a 50th cousin. Now, it's not just ancestors we share, it's descendants. If you have kids, and they have kids, look how quickly the descendants accumulate. So in ten, twelve generations, you're going to have thousands of offspring, and millions of offspring.*

*Number four, a kinder world. Now, I know that there are family feuds. I have three sons, so I see how they fight. But I think that there's also a human bias to treat your family a little better than strangers. I think this tree is going to be bad news for bigots, because they're going to have to realize that they are cousins with thousands of people in whatever ethnic group they happen to have issues with, and I think you look back at history, and a lot of the terrible things we've done to each other is because one group thinks another group is sub-human, and you can't do that anymore. We're not just part of the same species. We're part of the same family. We share 99.9 per cent of our DNA.*

### Answers
1 d   2 c   3 a   4 b

## 4

- ▶ 2.14 Students are now going to watch Part 3 of the talk, in which Jacobs talks about an event he wants to organize. Ask students to read the notes and consider what the missing words could be.

- Play Part 3 of the talk and ask students to listen for information about each of the headings in bold and complete the notes. They can then check answers in pairs before you check answers in class.

**2 Family connections**   **27**

### Transcript

*So I have all these hundreds and thousands, millions of new cousins. I thought, what can I do with this information? And that's when I decided, why not throw a party? So that's what I'm doing. And you're all invited. Next year, next summer, I will be hosting what I hope is the biggest and best family reunion in history. Thank you. I want you there. I want you there. It's going to be at the New York Hall of Science, which is a great venue,*

*[…] There's going to be exhibits and food, music. Paul McCartney is eleven steps away, so I'm hoping he brings his guitar. He hasn't RSVP'd yet, but fingers crossed. And there is going to be a day of speakers, of fascinating cousins.*

*[…] And, of course, the most important is that you, I want you guys there, and I invite you to go to GlobalFamilyReunion.org and figure out how you're on the family tree, because these are big issues, family and tribe, and I don't know all the answers, but I have a lot of smart relatives, including you guys, so together, I think we can figure it out. Only together can we solve these big problems. So from cousin to cousin, I thank you. I can't wait to see you. Goodbye.*

> **Answers**
>
> family reunion, food, music, speakers, Everyone

## CRITICAL THINKING

**5** `21st CENTURY OUTCOMES`

**Listen effectively to decipher meaning, including knowledge, values, attitudes and intentions**

- Tell students that in this activity the critical thinking skill they'll be using is the ability to identify when humour is being used. Tell them that this is a useful ability to have when you're interacting with native speakers of English.

- Have students read the sentences and identify what makes them funny. Then, ask them to decide which one they find the funniest. Put students into pairs to discuss their answers. In order to fulfil the 21st CENTURY OUTCOMES, students should be able to show that they understand where the humour comes from and why Jacobs uses it.

- Conduct whole-class feedback on students' answers. A possible answer would be that the humour in both sentences comes from the contrast between the fame of Gwyneth Paltrow and Albert Einstein's fame, which usually makes them seem distant and set apart from 'ordinary people', and the familiar way Jacobs talks about them, saying that they're his cousin or his uncle.

## VOCABULARY IN CONTEXT

**6**

- ▶ 2.15 Play the clips from the TED Talk. When each multiple-choice question appears, pause the clip so that students can choose the correct definition. Discourage the more confident students from always giving the answer by asking students to raise their hand if they think they know.

### Transcript and subtitles

**1** *… it **turns out** it's going through a fascinating revolution, and a controversial one.*

If it **turns out** that something is happening, _____.
  a it stops being true
  b you discover it is true
  c you want it to be true

**2** *… it turns out it's going through a fascinating **revolution**, and a controversial one.*

A **revolution** is _____.
  a an important change
  b a strange experience
  c a busy period

**3** *And there's my cousin Barack Obama. And he is my aunt's fifth great-aunt's husband's father's wife's seventh great-nephew, so **practically** my older brother.*

What does **practically** mean?
  a nearly
  b oddly
  c distantly

**4** *Now, I'm not **boasting**, because all of you have famous people and historical figures in your tree …*

When people **boast** they _____.
  a are not telling the full truth
  b say something to make you change your mind
  c talk about how good they are at something

**5** *Paul McCartney is eleven steps away, so I'm hoping he brings his guitar. He hasn't RSVP'd yet, but **fingers crossed**.*

What does **fingers crossed** mean?
  a Just kidding!
  b We're best friends!
  c I hope it happens!

> **Answers**
>
> 1 b  2 a  3 a  4 c  5 c

**7**

- Students are now going to use two of the expressions they heard Jacobs use in the TED Talk – *it turns out that …* (I have discovered that it's true) and *to boast* (to talk about how good you are at something) – to talk about their personal experiences, so check that students know what they refer to.

- Put students into pairs and ask them to say their own answers to the questions, giving as much detail as they can. Monitor students' discussions and give them feedback when they've finished.

## PRESENTATION SKILLS Personalizing a presentation

### 8

• ▶ 2.16  Direct students to the Presentation skills box and check the meaning of *personalize* (to make something personal to you).

• Ask students to read the options and then play the clip so that they can watch and tick the thing that Jacobs does. Check answers in class.

| Answer |
|---|
| c |

### 9

• ▶ 2.17  Ask students to read the statements on the left and the examples of personalization on the right and match them. Check the meaning of *feud* (a serious disagreement which usually lasts for a long period of time). Then play the clips and ask students to and check their answers.

| Answers |
|---|
| 1 c  2 a  3 b |

### 10

• Ask students to make a list of three points that they would make in presentations about each of the three topics in the box and then think of an example or write a sentence they could use to personalize each point. Encourage students to look back at the examples of personalization that Jacobs used to help them do this. If time is short, students could just choose and make notes on one of the three topics.

• Monitor students and give them feedback on how successfully they personalized the points they made in the presentations when they've finished.

▶ Set Workbook page 18 for homework.

## 2.5 Who's that?

### COMMUNICATE Making a family tree

### 1

• Put students into groups of four and ask them to decide who will be Student A, B, C and D. Tell them that they're going to work together to draw a family tree. Direct students to their file and have them read the information about how the people in the family they're going to draw a family tree for are connected to each other.

### 2  21st CENTURY OUTCOMES

*Demonstrate ability to work effectively and respectfully with diverse teams*

• Tell students that they're now going to share the information in their files and use all four sets of information to draw a family tree for the family they read about. Students may want to designate one group member to be the person who draws the family tree.

• Direct students to the Checking information box and ask them to use the phrases in it when they need to. In order to fulfil the 21st CENTURY OUTCOMES, students should be able to present the information in their file clearly, listen to the information other students give, check information, be polite and respectful to the other members of the group and divide up the work on the family tree fairly.

### WRITING Inviting people to a family reunion

### 3

• Ask students to read the example invitation to a family reunion and notice the information it contains. Tell students to include this information in their invitation and also add any other information they think is relevant. Encourage students to use some of the useful phrases for invitations in the model text, e.g. *I have great news! You're all invited! I hope you're free then*.

• Students then write their invitations. Circulate and monitor while they're writing, offering assistance and feedback where appropriate.

| Answers |
|---|
| Students' own answers. |

▶ Set Workbook page 19 for homework.

▶ Photocopiable communicative activity 2.2. Go to page 166 for further practice of talking about future plans and arrangements and family vocabulary. The teaching notes are on page 188.

2  Family connections   29

# 3 Global stories

**UNIT AT A GLANCE**

**THEME:** Stores from around the world
**VOCABULARY:** Describing stories
**LISTENING:** Interview with an author
**SPEAKING:** Talking about books, Can you guess?
**GRAMMAR:** Defining relative clauses
**PRONUNCIATION:** Word stress, Sentence stress
**READING:** *Top picks*
**TED TALK:** *My year reading a book from every country*. In this talk, Ann Morgan shares her experiences from a year when she read a book from every country.
**PRESENTATION SKILLS:** Closing a presentation
**WRITING:** Writing a book review

## WARM UP

- Books open. Draw students' attention to the unit title, the photo and the caption on page 29.
- Put students into pairs or small groups (three to four students) to discuss the questions.
- **Question 1**. Direct students to the photo and ask them to spend a minute looking closely at it. Check the meaning of *puppet* (a movable model or doll controlled by a person). Then, ask them to consider and discuss whether they think puppets are a good way to tell a story, giving reasons for their answers.
- **Question 2**. Encourage students to bring in their own experiences of watching puppet shows and say where the show took place, what type of puppets were used, whether the show was just for children or for adults and what their impressions of the puppet show were. Encourage students to mention any puppet shows they've seen in other countries and how these compared with those in their home country.
- **Question 3**. Ask students to brainstorm other possible ways in which people can tell stories. Encourage them to think creatively and go beyond stories in books. Possible answers could be: *novels, poems, oral storytelling, dance, plays, opera, songs, paintings*.

## 3.1 It's a great story

### VOCABULARY Describing stories

**1**

- **Optional step.** Draw students' attention to the photo of The Abbey Library of Saint Gallen, Switzerland, and ask them if they've ever visited this library or a similar one and whether they'd like to if they haven't.
- Ask students to match the adjectives in each set of three with their definitions. Students can refer to a dictionary if they need to. Weaker students could work in pairs.
- Check answers in class.

**Answers**
1 c   2 b   3 a   4 b   5 c   6 a   7 a   8 c   9 b

**TEACHING TIP**

**Using definitions to record vocabulary**

It can be useful to record the new words they learn with their definitions. It helps you to remember the meanings of the words when you look back at them and writing the definitions helps you to consolidate your understanding of the words. If students find this strategy helpful, suggest they use it the next time they encounter new vocabulary.

### Pronunciation Word stress

**2**

- ▶3.1 Elicit or explain that word stress involves stressing one or several syllables in a word by saying them more loudly or strongly. It's usually one syllable that's stressed in each word, but it may be two or three in long words.
- Model *charming* with exaggerated stress on the first syllable and elicit that the first syllable is stressed. Then, have students read the other adjectives in Exercise 1 and underline where they think the stress goes in each one. Saying the words out loud should help them to do this.
- Play the recording and ask students to listen and check that they underlined the correct syllables. Play it more than once if necessary. Conduct whole-class feedback.
- Then, play the recording again so that students can listen and repeat the adjectives with the correct syllable stress.

**Answers**
1 <u>char</u>ming   2 <u>pow</u>erful   3 re<u>al</u>istic   4 my<u>ste</u>rious
5 sur<u>pris</u>ing   6 <u>com</u>plicated   7 <u>mov</u>ing
8 dra<u>ma</u>tic   9 <u>ter</u>rifying

## 3

- Put students into pairs. Ask them to think of books which they could describe with the adjectives from Exercise 1. Tell them these could be any books they know of or have read in any language. Have them tell their partner the books they've thought of, using the example sentence as a model.

- Monitor students' conversations and notice whether they're using the adjectives appropriately. Conduct whole-class feedback.

> **TEACHING TIP**
>
> **Mining authentic book reviews for vocabulary**
>
> Have students go online and find a few reviews in English of a book they've read and liked. If students don't have access to the Internet in class, they could do this as a self-study task. Ask students to read the reviews and identify all the adjectives used in them to describe the books. They can then check if any of these adjectives were also given in Exercise 1 and find out the meaning of any adjectives that they haven't seen before. Students could also identify phrases in the reviews that their writers have used to give their opinion. They can note these down and use them while they're discussing which book to choose in 3.5, Exercise 2 and while writing a book review in 3.5, Exercise 4.

## 4

- Check the meaning of: *characters* (the people who do things in a book), *plot* (the basic story), *setting* (where the things in the book happen) and *theme* (what the book is about / the important aspects of the story). Then, ask students to think of a book they've read, ideally one they've read recently.

- Have students make some notes about the book's characters, plot, setting and theme to organize their ideas before they talk about the book. Then, put students into pairs and have them use their notes to describe the book.

## LISTENING Interview with an author

## 5

- ▶ 3.2 Direct students to the photo of Madeleine Thien, who they can see in the photo, and find out whether students have heard of her or read any of her books. Ask students to read the three sentences and check the meaning of *novel* (a longer work of fiction).

- Play the recording and ask students to listen and circle T for true or F for false. Students can then compare their answers in pairs before you check answers in class.

### Transcript

*I knew I wanted to be a writer from a very young age. I read a lot as a child, and I fell in love with imagining the lives of other people, the things they hope for and the experiences that change them. Empathy and imagination help a lot when you start to write stories of your own.*

*My first book was published in 2001, and it's called* Simple Recipes. *It's a collection of seven short stories, and it revolves around family relationships – all the acts of trust or betrayal or love between parents and children, and between people whose lives are bound together.*

*One of the stories is about a Malaysian immigrant family who now live in Canada. The story is told from the perspective of the youngest child – a girl born in Canada after the family's arrival. She describes a misunderstanding between her father and brother – a result of the cultural, and also language, differences between the two generations that is an inescapable part of the immigrant experience.*

*Simple Recipes received a great deal of praise, which gave me the confidence to keep doing what I loved. Since then, I've published three more books.*

*Writing stories and novels is an unusual way of life. Writing allows me to imagine and inhabit many different kinds of lives, and to expand the way I understand the world.*

> **Answers**
>
> 1 T  2 F  3 T

## 6

- ▶ 3.2 Tell students they're going to listen to the recording again and practise making notes on what they hear. Direct students to the Taking notes while listening box and ask them to keep the tips it gives in mind.

- Ask students to read the list of points. Then, play the recording and ask them to make notes on each one.

- Students then compare their answers in pairs before you check answers in class.

> **Answers**
>
> Date first book published: 2001
>
> Title of book: *Simple Recipes*
>
> Number of stories: seven
>
> Main theme: family relationships
>
> Reviews? the book received a great deal of praise
>
> How many other books? three

## 7

- Put students into pairs to discuss the questions. Ask them to say as much as they can in response to the questions and remember to use the hypothetical *would*, e.g. *I think I'd enjoy this book because ...*

- **Optional step.** Briefly review language for giving opinions in English before students start to discuss the questions. You could elicit phrases for giving opinions that students already know, e.g. *I think ..., I feel that ..., In my opinion ...*, etc. and write them up on the board. Students can then refer to these while they're speaking.

- Conduct whole-class feedback on students' answers and establish what proportion of the group would/wouldn't want to read *Simple Recipes*.

## SPEAKING  Talking about books

**8**

- ▶ 3.3  Ask students to read the conversation through once before they listen to it. Tell students to ignore the word choices on the right for the moment as they will focus on those in Exercise 9.
- Play the recording and ask students to read and listen to the conversation at the same time. Tell them to identify what the book is about.
- Check answers and elicit that when you're 'stuck' in a place, you cannot leave it.

> **Answer**
> It's about a group of people who are stuck on an island.

**9**

- Check the meaning of *be worth* + verb + *-ing* (if something is worth doing, there's a good reason for doing it or you will get something out of doing it). Then, model the conversation that students have just listened to aloud with a student before having them work in pairs to practise the conversation together. Make sure they alternate between A and B roles.
- Have students practise the conversation again using the words on the right instead of the words in bold in the conversation.

**10**

- Put students into pairs. Ask them to decide what their favourite book is. If they don't have a favourite book, they can think of any book they like. Have students read the example sentences and use these as a model. Weaker students will need some time to prepare and make notes on what they want to say about the book, whereas stronger students should be able to speak more spontaneously.
- Circulate and monitor students while they're talking to each other and give them feedback when they've finished.

▶ Set Workbook pages 20 and 21 for homework.
▶ Photocopiable communicative activity 3.1. Go to page 167 for further practice of describing stories vocabulary. The teaching notes are on page 189.

## 3.2  What's it about?

### GRAMMAR  Defining relative clauses

**1**

- ▶ 3.4  Direct students to the infographic. Ask them to read the titles of the books and the names of the authors in it and say which books they've read in their first language.
- Put students into pairs to compare which ones they've read. Conduct whole-class feedback.

> **Answers**
> Students' own answers.

### Extra activity

### Extending the discussion

Have students extend their discussion about the books in the infographic by giving them some further questions to discuss in pairs, e.g. *How old were you when you read them? Why did you read them?* e.g. because you had to read them at school or for pleasure. *Did you enjoy them and would you recommend them to other people?*

> **TEACHING TIP**
>
> **Reading English books**
>
> After finding out about what the best-selling English language books are, students may well be keen to try reading something in English themselves. Discourage students at this level from tackling a novel as this may be too challenging. Instead you could suggest that they try an A2-level graded reader and perhaps start with a collection of short stories. Direct students to shops or websites where they can buy graded readers, have them choose one which they think looks interesting and read it as a self-study task. Agree on a date of a future lesson where students will report back on what they've read, saying something about the plot, characters, setting and theme and what their opinion of it is.

**2**

- ▶ 3.5  Tell students that they're now going to listen to two people talking about *The Lion, the Witch and the Wardrobe*, which is one of the books in the infographic. Find out whether students have read it or heard of it. Have students read the text and predict the missing words.
- Play the recording and have students complete the sentences. Then, ask students to compare answers in pairs before checking answers in class.

### Transcript

**A:** *How many of these books have you read?*
**B:** *I've actually read them all except for* The Lion, the Witch and the Wardrobe. *Do you know it?*
**A:** *Yeah, it was one of my favourites when I was young.*
**B:** *What's it about?*
**A:** *Well, it's a children's story. It's about four brothers and sisters who live in an old house in England. They find an old wardrobe upstairs and it's magic.*
**B:** *How is it magic?*
**A:** *They can go through the wardrobe to visit a magical place called Narnia where they meet some talking animals.*
**B:** *Sounds interesting!*

> **Answers**
>
> 1 fantasy/children's   2 brothers and sisters   3 animals

## 3

- ▶3.6  Direct students to the Grammar box. They can check their answers and overall understanding of defining relative clauses by turning to the Grammar summary on page 140. Make sure students are aware that either *that* or *which* can be used to define things. *That* tends to be used more often than *which* in British English and *which'* tends to be used more often than *that* in American English.

- If you feel that students need more controlled practice before continuing, they could do the exercises in the Grammar summary. Otherwise, you could continue on to Exercise 4 in the unit and set the Grammar summary exercises for homework

> **Answers**
>
> a people   b things   c places

> **Answers to Grammar summary exercises**
>
> **1**
>
> 2 It's about a young boy who's a wizard
> 3 Hogwarts is a school where they train wizards
> 4 Harry has some friends who/that are called Ron and Hermione
> 5 Hedwig is an owl who/that/which helps Harry
> 6 There's a studio in London where you can see the Harry Potter sets
>
> **2**
>
> 1 who   2 that/which   3 that/which   4 who
> 5 that/which   6 who   7 where   8 that/which
> 9 that/which   10 who   11 that/which
>
> **EXTRA INFORMATION**
>
> **1**
>
> 1 b
> 2 He's the man who wrote the best-selling French book *Le Petit Prince*     d
> 3 It's a word that means 'very scary'     f
> 4 She's the actress who/that played the White Witch in the Narnia films   c
> 5 It's the country where they filmed *The Lord of the Rings*   e
> 6 They're the most famous plays that/which Shakespeare wrote     a
>
> **2**
>
> Relative pronouns not needed: 3, 4, 7 and 8.

## 4

- Have students match the sentence halves. Tell them that identifying whether the last word of the first sentence half is a thing, person or place will help them.
- Check answers in class.

> **Answers**
>
> 1 d   2 c   3 e   4 b   5 a

## 5

- ▶3.7  Tell students they're now going to read a text about a novel called *The Alchemist* by Paulo Coelho. Find out whether students have heard of this book or read it in their first language. If students have read it, elicit what it's about. Have students read the text and find and correct four mistakes in the use of defining relative clauses.

- Have students compare their answers in pairs before checking answers in class.

> **Answers**
>
> *The Alchemist*, by Brazilian novelist Paulo Coelho, is a story about a shepherd boy ~~where~~ **who** goes on a long adventure. After many years of having the same dream, he travels to the pyramids in Egypt to look for the treasure ~~what~~ **that/which** his dreams told him about. Along the way, he meets people who ~~teaches~~ **teach** him many life lessons. It's a novel ~~who~~ **that/which** is both charming and dramatic. I would recommend this book to anyone who wants to read a powerful and moving story about becoming who you want to be.

## 6

- Ask students to read the sentences and complete them with the correct words according to whether there's a thing, a person or a place before the gap.
- Don't check students' answers at this stage as they will check them in Exercise 7a.

> **Answers**
>
> 1 that   2 who   3 that   4 who   5 where   6 who

## Pronunciation  Sentence stress

### 7a

- ▶3.8  Play the recording once so that students can listen and check their answers to Exercise 6. Then, ask them to underline the important words in the sentences. Play the recording and ask students to listen and notice which words are stressed. You can then elicit that we stress the important words in a sentence.

- Conduct whole-class feedback on which words are stressed.

> **Answers**
>
> 1 It's the name for a <u>non-fiction</u> book that gives you <u>factual</u> information.
> 2 He's the <u>man</u> who wrote the <u>best-selling book</u> in the <u>world</u>.
> 3 It's a <u>Japanese</u> <u>word</u> that means to <u>buy</u> a book and then not <u>read</u> it.
> 4 He's a <u>famous fictional detective</u> who lives in <u>London</u>.
> 5 It's the <u>country</u> where people spend the <u>most</u> time <u>reading</u>.
> 6 It's a <u>story</u> about a <u>girl</u> with long <u>hair</u> who falls down a <u>hole</u>.

## 7b

- Put students into pairs to practise saying the sentences from Exercise 6 with the appropriate sentence stress. Then, have them look at the options and decide which thing, person or place each sentence refers to.

- Monitor students' use of sentence stress and then check that they've correctly matched the things, people and places with the sentences.

> **Answers**
>
> 1 a reference book   2 Dickens   3 tsundoku
> 4 Sherlock Holmes   5 India   6 *Alice in Wonderland*

**TEACHING TIP**

**Practice with sentence stress**

For more practice with sentence stress, write the following sentence on the board: *You didn't tell me Stephanie's flying home.* Tell students that the meaning of this sentence changes depending on which word is stressed. With weaker students, model the sentence seven times, stressing a different word each time, and elicit how the meaning changes each time in class. With stronger students, put them into pairs, ask them to say the sentences themselves seven times and have them discuss with their partner how they think the meaning changes each time. Then, conduct whole-class feedback.

Answers: *You* (why didn't you tell me? / someone else told me) *didn't* (I'm unhappy about the fact you didn't do this), *tell* (I'm unhappy about the fact that you didn't give me this information) *me* (you told other people, but not me) *Stephanie's* (You told me about other people flying home, but not about Stephanie) *flying* (I thought she was using another form of transport) *home* (I thought she was flying somewhere else).

## 8

- Ask students to complete the notes with their own opinions about books. If students don't have specific likes and dislikes when it comes to books or aren't regular readers, tell them they can always write something which isn't completely true.

- Put students into pairs to share and compare their notes. Ask some students to summarize their likes and dislikes in class.

> **Answers**
>
> Students' own answers.

### SPEAKING  Can you guess?

## 9

- Ask students to think of a book or story in any language and write three sentences that say what it's about. It should be one that they think other students are likely to have heard of and nothing too obscure.

- The purpose of this activity is to give students some freer practice with defining relative clauses so remind them to use these in their sentences.

## 10

- Put students into pairs. They take it in turns to read the three sentences they wrote in Exercise 9 out loud, pausing after each one to give their partner a chance to guess what the book or story is. If their partner is unable to correctly guess what it is after hearing all three sentences, students can give some extra information about the book or story's plot, characters, setting or theme.

- Give students feedback when they've finished.

▶ Set Workbook pages 22 and 23 for homework.

▶ Photocopiable communicative activity 3.2. Go to page 168 for further practice of defining relative clauses. The teaching notes are on page 189.

## 3.3 A world in books

### READING  Top picks

## 1

- ▶ 3.9  Tell students they're going to read reviews of three books by Ann Morgan, a writer and author whose TED Talk they're going to watch. Ask students to scan each of the reviews to identify the main reason why Morgan liked each book and make notes on this.

- Ask students to compare answers in pairs before checking answers in class.

> **Suggested answers**
>
> *Lake Como* was very funny. *Crowfall* had clear, powerful language. *The Blue Sky* made her feel connected to the world.

## Understanding details

**2**

- Students are now going to read the article more closely and focus on understanding what each book is about. Ask students to read the incomplete sentences and then read the text again to find out which book matches with each one.
- Check answers in class.

> **Answers**
>
> 1 *Crowfall*  2 *The Blue Sky*  3 *Lake Como*

**3**

- Have students read the reviews again, identify each book's setting and characters, and make brief notes on them in the table. Weaker students could do this in pairs.
- Point out the glossary at the bottom of the text and tell students to refer to it as they read or to look at the words and definitions before they start reading.
- Ask students to compare their notes in pairs before you check answers in class.

> **Answers**
>
> | Title | Setting | Characters | Theme |
> |---|---|---|---|
> | *Lake Como* | Italy | a Serbian writer named Frank | culture, identity |
> | *Crowfall* | Mumbai, India | three painters, a musician, a journalist and a teacher | art, music, loss |
> | *The Blue Sky* | Mongolia | a young boy named Dshurukuwaa | changing traditions |

## Making inferences

**4**

- Start by explaining that when you make an inference you decide what a speaker or writer is referring to or what they really mean. Check the meaning of *customs* (things that a group of people usually do and have been doing for a very long time).
- Have students read the comments and infer from them which books they refer to. Check answers in class.

> **Answers**
>
> 1 c   2 b   3 a

## Understanding vocabulary

**5**

- Ask students to read the bold words and match them with their definitions. Students may find it helpful to look back at the text to see how the words are used in context.
- Check answers in class. Model and drill the pronunciation of *ambitious* /æmˈbɪʃəs/ and *glimpse* /glɪmps/.

> **Answers**
>
> 1 c   2 d   3 a   4 e   5 b

**6**

- Put students into pairs and ask them to decide which of the three books they'd most like to read and why. They may find it helpful to refer back to the article and the review of the book they've chosen as they do this. Students can then tell each other which book they'd like to read and why.
- Conduct whole-class feedback on students' ideas and establish which book is the most popular in your class and why.

### Extra activity

#### Read the book, watch the film

Put students into pairs or small groups. Ask them to think of a story that they've both read as a book and watched as a film. Then have them discuss how the book compares with the film: What was the same and what was different? Which did they prefer and why? Would they recommend watching the film to people who've read the book? If the other student(s) in the pair or group have either read the book, but not seen the film, or seen the film, but not read the book, have them ask questions to find out more information about what they haven't seen or read.

▶ Set Workbook pages 24 and 25 for homework.

## 3.4 My year reading a book from every country

**TED**TALKS

**1**

- Tell students that they're now going to watch a TED Talk by Ann Morgan whose book reviews they read in **3.3**.

3   Global stories   35

- Have students read the summary of the talk and match the words in bold with their definitions or synonyms.
- Students can compare their answers in pairs before you check answers in class.

> **Answers**
> 1 narrow   2 alarming   3 extraordinary   4 blind spots

**2**

- ▶ 3.10  Tell students they're now going to watch the first part of Morgan's talk in which she introduces her reading project. Ask students to read the questions and answer options. Then, play Part 1 of the talk and ask students to focus on understanding the main ideas in it so they can circle the correct answers to the questions.
- Ask students to compare their answers in pairs before you check answers in class.

### Transcript

*It's often said that you can tell a lot about a person by looking at what's on their bookshelves. What do my bookshelves say about me? Well, when I asked myself this question a few years ago, I made an alarming discovery. I'd always thought of myself as a fairly cultured, cosmopolitan sort of person. But my bookshelves told a rather different story. Pretty much all the titles on them were by British or North American authors, and there was almost nothing in translation. Discovering this massive, cultural blind spot in my reading came as quite a shock.*

*And when I thought about it, it seemed like a real shame. I knew there had to be lots of amazing stories out there by writers working in languages other than English. And it seemed really sad to think that my reading habits meant I would probably never encounter them. So, I decided to prescribe myself an intensive course of global reading. 2012 was set to be a very international year for the UK; it was the year of the London Olympics. And so I decided to use it as my time frame to try and read a novel, short story collection or memoir from every country in the world. And so I did. And it was very exciting and I learned some remarkable things and made some wonderful connections that I want to share with you today.*

> **Answers**
> 1 a   2 b

### Extra activity

#### What's on your bookshelf?

As a self-study task, ask students to look at the books on their bookshelves at home and work out roughly what percentage of them were written by authors from their home country, identify which countries the other books are from and decide whether they generally prefer the books from their home country or the other books. Have students share this information in pairs in class and discuss whether or not they think they should read more books from other countries, giving reasons from their answers.

**3**

- ▶ 3.11  Tell students they're now going to listen to Part 2 of Morgan's talk. Ask them to read the events and consider what the correct order is.
- Then, play Part 2 of the talk and ask students to focus on the order of the events and number them.
- Check answers in class.

### Transcript

*So how on earth was I going to read the world? I was going to have to ask for help. So in October 2011, I registered my blog, ayearofreadingtheworld.com, and I posted a short appeal online. I explained who I was, how narrow my reading had been, and I asked anyone who cared to to leave a message suggesting what I might read from other parts of the planet. Now, I had no idea whether anyone would be interested, but within a few hours of me posting that appeal online, people started to get in touch. At first, it was friends and colleagues. Then it was friends of friends. And pretty soon, it was strangers.*

*Four days after I put that appeal online, I got a message from a woman called Rafidah in Kuala Lumpur. She said she loved the sound of my project, could she go to her local English-language bookshop and choose my Malaysian book and post it to me? I accepted enthusiastically, and a few weeks later, a package arrived containing not one, but two books – Rafidah's choice from Malaysia, and a book from Singapore that she had also picked out for me. Now, at the time, I was amazed that a stranger more than 6,000 miles away would go to such lengths to help someone she would probably never meet.*

*But Rafidah's kindness proved to be the pattern for that year. Time and again, people went out of their way to help me. Some took on research on my behalf, and others made detours on holidays and business trips to go to bookshops for me. It turns out, if you want to read the world, if you want to encounter it with an open mind, the world will help you.*

> **Answers**
> a 4   b 2   c 3   d 1   e 5

**4**

- ▶ 3.11  Students are now going to watch Part 2 of the talk again and focus specifically on listening out for what surprised Morgan about the response to her project. Elicit what students think surprised Morgan the most at this stage, based on what they can remember from their previous viewing(s).
- Play Part 2 again and have students note down their answer to the question. Then, put them into pairs to discuss their answers.

> **Answer**
> She was surprised that so many people went out of their way to help her.

## 5

- ▶3.12 Students are now going to watch Part 3 of the talk. Ask students to read the statements and predict which ones Morgan agrees with.

- Play the recording and ask students to listen out for the information in the statements and tick the ones that Morgan would agree with. You could then either check answers in class or refer students to the transcript for this part of the talk to check their answers.

### Transcript

*The books I read that year opened my eyes to many things. As those who enjoy reading will know, books have an extraordinary power to take you out of yourself and into someone else's mindset, so that, for a while at least, you look at the world through different eyes. That can be an uncomfortable experience, particularly if you're reading a book from a culture that may have quite different values to your own. But it can also be really enlightening. Wrestling with unfamiliar ideas can help clarify your own thinking. And it can also show up blind spots in the way you might have been looking at the world.*

*When I looked back at much of the English-language literature I'd grown up with, for example, I began to see quite how narrow a lot of it was, compared to the richness that the world has to offer. And as the pages turned, something else started to happen, too. Little by little, that long list of countries that I'd started the year with, changed from a rather dry, academic register of place names into living, breathing entities.*

*Now, I don't want to suggest that it's at all possible to get a rounded picture of a country simply by reading one book. But cumulatively, the stories I read that year made me more alive than ever before to the richness, diversity and complexity of our remarkable planet. It was as though the world's stories and the people who'd gone to such lengths to help me read them had made it real to me. These days, when I look at my bookshelves or consider the works on my e-reader, they tell a rather different story. It's the story of the power books have to connect us across political, geographical, cultural, social, religious divides. It's the tale of the potential human beings have to work together.*

*[...] And I hope many more people will join me. If we all read more widely, there'd be more incentive for publishers to translate more books, and we would all be richer for that.*

*Thank you.*

> **Answers**
> a, b, d

## CRITICAL THINKING

### 6  21st CENTURY OUTCOMES

***Understanding other nations and cultures, including the use of non-English languages***

- Tell students that the critical thinking skill they'll be using in this activity is the ability to reflect on their own experiences and the effect they've had on their world view.

- Put students into pairs and ask them to discuss the questions, giving specific examples from their own experiences. Things which may have opened their eyes to other cultures include: travelling, watching films from other cultures, eating food from other cultures, etc. In order to fulfil the 21st CENTURY OUTCOMES, students should show that they've gained understanding of other cultures by saying what they've learned from them.

- Conduct whole-class feedback.

## VOCABULARY IN CONTEXT

### 7

- ▶3.13 Play the clips from the TED Talk. When each multiple-choice question appears, pause the clip so that students can choose the correct definition.

### Transcript and subtitles

*1 Discovering this massive, cultural blind spot in my reading came as quite a shock. And when I thought about it, it seemed like **a real shame**.*

A person might say something is **a real shame** when they feel _____ it.
 a  happy and excited about
 b  tired or bored with
 c  sad or sorry about

*2 Now, I had no idea whether anyone would be interested, but within a few hours of me posting that appeal online, people started to **get in touch**.*

If people **get in touch**, they _____ you.
 a  contact
 b  hold hands with
 c  wait for

*3 She said she loved **the sound of** my project...*

If you like **the sound of** something, you like _____.
 a  the music it has
 b  the idea of it

*4 It turns out, if you want to read the world, if you want to encounter it with **an open mind**, the world will help you.*

If you approach something with **an open mind**, you do it _____ .
 a  without making mistakes
 b  only after a lot of research
 c  without having a fixed opinion

3  Global stories

**5** *Little by little*, that long list of countries that I'd started the year with, changed from a rather dry, academic register of place names into living, breathing entities.

If something changes **little by little**, it happens _____.
  a  in a surprising way
  b  in a slow and gradual way
  c  in a not very important way

> **Answers**
> 1 c   2 a   3 b   4 c   5 b

**8**

- Students are now going to use two terms from Morgan's talk – *get in touch* and *little by little* – which they looked at in the Vocabulary in context section, to talk about their own personal experiences.
- Put students into pairs and ask them to say their own answers to the questions, giving as much detail as they can.

## PRESENTATION SKILLS Closing a presentation

**9**

- ▶ 3.14 Tell students that they're now going to watch the end of Morgan's talk again and focus on what she does at the end. Direct students to the Presentation skills box and ask them to read the different ways in which a presenter can end a talk.
- Have students read the three options and then play the clip so that they can watch and choose the correct option. Check answers in class.

> **Answer**
> c

**10**

- ▶ 3.15 Ask students to read the options and think back to the end of Virani's talk. Then, play the clip and ask students to tick the things that Virani does. You could make this easier for weaker students by telling them that he does three of the four things. Check answers in class.

> **Answers**
> a, b, d

**11**

- Put students into groups. Ask them to compare Virani and Morgan's closings and discuss which one they think is better and why.

- Stop students after about five minutes and find out what proportion of the class preferred Virani's closing and what proportion preferred Morgan's. Conduct feedback on the reasons for their preferences.

▶ Set Workbook page 26 for homework.

## 3.5 A good read

### COMMUNICATE  A book recommendation

**1**  **21st CENTURY OUTCOMES**

*Use a wide range of idea creation techniques (such as brainstorming)*

- Put students into groups of three or four and ask them to work together to brainstorm books from their country which they think people from other countries should read. In order to fulfil the 21st CENTURY OUTCOMES, students should come up with what you consider to be a wide range of different books while they're brainstorming.
- If students come from different countries, you could put them into groups or pairs with students from the same country. If this isn't possible, students can think of their ideas for books and then choose a book to recommend to Morgan (in Exercise 2) individually and then get together in groups to talk about the book they've chosen after completing Exercise 2.

**2**

- Ask students to discuss and decide which book from Exercise 1 they would recommend to Ann Morgan. Encourage them to think of the book which best shows what their country or culture is like. Direct students to the model conversation and the Asking for opinions box and have them use these questions during their discussions.

**3**

- Ask the groups to take it in turns to present the book they've chosen in class. Weaker students can look at the notes they made in Exercise 2, whereas stronger students should be able to speak more spontaneously.

### Extra activity

#### A comment on Ann Morgan's blog

Have students write a comment on Ann Morgan's blog in which they recommend the book they decided best represents their country in Exercise 2, giving reasons why Ann Morgan and other people who are interested in reading books from their country should read it. The address of Ann Morgan's blog is: www.ayearofreadingtheworld.com.

## WRITING Writing a book review

### 4  21st CENTURY OUTCOMES

*Articulate thoughts and ideas effectively using oral, written and nonverbal communication skills in a variety of forms and contexts*

- Ask students to read the example book review. Then, have them choose a book they've read and write a review of it. In order to fulfil the 21st CENTURY OUTCOMES, students should clearly communicate information about the book and clearly express their opinion of it.

- Circulate and monitor while students are writing.

### 5

- Put students into groups of four or five and have them read the reviews that the other members of their group wrote in Exercise 4. They then decide which book they think sounds the most interesting and take it in turns to say which one they chose and why. Tell students to think of two or more reasons why the book sounds interesting.

> **Answers**
> Students' own answers.

▶ Set Workbook page 27 for homework.

# Presentation 1 | UNITS 1–3

## MODEL PRESENTATION

**1**

- Tell students they're going to read the text of a presentation. The aim of the presentation is to tell people about an endangered animal, why we should try to save it and how we can help.

- Ask students to read the text of the presentation all the way through and think about what the missing words could be as they do so. Then, ask them to look at the words in the box, read the text all the way through again and complete it with the correct words. Encourage students to look at what comes before and after the gaps to help them decide which words should go in them.

- Students can compare their answers in pairs, but don't confirm answers at this stage as they will find out what the correct answers are when they watch the presentation in Exercise 2.

> **Answers**
> 1 reptile   2 cousin   3 that   4 endangered   5 where
> 6 help   7 travelling   8 work   9 going to   10 facing

**2**

- ▶ P.1 Play the recording of the presentation and ask students to listen closely for the words the presenter says in the gaps so they can check their answers from Exercise 1. Check answers in class.

- **Optional step.** Draw students' attention to some of the 'signposting' language the presenter uses to guide the audience through her presentation and elicit that 1) *I'd like to talk to you about ...* is used to introduce the topic of the presentation, 2) *firstly*, *secondly* and *finally* are used to show when the presenter starts talking about each of the three points she wants to make and 3) *Thank you so much* is used to thank the audience and show that this is the end of the presentation.

**3**

- ▶ P.1 Ask students to read the list of presentation skills and think back to when they looked at using questions to signpost (Unit 1), personalizing the presentation (Unit 2) and closing the presentation effectively (Unit 3). Students can look back at the Presentation skills boxes from those units to refresh their memory of how presenters can do these things. Put students into pairs and ask them to discuss which of these skills they remember the speaker using in her presentation.

- Play the recording again so students can watch and check their answers.

- **Optional step.** Weaker students could do this activity as a collaborative viewing task. Students work in pairs and one student (which could be the stronger student) focuses on two of the skills, while the other student focuses on one of them. They then compare which skills they noticed the speaker using in their pairs.

- Elicit or explain that you need to do more than just say *Thank you so much* at the end of a presentation, as this speaker does, to close it effectively. Elicit the things that you can do to close a presentation effectively and/or refer students back to the list of them in the Presentation skills box on page 37.

> **Answers**
> She uses questions to signpost and personalizes the presentation, but she doesn't close the presentation effectively.

**4**

- Ask students to read the notes and then re-read the presentation transcript to identify any information in the notes that isn't in the presentation.

> **Answers**
> She didn't say: be careful what you eat when you're abroad.

## YOUR TURN

**5**

- Ask students to think of an endangered animal. This could be one of the animals they read and talked about in Unit 1 or another endangered animal that they could do some online research to find out more about.

- Give students some time to prepare their presentations. Tell them to re-read the notes in Exercise 4 and use these to structure their own notes. Remind them to include some information about the animal, what makes it special or different to other animals, any personal experiences they've had with it, e.g. while they were on holiday, and what people can do to save it.

- Direct students to the list of presentation skills in Exercise 3 and tell them that the objective is to use all of them in their own presentations. They will, therefore, also need to think about how they can include these three points in their presentations while they're preparing to speak.

**6**

- Direct students to the Useful phrases box. Ask them to read its contents and note down the words and phrases they want to use in their presentations. Tell students to use at least one word or phrase from each of the five categories in the box.

**TEACHING TIP**

**From the page to your tongue**

Students may find some of the words in the Useful phrases box, such as *amphibian*, *threatened* and *vulnerable*, or other words they've read and want to use in their presentations, difficult to pronounce. If this is the case, tell them to look up the words in an online dictionary where they can also listen to the words being pronounced and then practise saying the words themselves. Students could also support each other with their pronunciation in pairs by practising saying the words together and giving each other feedback. Remind students of the importance of being able to correctly pronounce words they read and decide to use in a presentation and ask them to remember the strategy/strategies they've used to help them do this for future reference.

**7**

- Put students into pairs and tell them they're now going to take it in turns to give their presentations.

- Have students give their presentations and tick the skills their partner uses while they're listening to them. Make sure students are aware that when they're giving their partner feedback they're going to say two things they liked about it and one thing that could be improved, so they will also need to be thinking about this while they're listening.

**8**

- Ask students to read the example feedback in the speech bubble and use it as a model for giving their own feedback to their partner. Encourage them to start with a positive comment, as in the example, and then mention the good things that their partner did, using the ticks they made in their checklist, before saying something that their partner could improve.

- **Optional step.** When students have finished giving each other feedback, add your global feedback on students' presentations to their comments and highlight some areas for improvement for next time.

# 4 Music

**UNIT AT A GLANCE**

**THEME:** Music
**VOCABULARY:** Music
**LISTENING:** A traditional singer
**SPEAKING:** Talking about music, Discussing musical preferences
**GRAMMAR:** Countable and uncountable nouns
**PRONUNCIATION:** /ŋ/, Stress with quantifiers

**READING:** *Music and the brain*
**TED TALK:** *Why I take the piano on the road ... and in the air*. In this talk, Daria van den Bercken tells us why we should try to experience music as a child does – full of awe and wonder.
**PRESENTATION SKILLS:** Providing background information
**WRITING:** Describing a favourite song

## WARM UP

- Books open. Draw students' attention to the unit title, the photo and the caption on page 41.
- Put students into pairs or small groups (three to four students) to discuss the questions.
- **Question 1**. Direct students to the photo and elicit that the women in it are singing and one of them is playing an instrument called an accordion. Ask them to spend a minute looking closely at the photo and then consider and discuss how the women feel about music. Draw students' attention to the significance of the fact that they're making music together as a group. You could also bring in students' own experiences by asking them to say whether the women in the photo remind them of any people they know or have met and what music means to these people.
- **Question 2**. Ask students to describe any experiences of playing or singing music in a group that they've had, e.g. in a choir as a child or adult, or playing in a band. Remind them to use the past simple when they're talking about the past, the present continuous for activities they're doing now and the present simple for any regular activities they do.
- **Question 3**. Here students are considering and discussing how important music is to them and how much of it there is in their lives. You could draw students' attention to the fact that even if they're not involved in music by doing something like singing in a choir, music may still play an important part in their life because they always listen to it on their way to work, for example.

## 4.1 Feel the music

### VOCABULARY Music

**1**

- ▶ 4.1 Review the meaning of *genre* (a type or style) and then ask students to read the list of musical genres and check that they understand what type of music each one is.

Tell students that they're going to listen to six tracks, each of which is a different genre. They have to identify the genre and then write the number of the track next to it. Play the recording more than once if necessary.

- Ask students to compare their answers in pairs before you check answers in class. Explain that there is often a certain amount of crossover between musical genres, for example, track 5 is a piece of easy listening music, but it has an electronic feel.
- **Optional step**. Elicit any other musical genres that students know and write them on the board.

**Answers**

a 2   b 3   c 1   d 5   e 4   f 6

**2**

- Ask students to read the adjectives in the box and look up the meanings of any words they don't know. Students then decide whether the words could be used to describe music, feelings or both, and write them in the correct column in the table. Encourage students to think about how the words would be used, e.g. which adjectives could follow *The music is* ..., which could follow *I feel* ... and which could follow both.
- Ask students to compare their answers in pairs before checking answers in class. Model and drill the pronunciation of the words students are likely to find challenging, e.g. *gentle* /ˈdʒent(ə)l/, *lively* /ˈlaɪvli/ and *rhythmic* /ˈrɪðmɪk/.

**Suggested answers**

| Music | Feeling | Both |
|---|---|---|
| loud | relaxed | lively |
| rhythmic | sleepy | peaceful |
| soft | | romantic |
| | | upbeat |

## 3

- ▶ 4.1 Tell students that they're now going to listen to the music they listened to in Exercise 1 again and use the vocabulary from Exercise 2 to describe how the different pieces of music sound to them and how they make them feel. Encourage them to look at the vocabulary in the table in Exercise 2 as they're listening and then choose the words in it that come to mind for each track.

- Put students into pairs. They can then take it in turns to share their feelings about each piece of music and give their reaction to their partner's ideas. Encourage them to read the model conversation and use it to help them do this in a natural and interactive way.

### TEACHING TIP

**Spaced repetition**

Students are likely to forget a lot of the new vocabulary they've learned very quickly unless they keep returning to it. In this unit, students will frequently need to re-use the vocabulary for music and feelings that they've looked at in this section, so these occasions provide an ideal opportunity for reviewing and repeating it.

If spaced repetition isn't built into the unit that students are working on, however, you can test them on new vocabulary at intervals, e.g. by allocating two minutes at the end of the lesson to check which words students can remember from it. Put students into pairs, ask them to choose a word and describe it or say an example or synonym to their partner who has to say what they thing that word is. After looking at vocabulary for a specific topic in one lesson, e.g. music, you could challenge students to write down as many words or expressions as they can related to that topic in 30 seconds at the start of the next lesson.

## LISTENING  A traditional singer

## 4

- ▶ 4.2 Direct students to the Understanding accents box and check the meaning of *accent* (how you say the sounds in words). Elicit or explain the difference between *accent* and *dialect* (words which are only used by people in/from a specific geographical area) as some students may confuse the two terms.

- Tell students they're going to practise using strategies to understand unfamiliar accents by listening to Iarla Ó Lionáird, who they can see in the photo. Don't reveal that he's from Ireland, but ask students to consider which country sean-nós singing could be from, based on its name.

- Play the recording and ask students to listen out for words for countries or nationalities to help them identify which country sean-nós singing is from. They can then compare their answers in pairs before you check answers in class.

### Transcript

*I* = Iarla Ó Lionáird; *N* = narrator

**I:** My name is Iarla Ó Lionáird, and I'm an Irishman. I come from Cork – west Cork. And I'm a person who sings.

**N:** Ó Lionáird sings in a traditional style called sean-nós. He sings in Gaelic, which was Ó Lionáird's first language as a child. He was five years old before he learned English. Ó Lionáird was the eighth of twelve children. His mother and grandmother were also singers in the sean-nós style.

**I:** I remember my first day in school. Mrs McSweeney – Mrs Mac – was my teacher. I remember she lifted me up and she stood me on a desk, the first day I was ever in school, I was about five, and she said, 'sing'. It was almost as if there was shoes there waiting for me to put my feet into.

**N:** Ó Lionáird released his first of three solo albums in 1997. He is now a member of a group called The Gloaming. The group released its award-winning first album in 2014.

#### Answer
Ireland

## 5

- ▶ 4.2 Tell students that they're going to listen to the recording again and focus on some of the specific pieces of information that Iarla Ó Lionáird gives about his background and musical career. Have students read the sentences before they listen and speculate about whether they're true or false, based on what they can remember from their first listening.

- Play the recording and ask students to decide if the sentences are true or false. Check answers in class.

#### Answers
1 F   2 T   3 T   4 F

## 6

- ▶ 4.3 Students are now going to listen again and focus on which words are used in three example sentences taken from the recording.

- Ask students to read the sentences and predict the missing words. Then, play the recording and have them complete the sentences with the correct words. Ask students to compare their answers in pairs before checking answers in class.

#### Answers
1 first   2 up, on   3 about

### Extra activity

**Traditional music**

Ask students to think about what traditional music comes from their home country. If the students in one group come from several different countries, they could prepare a short presentation each about traditional music from their home country. If possible, they could play some examples of this music in their presentation, e.g. on their smartphones or computers. They then take it in turns to give their presentations in class and at the end of each one, the other students can use the vocabulary from Exercise 2 to comment on how the music presented sounds to them and how it makes them feel.

## Pronunciation /ŋ/

**7**

- ▶ 4.4 **Optional step.** Model and drill the pronunciation of the /ŋ/ sound.

- Play the recording and ask students to listen and notice where the /ŋ/ sound is in each word. With weaker students, you could stop the recording after each word and elicit which letters spell the /ŋ/ sound before moving on to the next one.

- Conduct whole-class feedback on where the /ŋ/ sounds are. Then, play the recording again and have students repeat the words they hear with the correct pronunciation of the /ŋ/ sounds.

| Answers |
|---|
| 1 si**ng**er  2 E**ng**lish  3 la**ng**uage |
| 4 waiti**ng**  5 award-winni**ng** |

> **TEACHING TIP**
>
> **The /ŋ/ sound**
>
> You make the /ŋ/ sound by curling your tongue up against the back of your mouth and letting the air come out of your nose. The technical term for the sound is *velar nasal* for this reason. The /ŋ/ sound is most frequently spelled as *ng*, in the words it's used in, e.g. *long, bring, morning*, but it can also be spelled as just 'n' when it is in the middle of a word, like *thank*. Ask students to be aware of where the /ŋ/ sound will need to be used in the words that they use during the Speaking section that follows.

## SPEAKING Talking about music

**8**

- ▶ 4.5 Ask students to read the conversation through once before they listen to it. Tell students to ignore the word choices on the right for the moment as they will focus on those in Exercise 9.

- Play the recording and ask students to read and listen to the conversation at the same time. Tell them to identify what the book is about.

- Check answers in class. Both *rock* and *gentle rock* would be acceptable answers. We can define *gentle rock* as rock music which is more rhythmic than rock music usually is and isn't as upbeat/lively as it usually is.

| Answer |
|---|
| (gentle) rock |

**9**

- Model the conversation that students have just listened to out loud with a student. Elicit that the word *stuff* is commonly used in British English to mean a general type of something. Then, have students work in pairs to practise the conversation together. Make sure they alternate between A and B roles.

- Have students practise the conversation again using the words on the right instead of the words in bold in the conversation.

**10**

- Put students into pairs and ask them to think of a band or singer they like and a reason why they like them. Every student should be able to think of at least one band or singer that they like or liked in the past. If time allows, students could talk about several bands and singers they like with their partner.

- Direct students to the example sentence and have them use it as a model to tell their partner who they like and why.

- Circulate and monitor students while they're talking to each other and give them feedback when they've finished.

▶ Set Workbook pages 28 and 29 for homework.

▶ Photocopiable communicative activity 4.1. Go to page 169 for further practice of music vocabulary. The teaching notes are on page 190.

## 4.2 Getting into a good rhythm

### GRAMMAR Countable and uncountable nouns

**1**

- ▶ 4.6 Direct students to the infographic and ask them to scan the text in it for *classical music*, so they can find the answer to the question. Check answers in class.

- **Optional step.** Ask students whether they agree that it's good to listen to classical music while studying and going to sleep and whether they ever do this. If they don't, ask them what type of music they like to listen to while they're doing these things.

#### Answer

while studying and when you're trying to get to sleep

### 2

- ▶ 4.7 Tell students that they're now going to listen to a music expert talking about the best music to listen to while studying. Ask students to predict what the expert will say and then have them read the phrases.
- Play the recording and ask students to listen out for the options and circle the correct one. Then, have them compare their answers in pairs before checking answers in class.
- **Optional step**. Elicit whether students agree or disagree with the expert's opinions and have them give reasons for their point of view.

#### Transcript

*Many students listen to music when they study. Is this a good idea? Well, it depends on what they listen to. Songs without lyrics are generally OK, such as classical music. Songs with lyrics can distract you from studying, so it's best to avoid those. Some research also suggests that we study better when we listen to songs we like. Songs that we like help us to relax. Songs we dislike are going to annoy and distract us from our studies. So it may be best to listen to your favourite album rather than the radio.*

#### Answers

1 without  2 like  3 an album

### 3

- Ask students to read the example sentences and identify the difference between countable and uncountable nouns, and which words are examples of each one. Students may also find it helpful to think of countable nouns as nouns which you can put a number in front of, e.g. *two students*, and uncountable nouns as nouns which you can't put a number in front of, e.g. *money*.
- Students can check their answers and overall understanding of how to use countable and uncountable nouns by turning to the Grammar summary on page 141.
- If you feel that students need more controlled practice before continuing, they could do the exercises in the Grammar summary. Otherwise, you could continue on to Exercise 4 in the unit and set the Grammar summary exercises for homework.

#### Answers

a countable  b uncountable  c countable
d uncountable

#### Answers to Grammar summary exercises

**1**

1 a few  2 a lot of  3 much  4 some  5 many

**2**

1 some  2 any  3 a lot of  4 much  5 many, a few

> **TEACHING TIP**
>
> **Both countable and uncountable**
>
> If you have a group of stronger students, you could draw their attention to the fact that some nouns can be both countable and uncountable. These are usually words that can have two different meanings and they have one meaning when they're used as a countable noun and another one when they're used as an uncountable noun. Some common examples include: *light* (a light (C) and light from the sun (U)); *room* (a room in a building (C) or the synonym for *space* (U)); *hair* (a hair (C) and hair on your whole head (U)) and *paper* (a paper (C) and paper as a material (U)). You could give students some example sentences which include either the countable or uncountable version of the nouns above and ask them to identify which type of noun is being used in each one. Or, for an extra challenge, ask students to write these sentences themselves and then exchange them with a partner who then identifies which type of noun their partner has used in each one.

### 4

- Have students read the words and put them into the correct columns. Make sure they're aware that some of the words can be used with both types of nouns and they should put these in the *C/U* column. Encourage students to think of some examples of how the words in the box could be used in sentences or questions if they're unsure about how to categorize them, e.g. *How many CDs do you have?*
- Have students compare their answers in pairs before you check answers in class.

#### Answers

| C | U | C/U |
|---|---|---|
| a few | a little | any |
| many | much | a lot of |
|  |  | some |

### Pronunciation Stress with quantifiers

### 5

- ▶ 4.8 Check the meaning of *quantifier* (a word which tells you how much/many of something there is/are). You could make this slightly easier for students by telling them that the stress falls on different words in each of the two examples.

4  Music  45

- Play the recording and have students read the sentences while they listen and identify the words that are stressed in each one. Have students compare their answers in pairs before you check answers in class. Elicit or explain that in the longer sentences the focus is on the thing that you're giving the quantity of, e.g. *music, CDs*, and that's why these words are stressed, whereas in the shorter sentences, the focus is on the quantity of the thing.
- Put students into pairs to practise saying the sentence pairs with the correct word stress.

### Answers
1 a I have a lot of <u>music</u>.
  b I have a <u>lot</u>.
2 a We only have a few <u>CDs</u>.
  b We only have a <u>few</u>.
3 a I don't listen to any <u>jazz music</u>.
  b I don't listen to <u>any</u>.

## LANGUAGE FOCUS  Talking about quantity

### 6
- ▶ 4.9  Ask students to read the Language focus box and to notice how quantifiers are used. Draw students' attention to the use of *were* in the sentences with countable nouns, which contrasts with the use of *was* in the equivalent sentences with uncountable nouns. Elicit that the reason for this is that countable nouns have plural forms, but uncountable nouns only have singular forms.
- Students can check overall understanding of the language focus by turning to the Grammar summary on page 142.
- If you feel that students need more controlled practice before continuing, they could do the exercises in the Grammar summary. Otherwise, you could continue on to Exercise 7 in the unit and set the Grammar summary exercises for homework.

### Answers to Grammar summary exercises
**1**
1 too much   2 too   3 too many   4 How much
5 too many   6 How many

**2**
1 much   2 any   3 lots, a little   4 much   5 a few, too much   6 much, a little

### 7
- Ask students to look at the sentences and identify whether they're positive statements, negative statements or questions and whether they contain countable or uncountable nouns. Then, have them identify the correct option in each one. Tell students to refer back to the examples in the Language focus box to help them choose the correct options if they need to.
- Students can compare their answers in pairs before you check answers in class.

### Answers
1 any, some   2 much, many   3 Was, few

### 8
- ▶ 4.10  Have students read the text about the benefits of listening to classical music all the way through and then focus on each pair of options and choose the correct one. Paying attention to the type of noun that each quantifier refers to should help them do this.
- Have students compare their answers in pairs before playing the recording so they can check them.

### Answers
1 many   2 little   3 many   4 many   5 much   6 much

### 9
- Tell students to read the sentences and focus on the part of it which contains a quantifier. They can then identify the mistake in the use of the quantifier in each sentence and correct it. Weaker students could do this in pairs.
- Check answers in class.

### Answers
1 I love this band, but they don't do many live concer**ts** these days.
2 The performer stopped because there was too ~~many~~ **much** noise coming from the crowd.
3 I was amazed by how ~~few~~ **little** equipment the band had on stage.
4 After the band finished their last song, there ~~were~~ **was** a lot of applause.

### Extra activity

#### What's in your fridge?
For freer practice of using countable and uncountable nouns, and quantifiers in a real-world context:
- Put students into pairs and ask them to make a list of eight food or drink items they currently have in their fridge at home. Encourage them to think of a mixture of countable and uncountable nouns so that they have at least three examples of each.
- They then look at each other's lists and take it in turns to ask their partner questions about the quantity of each item using: *How much ... ?* or *How many ... ?* They can then ask their partner if they have any of the items that they have in their fridge using: *Do you have any ... ?*
- Monitor students' conversations and give them feedback on how accurately they used countable and uncountable nouns, and quantifiers when they've finished.

## SPEAKING  Discussing musical preferences

### 10  21st CENTURY OUTCOMES

**Listen effectively to decipher meaning, including knowledge, values, attitudes and intentions**

- Ask students to read the questions and decide what their own answers to them are. They may want or need to refer back to the list of musical genres given in **4.1** Exercise 1 to help them do this.

- Put students into pairs and have them take it in turns to ask and answer the questions. In order to fulfil the 21st CENTURY OUTCOMES, students need to listen to the information their partner tells them carefully and note down anything interesting that they learn from them during their discussion.

- Direct students to the model question and ask them to use it to ask each other the questions and share a piece of interesting information they heard in response to each one.

- **Optional step**. Tell students to give a reason why they think a certain type of music is the best one for each activity and/or bring in their own experiences, e.g. *I listened to a lot of electronic music while I studied for my last exams at school and it helped me to concentrate*. They can also respond to each other's answers by showing interest and/or asking follow-up questions, e.g. *What's your favourite rock band?*

- Monitor students and give them feedback on how successfully they've used quantifiers and vocabulary for musical genres when they've finished.

▶ Set Workbook pages 30 and 31 for homework.

## 4.3  It's our song

### READING  Music and the brain

**1**

- ▶ 4.11  Tell students they're now going to listen to Johannes Brahms' Hungarian Dance No. 5. Ask students if they've heard this piece of music or other music by Brahms before. Then, play the recording and have students note down adjectives which describe how the music makes them feel. They may find it helpful to refer back to the adjectives in **4.1** Exercise 2 as they listen.

- Ask students to compare their notes in pairs.

| Answers |
|---|
| Students' own answers. |

### Understanding gist

**2**

- ▶ 4.12  Ask students to read the four questions and check the meaning of the verb *affect* (to have an effect on). Then, give them 20 or 30 seconds to scan the article and identify the two questions that it discusses.

- Ask students to compare their answers in pairs before you check answers in class.

| Answers |
|---|
| a, d |

### Understanding details

**3**

- Students are now going to focus on understanding some of the details given in the article. Ask them to read the questions and answer options, and then read the article all the way through and focus on finding information about the things the questions refer to. They can then circle their answers.

- Point out the glossary at the bottom of the text and tell students to refer to it as they read or to look at the words and definitions before they start reading.

- Check answers in class.

| Answers |
|---|
| 1 b   2 a   3 b   4 a   5 a |

### Understanding vocabulary

**4**

- Ask students to read the sentences. They can then look back at the words in bold in the article and use them to complete the sentences. If students are unsure about the meaning of any of the items in bold, they may find it helpful to look at how the words are used in context in the article. Students can also look at the words that come before and after the gaps and identify which type of word (verb, noun or adjective) goes in them.

- Check answers in class.

| Answers |
|---|
| 1 research   2 chemicals   3 registered |
| 4 unfamiliar   5 analysed |

**5**

- Put students into pairs and have them read and discuss the questions. Draw their attention to the phrases *... has had an effect on me* and *... has affected me*, elicit that they have the same meaning and encourage students to use them during their conversations.

- Monitor students' discussions and give them feedback when they've finished.

▶ Set Workbook pages 32 and 33 for homework.

## 4.4 Why I take the piano on the road ... and in the air

**TEDTALKS**

**1**

- Tell students that they're now going to watch a TED Talk by Daria van den Bercken, who they can see in the photo. Before students read the summary of the talk, direct them to the photo of van den Bercken playing her piano in the air. Ask them what their reaction to this photo is and have them speculate about why anyone would decide to play their piano in the air.

- Have students read the summary of the talk and choose the correct options in the definitions. If students are unsure about which words to match with which items, encourage them to use deduction or simply have a guess.

- Students can compare their answers in pairs before you check answers in class. Draw students' attention to the pronunciation of *awe* /ɔː/ and *unprejudiced* /ˌʌnˈpredʒʊdɪst/ as they may find these challenging.

> **Answers**
> 1 admire   2 on a beautiful mountain   3 an open

**2**

- ▶ 4.13 Tell students that they're now going to listen to van den Bercken playing two pieces of music and identify which of the two options best describes how each piece sounds. Check the meaning of *melancholic* (feeling sadness).

- Play the recording and ask students to listen and circle the correct options. Students can then check answers in pairs before you check answers in class.

> **Answers**
> Piece 1: a   Piece 2: a

**3**

- ▶ 4.14 Tell students that they're now going to watch Part 1 of van den Bercken's talk, in which she talks about a discovery of new music she made. You may want to let students know before they watch that this section of the talk also contains a small amount of spoken Dutch because this is van den Bercken's first language.

- Ask students to read the questions and answer options. Then, play Part 1 and tell students to focus on understanding the gist of what the speaker is saying so they can answer the questions. Check answers in class.

**Transcript**

*Recently, I flew over a crowd of thousands of people in Brazil, playing music by George Frideric Handel. I also drove along the streets of Amsterdam, again playing music by this same composer. Let's take a look.*

*[Music: George Frideric Handel, 'Allegro'. Performed by Daria van den Bercken.]*

*[Video] Daria van den Bercken: I live there on the third floor. [In Dutch] I live there on the corner. I actually live there, around the corner ... and you'd be really welcome.*

*Man: [In Dutch] Does that sound like fun?*

*Child: [In Dutch] Yes!*

*Daria van den Bercken: All this was a real magical experience for hundreds of reasons. Now you may ask, why have I done these things? They're not really typical for a musician's day-to-day life. Well, I did it because I fell in love with the music and I wanted to share it with as many people as possible.*

*It started a couple of years ago. I was sitting at home on the couch with the flu and browsing the Internet a little, when I found out that Handel had written works for the keyboard. Well, I was surprised. I did not know this. So I downloaded the sheet music and started playing. And what happened next was that I entered this state of pure, unprejudiced amazement. It was an experience of being totally in awe of the music, and I had not felt that in a long time. It might be easier to relate to this when you hear it. The first piece that I played through started like this. [Music] Well, this sounds very melancholic, doesn't it? And I turned the page and what came next was this. [Music] Well, this sounds very energetic, doesn't it? So within a couple of minutes, and the piece isn't even finished yet, I experienced two very contrasting characters: beautiful melancholy and sheer energy. And I consider these two elements to be vital human expressions. And the purity of the music makes you hear it very effectively.*

> **Answers**
> 1 a   2 b

**4**

- ▶ 4.15 Tell students that they're now going to watch Part 2 of the talk, in which van den Bercken talks about how children in two different age groups react to her music.

- Check the meaning of *claim* (here: a statement that something is true), *willing* (ready or prepared to do something) and *to get someone to do something* (to do something that makes someone do it). Then, direct them to the table and have them read the list of claims. Ask students to think about the things they know about 7- and 8-year-olds and 11- and 12-year-olds and use this to predict which statements van den Bercken will make about each of these groups.

48   4   Music

- Then, play Part 2 of the talk and ask students to identify the age group that each statement describes. Check answers in class.

## Transcript

*I've given a lot of children's concerts for children of seven and eight years old, and whatever I play, whether it's Bach, Beethoven, even Stockhausen, or some jazzy music, they are open to hear it, really willing to listen, and they are comfortable doing so. And when classes come in with children who are just a few years older, eleven, twelve, I felt that I sometimes already had trouble in reaching them like that. The complexity of the music does become an issue, and actually the opinions of others – parents, friends, media – they start to count. But the young ones, they don't question their own opinion. They are in this constant state of wonder, and I do firmly believe that we can keep listening like these seven-year-old children, even when growing up. And that is why I have played not only in the concert hall, but also on the street, online, in the air: to feel that state of wonder, to truly listen, and to listen without prejudice. And I'd like to invite you to do so now. [music]*

*Thank you.*

> **Answers**
>
> 1 7- and 8-year-olds   2 11- and 12-year-olds
> 3 11- and 12-year-olds   4 7- and 8-year-olds

## CREATIVE THINKING

### 5   21st CENTURY OUTCOMES

***Develop, implement and communicate new ideas to others effectively***

- Tell students that in this activity the creative thinking skill they'll be using is the ability to think of a way of sharing a passion with other people.

- Give students a few minutes to choose a passion and brainstorm their ideas for ways of sharing it. If students say that they aren't passionate about anything, ask them to simply think of something that they like doing. After they've finished brainstorming, ask students to choose the best idea and make some more detailed notes on it.

- Then, put students into pairs and have them present their ideas to each other and ask and answer questions about them. In order to fulfil the 21st CENTURY OUTCOMES, students need to show that they've thought of an original idea and to effectively communicate what it is to their partner so that he/she understands what it involves. Conduct whole-class feedback on students' ideas.

## VOCABULARY IN CONTEXT

### 6

- ▶ 4.16  Play the clips from the TED Talk. When each multiple-choice question appears, pause the clip so that students can choose the correct definition. Discourage the more confident students from always giving the answer by asking students to raise their hand if they think they know.

### Transcript and subtitles

*1 Now you may ask, why have I done these things? They're not really typical for a musician's **day-to-day** life.*

What does **day-to-day** mean?
  a *usual*
  b *difficult*
  c *early*

*2 It started **a couple of** years ago.*

How many is **a couple of**?
  a *lots*
  b *four or five*
  c *about two*

*3 … they are open to hear it, really willing to listen, and they are **comfortable** doing so.*

If you are **comfortable** doing something, you are _____.
  a *relaxed about it*
  b *sitting down*
  c *unsure about it*

*4 The complexity of the music does become an issue, and actually the opinions of others – parents, friends, media – they start to **count**.*

What does **count** mean?
  a *say numbers*
  b *become important*
  c *become unimportant*

*5 They are in this constant state of wonder, and I do **firmly** believe that we can keep listening like these seven-year-old children, even when growing up.*

If you **firmly** believe something, you _____ believe it.
  a *strongly*
  b *sometimes*
  c *want to*

> **Answers**
>
> 1 a   2 c   3 a   4 b   5 a

### 7

- Students are now going to use two of the terms they looked at in Exercise 6 – *comfortable* and *to count* – to discuss their opinions about issues related to work and work-life balance.

- Put students into pairs and ask them to say their own answers to the questions, giving as much detail as they can. Circulate and monitor students' discussions and give them feedback when they've finished.

## PRESENTATION SKILLS Providing background information

### 8

- ▶ 4.17 Direct students to the Presentation skills box and check the meaning of *background information* (information about what has happened (to someone) up to now).

- **Optional step.** Ask students what background information they've given about themselves in presentations and what they've heard other presenters give about themselves – can they think of any unusual or surprising information presenters have given?

- Ask students to read the three pieces of information and check the meaning of *composer* (a person who writes music). Then play the clip and ask students to identify the piece of information that van den Bercken provides.

> **Answer**
> b

### 9

- ▶ 4.18 Ask students to read the names of the speakers whose TED Talks they watched in Units 2 and 3 respectively and the three options. Ask students to think back to these speakers' TED Talks and remember which piece of background information each speaker gave. Then, play the clip and have students match the speakers with the pieces of information. Make sure students are aware that one option is extra.

- Ask students to compare their answers in pairs before you check answers in pairs.

> **Answers**
> 1 b   2 c

### 10

- Put students into small groups (three to four students). Ask them to discuss what background information they would include in a presentation about the passion they thought of in Exercise 5. Encourage them to consider what background information would be specifically relevant to a presentation about the passion they chose.

- **Optional step.** Students could then prepare an introduction to the talk in which they give their background information and take it in turns to present it to the rest of the group, who could then give them feedback.

- Conduct whole-class feedback on what background information students decided they should include.

▶ Set Workbook page 34 for homework.

## 4.5 Musical choices

### COMMUNICATE Desert island discs

#### Extra activity

#### Listening to Desert Island Discs

Tell students that the title of this section – Desert island discs – refers to a long-running British radio programme with the same name that's broadcast on BBC Radio 4. In this programme, famous and distinguished guests from around the world choose eight records that they would like to take to a desert island with them and introduce each one while talking about their lives.

Ask students to search for the programme's website online by googling 'Desert island discs' and then choose an episode with a person they are interested in. Tell students to be aware of the fact that they may find some of the natural speech difficult to understand, but they should focus on listening for gist. They can use this as an opportunity to hear different accents as the host has a Scottish accent and the guests have a range of different accents.

### 1

- Check the meaning of *desert island* (an island far away from other countries where there's no civilization). Then, ask students to choose four songs that they would like to take with them to listen to on a desert island and write them in the table.

### 2

- Ask students to read the questions and prepare answers to them for each song on the list in Exercise 1. If time is short, students could just prepare answers for one of the songs. If they need to, have students do some research online to find out any information they don't already know. Students can also refer back to **4.1** to remind themselves of the vocabulary they can use to describe the songs.

### 3   21st CENTURY OUTCOMES

*Respond open-mindedly to different ideas and values*

- Put students into pairs and have them take it in turns to ask and answer the questions from Exercise 2 about the songs they chose. In order to fulfil the 21st CENTURY OUTCOMES, students also need to show that they're willing to accept musical preferences that are different to their own by showing interest in what their partner tells them and asking follow-up questions to find out more information about their partner's song choices.

- Monitor students' interviews and give them feedback on how successfully and accurately they communicated when they've finished.

### 4

- It may be more appropriate for students to listen to the songs their partner from Exercise 3 chose as a self-study task. Students could watch the videos for the songs online or listen to previews of them in online music stores.

- Direct students to the Describing music box and check the meaning of *remind* (to make someone remember something that happened earlier). Ask students to use the phrases in the Describing music box to talk about the songs.
- **Optional step**. Encourage students to react to what their partner says, e.g. by agreeing or disagreeing with them (*I agree., I'm not sure about that*.), saying that they understand what their partner means (*I know what you mean*.) or giving an example of something from the song that their partner is describing (*That's the sound of African drums*.) or an explanation of it (*That's because the band used a sample from that song*.).

## WRITING  Describing a favourite song

### 5

- Ask students to choose another song that they really like and think about how it makes them feel and why they like it. Ask students if the song reminds them of anything or anyone special in their lives. Then, ask students to read the example text about a favourite song and use it as a model to write their own text.
- Circulate and monitor while students are writing, offering assistance and feedback where appropriate.

> **Answers**
> Students' own answers.

▶ Set Workbook page 35 for homework.

▶ Photocopiable communicative activity 4.2. Go to page 170 for further practice of countable and uncountable nouns, talking about quantity and vocabulary from Unit 4. The teaching notes are on page 191.

# 5 Good design

**UNIT AT A GLANCE**

**THEME:** Design
**VOCABULARY:** Design elements
**LISTENING:** A designer's advice
**SPEAKING:** Talking about design, Describing a coat of arms
**GRAMMAR:** Prepositions and adverbs of place
**PRONUNCIATION:** Sound and spelling, Word linking
**READING:** Chicago's much-loved flag
**TED TALK:** *The worst-designed thing you've never noticed*. In this TED Talk, Roman Mars talks about how to design a great flag.
**PRESENTATION SKILLS:** Numbering key points
**WRITING:** Describing your country's flag

## WARM UP

- Books open. Draw students' attention to the unit title, the photo and the caption on page 51. Make sure students are aware that when we use the word *design*, we mean how visual elements are put together to create a specific look.

- Put students into pairs or small groups (three to four students) to discuss the questions.

- **Question 1**. Direct students to the photo of a stairwell at Rivers Academy, which is a secondary school in London, and ask students how similar to their own secondary school it looks. Then, ask students to look at the photo more closely, focusing on the design, and decide whether or not they like it and why.

- **Question 2**. Bring in students' own experiences by asking them to think of buildings where they've worked or studied, how well-designed these buildings are/were and what effect their design had on them. Tell students to share any specific examples of good or bad design and the positive or negative effects it had on them.

- **Question 3**. Ask students to think of buildings they've enjoyed being in, such as schools, religious buildings, shopping centres, stadiums, theatres, and consider whether the design of these buildings made them enjoy being there.

## 5.1 Does it go?

### VOCABULARY Design elements

**1**

- Have students read the names of the categories on the left and look up the meanings of any words they don't already know – *texture* may be unfamiliar, for example. Then, ask them to read the words in each line and identify the one which doesn't belong in each category. Again, students can look up the meaning of any unfamiliar words and note down those they want to remember for future use.

- Check answers in class.

| Answers |
|---|
| 1 short  2 happy  3 pale  4 orange  5 empty  6 tall |

**2**

- Put students into pairs and ask them to think of and write in one more word for each category. They may need to use a dictionary to help them.

- **Optional step**. Thinking of another word to describe texture may prove to be challenging, in which case you could suggest that students think of materials or objects they know which have an interesting texture and then think of a word that could be used to describe it, e.g. *woollen* (an item of clothing or a blanket made of wool), *fluffy* (a fluffy toy) or *scratchy* (a metal dish scourer).

- Conduct whole-class feedback on students' additional words and check that they're able to pronounce them correctly.

| Answers |
|---|
| Students' own answers. |

### Pronunciation Sound and spelling

**3**

- ▶5.1 Students are now going to focus on the pronunciation of some of the vocabulary items from Exercise 1.

- Play the recording and ask students to listen and read the words and notice how the underlined letters in the words in each pair are pronounced differently. Play the recording more than once if necessary.

- Conduct whole-class feedback and elicit the sounds that are used to say the underlined letters.

**4**

- Direct students to the photo of a painted car at the top of page 52 and ask them to spend about a minute looking closely at it. Then, have them look back at the words from Exercise 1, including the extra words that they added, and choose the ones that could be used to describe the car.

- Then, put students into pairs to share the words they've chosen and discuss whether they like the car, giving reasons. Direct students to the model conversation and ask them to interact with their partner in the same way, saying whether they agree or disagree with their partner's opinion.
- Conduct whole-class feedback on the words students choose and the reasons why they like or dislike the car.

### Extra activity

### Writing a design review

Ask students to write a review of the car in the photo on page 52 as an example of design, based on what they discussed in their conversations. Tell them to include a description of the car, using the relevant design vocabulary, their opinion of it and whether they would recommend going to the exhibition that this car is at, giving reasons.

## LISTENING  A designer's advice

### 5

- ▶ 5.2  Direct students to the Listening for changes in topic box. Elicit or explain that all the phrases in the box for introducing a new topic have the same meaning, but knowing a range of phrases can help you make what you say or write more interesting.
- Tell students that they're going to listen to an interior designer called Sarah Lafferty, who they can see in the photo, talking about the work she does and her design philosophy. Ask students to read the quotation and find out if students know who William Morris is.
- Play the recording and ask students to listen for the quotation and complete it with one word in each gap.
- Students can then compare their answers in pairs before you check answers in class.

### Transcript

*I've been an interior designer now for about sixteen years. My mother and father were both architects so it was always likely that I'd have a career in design. I enjoyed art a lot in school, and I studied textile design when I was at university. I really learned a lot there, not just about textiles, but about design in general.*

*Every home I design is very different because every client is unique. I spend a lot of time talking with clients and learning about their personal needs and tastes. I want the finished space to reflect them as individuals, not myself as a designer.*

*There is a quote from a famous British designer called William Morris which I use as a starting point for every project. He said, 'Have nothing in your houses that you do not know to be useful or believe to be beautiful.' I think it's really helpful to think about interior design in terms of those two factors. Everything in your home should be either useful, or beautiful. If it isn't either, it shouldn't be there! And, in regard to ideas about what's beautiful, it's really important to respect and value your client's personal taste.*

### Answers
useful, beautiful

### Background information

### William Morris

William Morris was a designer from England who lived in the 19th century. During his lifetime he was well known for his poetry, but after his death he was also recognized as one of the most influential designers in Victorian England. Morris was also a leading figure in the Arts and Crafts movement, which aspired to a return to a simpler pre-industrial age in life and in art. His company, Morris & Co, is still selling fabric and wallpaper today.

### 6

- ▶ 5.2  Ask students to read the sentences, and then play the recording and ask them to listen and circle the correct options.
- Students then compare their answers in pairs before you check answers in class.

### Answers
1 architects   2 textile   3 clients'

### Extra activity

### Working as an interior designer

Ask students whether they'd like to be an interior designer and say why/why not. Find out what they think the good and bad parts of this job would be.

### 7

- Ask students to re-read the quotation in Exercise 5 and then put them into pairs to discuss the question. They may find it helpful to refer back to the vocabulary in Exercise 1.
- Conduct whole-class feedback on students' ideas.

## SPEAKING  Talking about design

### 8

- ▶ 5.3  Ask students to read the conversation before they listen. Check the meaning of *stripes* (rectangular blocks of colour that run horizontally or vertically). Tell them to ignore the word choices on the right for the moment as they will focus on those in Exercise 9.
- Play the recording and ask students to read and listen to the conversation at the same time. Have them compare their answers in pairs before checking answers in class.

### Answer
probably not

5  Good design   53

**9**

- Model the conversation that students have just listened to aloud with a student. Then, have students work in pairs to practise the conversation together. Make sure they alternate between A and B roles.
- Have students practise the conversation again using the words on the right instead of the words in bold in the conversation.

**10  21st CENTURY OUTCOMES**

*Articulate thoughts and ideas effectively using oral, written and nonverbal communication skills in a variety of forms and contexts*

- Put students into pairs. Have them read the model conversation and notice the phrases for giving an opinion (*I like ...*, *I think ...*) and the phrase for agreeing (*I agree*). Then, ask them to turn to page 161, look at the two photos of unusual furniture and say whether they like or dislike them and why. In order to fulfil the 21st CENTURY OUTCOMES, students should be able to effectively communicate their thoughts about the furniture to their partner. Encourage them to re-use the vocabulary for design that they've learned.
- Circulate and monitor students while they're talking to each other and give them feedback when they've finished.

▶ Set Workbook pages 36 and 37 for homework.

▶ Photocopiable communicative activity 5.1. Go to page 171 for further practice of design elements vocabulary and talking about design. The teaching notes are on page 191.

## 5.2 Signs of the times

### GRAMMAR Prepositions and adverbs of place

**1**

- ▶ 5.4 Direct students to the infographic. Ask whether they've seen coats of arms before and, if so, where they've seen them. Find out if students know what their family's coat of arms is. Then, have them look at the example coat of arms and find the answer to the question in the text.
- Check answers in class and elicit or explain that a *battle* is a single fight between two armies which usually takes place over a period of a few days.

| Answer |
|---|
| to establish identity in battle |

**2**

- ▶ 5.5 Tell students that they're now going to listen to someone explaining the different parts of the coat of arms labelled in the infographic.

- Play the recording and tell students to listen for the information in the sentences and circle the correct options. Check answers in class.

**Transcript**

*Let me explain to you a little more about three of the main features of a coat of arms.*

*One of the first things people notice is the motto. It's a very common feature, but some coats of arms do not have it. This motto is in Latin. In English, it means, 'To be, rather than to seem'. The motto here is above the crest, but sometimes the motto appears below the shield.*

*The supporters are also a key element. Supporters are usually animals, but they can also be people. The two supporters can also be different – for example, in this coat of arms, you can see a unicorn and a lion.*

*And then, of course, there's the shield. The design on the shield is very important. The different symbols that are used all have meaning. Even the shape of the shield – which can vary – carries some kind of meaning.*

| Answers |
|---|
| 1 Not all   2 below   3 usually   4 has |

**3**

> **TEACHING TIP**
>
> **Differentiating between prepositions of place and adverbs of place**
>
> Students will most likely not know the difference between a preposition of place and an adverb of place. Words which describe where something is can be used as either a preposition of place or an adverb of place – these aren't two different sets of words.
>
> Tell students they can tell how a word is being used by looking at what comes after it in a sentence. If the word is followed by a noun that answers a question, such as *what? where? when? who?* the word is a preposition of place because it has an object (the noun that follows it), e.g. *She walked on water*. However, when the preposition isn't followed by an object because the answer to questions such as *what? where? when? who?* is clear from the context, the word describing place is an adverb of place, e.g. *She walked across*.

- ▶ 5.6 Ask students to read and listen to the example sentences and notice how the words in bold are used in them and what comes after them (if anything).
- Students can check their answers and overall understanding of *should* and *shouldn't* by turning to the Grammar summary on page 143.

54   5   Good design

- If you feel that students need more controlled practice before continuing, they could do the exercises in the Grammar summary. Otherwise, you could continue on to Exercise 4 in the unit and set the Grammar summary exercises for homework

> **Answers**
> a 1, 2, 4
> b 3
> c a noun

> **Answers to Grammar summary exercise**
>
> **1**
>
> 1 in front of   2 behind   3 Above   4 on the left
> 5 on   6 on the right   7 on   8 Below   9 Behind
> 10 on the right of   11 on top of   12 below
>
> **2**
>
> 1 ✗ At **the** top of the tower I can see a black bird.
> 2 ✓
> 3 ✗ 'Where is the mirror?' 'It's behind ~~of~~ the piano.'
> 4 ✗ The artist's name is at the bottom **of** the painting.
> 5 ✓

**EXTRA INFORMATION**

**1**

1 In the foreground
2 In the middle (of the picture)
3 In the top right corner
4 In the background
5 In the bottom left corner

**2**

1 across   2 opposite   3 in front of   4 through   5 at
6 over

**4**

- Ask students to complete the sentences. They will need to refer back to the infographic to do this. Make sure students are aware that they may need to add *of* after the words in the box, but tell them to be careful not to overuse it.
- Check answers in class.

> **Answers**
> 1 on the left of   2 at the bottom   3 in the shape of
> 4 on top of   5 in the middle of   6 around
> 7 in front of   8 above

**5**

- Ask students to read the sentences and try to see the thing(s) being described in their mind's eye. They can then refer back to the prepositions and adverbs of place in Exercise 4 and the Grammar box to help them complete the sentences.

In order to complete sentence 4, students will need to know that people in Britain drive on the left side of the road.
- Have students compare their answers in pairs before you check answers in class.

> **Answers**
> 1 behind   2 at the top of / in the middle of, below
> 3 in front of   4 on the left of

**Pronunciation** Word linking

**6**

- ▶ 5.7   Play the recording and ask students to read the sentences as they listen and notice how the linked words sound. Play the recording more than once if necessary.
- Then, play the recording again and have students listen and repeat the sentences with the same word linking they hear in it.

> **TEACHING TIP**
>
> **Word linking**
>
> Tell students that it's normal for native speakers of English to link (or connect) words when they speak and this is usually done by linking a consonant at the end of one word with the vowel at the start of the word that follows it. Native speakers do this because it enables them to speak more quickly and it makes their speech 'flow' better.
>
> Students can use this knowledge to help them understand which words someone is saying as this will improve their aural comprehension skills. It's less important that students are able to reproduce the word linking themselves, especially at this level.

**7**

- ▶ 5.8   Ask students to read the text about road signs all the way through first with the aim of understanding its main message. Then, have them circle the correct words. Tell students to look carefully at the traffic light sign in the photo as this will help them.
- Check answers in class.

> **Answers**
> 1 in   2 around   3 bottom   4 inside   5 at   6 in   7 on

**8**

- Have students look at the three road signs from around the world. Ask students which country they think each one is from and whether they've seen any of them before. Then, ask them to read the three texts and identify and correct the mistake in each one. Looking at the photo of the sign should help them do this. Tell students that all of the mistakes are with the use of prepositions of place.

**5   Good design**

- Have students compare their answers in pairs before checking answers in class.

> **Answers**
> 1 ~~behind~~ **around** the circle   2 ~~on~~ **in** the shape of
> 3 ~~below~~ **on** it

### Extra activity

**Describing a road sign**

Ask students to think of a road sign that is used in their home country, ideally this would be a road sign which is only used in their country. In pairs, students either write a description of the road sign and give it to their partner to read or give a spoken description of it to a partner. Tell them to use the texts in Exercise 8 as models and make sure that they don't write or say what the road sign's purpose is or what it's for. Students then guess what their partner's road sign is for. They may need to look up some words in a dictionary to help them find the right English words to describe what the signs are for.

## SPEAKING   Describing a coat of arms

**9**

- Tell students to look back at the infographic on page 54 and notice the different elements that a coat of arms consists of. They can then take some time to think about what these elements would be in their coat of arms.

- **Optional step.** If students aren't very familiar with coats of arms and what types of pictures, symbols and words they usually contain, they could do an online image search for coats of arms to give them some ideas.

- Students then design their coats of arms individually. Make sure that each student's coat of arms includes at least some of the design elements in the infographic and a motto. Also, tell students not to show their design to anyone else at this stage.

**10**   **21st CENTURY OUTCOMES**

*Use communication for a range of purposes (e.g. to inform, instruct, motivate and persuade)*

- Put students into groups of three or four students. Have them take it in turns to describe the coat of arms they designed and to draw the coats of arms that they hear the other members of their group describing. In order to fulfil the 21st CENTURY OUTCOMES, students should be able to effectively instruct their partner to draw the coat of arms, so that the version their partner draws is very similar to or the same as the original. If time is short, students could do this activity in pairs instead.

- Weaker students will need some time to prepare their descriptions, referring back to the vocabulary for the elements of coats of arms in the infographic and the examples of prepositions and adverbs of place in the Grammar box and Exercise 4.

- Monitor students so you can give them feedback on their descriptions at the end of Exercise 11.

**11**

- Students compare the coats of arms that they drew after listening to the other group members' descriptions with the original versions. They can then evaluate how accurately and effectively they described them.

- Give students the feedback you noted down during Exercise 10.

▶ Set Workbook pages 38 and 39 for homework.
▶ Photocopiable communicative activity 5.2. Go to page 172 for further practice of prepositions of place and describing a coat of arms. The teaching notes are on page 192.

## 5.3 Symbol of a city

**READING**   Chicago's much-loved flag

**1**

- **Optional step.** Bring in students' own experiences by asking them if they've ever been to Chicago in the USA and find out what they already know about the city. If they have been to Chicago, ask them if and where they saw the city's flag while they were there.

- Direct students to the photo on page 57 and draw their attention to the Chicago flag. Ask them to look closely at the flag and then read the third paragraph of the article to identify the meaning of the three parts of the Chicago flag.

- Check answers in class. Elicit or explain that it's the Chicago River that runs through the centre of Chicago, giving the city its name, and Lake Michigan which borders it.

> **Answers**
> 1 three Chicago neighbourhoods   2 the river and the lake   3 important events in Chicago's history

### Understanding main ideas

**2**

- ▶ 5.9  Have students read the sentences and then go through the whole article with the objective of understanding its gist and identifying the main idea in it.

- Students can compare their answers in pairs before you check answers in class.

> **Answer**
> a

**56**   **5   Good design**

## Understanding supporting quotes

### 3

• Check the meaning of *quote* (something that someone has said – usually one or two sentences – which is frequently repeated and re-used). A *supporting quote* is, therefore, information which shows that a quote is true.

• Have students scan the text for the quotes from the three people (1–3). Advise students to read the quotes two or three times to make sure that they understand them. They can then match the people with the statements that have the same meaning as their quotes. Point out the glossary at the bottom of the text and tell students to refer to it as they read or to look at the words and definitions before they start reading.

• Ask students to compare their answers in pairs before you check answers in class.

| Answers |
|---|
| 1 c   2 a   3 b |

## Understanding details

### 4

• Students are now going to focus on understanding some specific pieces of information in the article. Ask students to read the sentences. Draw their attention to the fact that some of the things mentioned in the sentences may not be in the article and, in this case, they should circle *NG*.

• Have students scan the article for information about the things each sentence mentions and circle the correct option for each one. Check answers in class.

| Answers |
|---|
| 1 F   2 NG   3 T   4 T   5 F |

## Understanding vocabulary

### 5

• Ask students to read the sentences and choose the correct option to complete them. If students are unsure about the meaning of any of the items in bold, they may find it helpful to look at how the words are used in context in the article.

• Check answers in class.

| Answers |
|---|
| 1 b   2 a   3 a   4 b   5 b |

### 6

• Put students into pairs. Ask them to discuss possible events in the history of the town or city where they currently are, or a town they both know well, which could be represented by a flag. Possible events could include: the founding of the town/city, a battle that happened in or near the town, the birth of a famous person in the town/city. If students don't have a town or city that they both know well, they could each choose a different town or city and tell each other which event from that place's history could be represented in a flag.

• Conduct whole-class feedback on students' ideas.

▶ Set Workbook pages 40 and 41 for homework.

## 5.4 The worst-designed thing you've never noticed

**TED**TALKS

### 1

• Tell students they're now going to watch a TED Talk by Roman Mars, who they read about in **5.3**. Have students read the summary of the talk and choose the correct options in their definitions. If they're unsure about which words to match with which items, encourage them to use deduction or simply have a guess.

• Students can compare their answers in pairs before you check answers in class. Draw students' attention to the pronunciation of *engage* /ɪnˈgeɪdʒ/ as they may find this challenging.

| Answers |
|---|
| 1 need   2 interesting and exciting   3 show interest in |
| 4 concentrate on |

### 2

• Put students into pairs. Ask them to look carefully at the two flags.

• **Optional step**. Bring in students' own experiences by asking them if they've ever visited Canada or San Francisco and, if they have, where they saw the country or city's flags while they were there and what their impressions of the place(s) they've been to were.

• Have them find two or three things that they like about each one and share these in pairs.

5   Good design

- Remind students to re-use the vocabulary for design that they looked at in **5.1** to describe the flag and the prepositions of adverbs of place they looked at in **5.2** to describe the position of the items on the flag.

- Conduct whole-class feedback on the things students liked about the flags. If time allows, ask them what they don't like about the flags too.

> **Answers**
>
> Students' own answers.

**3**

- ▶ 5.10 Students are now going to listen to Part 1 of Mars's talk, in which he explains his interest in flags and says what he thinks about the two flags students discussed in Exercise 2.

- Play Part 1 of the talk and ask students to make notes on the key points Mars makes about each of the two flags so they can identify which one he prefers. They can then check answers in pairs before you check answers in class.

**Transcript**

*I know what you're thinking: 'Why does that guy get to sit down?' That's because this is radio. I tell radio stories about design, and I report on all kinds of stories: buildings and toothbrushes and mascots and wayfinding and fonts. My mission is to get people to engage with the design that they care about so they begin to pay attention to all forms of design.*

*[…] And few things give me greater joy than a well-designed flag. Yeah! Happy 50th anniversary on your flag, Canada. It is beautiful, gold standard. Love it. I'm kind of obsessed with flags. Sometimes I bring up the topic of flags, and people are like, 'I don't care about flags', and then we start talking about flags, and trust me, 100 per cent of people care about flags. There's just something about them that works on our emotions.*

*[…] OK. So when I moved back to San Francisco in 2008, I researched its flag, because I had never seen it in the previous eight years I lived there. And I found it, I am sorry to say, sadly lacking. I know. It hurts me, too.*

> **Answer**
>
> He prefers the flag of Canada because it's well designed.

**4**

- Students are now going to compare the San Francisco flag with the Chicago flag, which they read about in **5.3**, and identify differences between them. Ask students to read the excerpt from Part 1 of the talk and deduce what it tells us about San Francisco's flag and how it's different to Chicago's flag.

- Put students into pairs to compare their answers, then check answers in class.

> **Answer**
>
> The Chicago flag appears everywhere in the city, but the San Francisco flag doesn't.

**5**

- ▶ 5.11 Students are now going to complete the five principles of flag design and the list of things that could be done to improve San Francisco's flag, using their knowledge of vocabulary for design. Check the meaning of *enlarge* (to make bigger) and *border* (here: a line that goes around the outside of something).

- Play Part 2 of the TED Talk and have students watch and check their answers. Note that there's a slide in the excerpt which contains the word *colors* and this is the American English spelling of the word because Roman Mars is American. As this is a British English course though, students are using the British English spelling *colours* here.

- **Optional step**. Draw students' attention to the fact that all of the verbs in the table are in the infinitive without *to* (or imperative) form. Elicit or explain that we use the imperative form to tell people what to do, i.e. give instructions.

**Transcript**

**Narrator:** *The five basic principles of flag design. Number one.*

**Ted Kaye:** *Keep it simple.*

**Narrator:** *Number two.*

**TK:** *Use meaningful symbolism.*

**Narrator:** *Number three.*

**TK:** *Use two to three basic colours.*

**Narrator:** *Number four.*

**TK:** *No lettering or seals.*

**Narrator:** *Never use writing of any kind.*

**TK:** *Because you can't read that at a distance.*

**Narrator:** *Number five.*

**TK:** *And be distinctive.*

**Roman Mars:** *All the best flags tend to stick to these principles. And like I said before, most country flags are OK. But here's the thing: if you showed this list of principles to any designer of almost anything, they would say these principles – simplicity, deep meaning, having few colours or being thoughtful about colours, uniqueness, don't have writing you can't read – all those principles apply to them, too.*

*[…] But here's the trick: if you want to design a great flag, a kickass flag like Chicago's or DC's, which also has a great flag, start by drawing a one-by-one-and-a-half-inch rectangle on a piece of paper. Your design has to fit within that tiny rectangle. Here's why.*

**TK:** *A three-by-five-foot flag on a pole 100 feet away looks about the same size as a one-by-one-and a-half-inch rectangle seen about 15 inches from your eye. You'd be surprised at how compelling and simple the design can be when you hold yourself to that limitation.*

**RM:** *Meanwhile, back in San Francisco. Is there anything we can do?*

**TK:** *I like to say that in every bad flag there's a good flag trying to get out. The way to make San Francisco's flag a good flag is to take the motto off because you can't read that at a distance. Take the name off, and the border might even be made thicker, so it's more a part of the flag. And I would simply take the phoenix and make it a great big element in the middle of the flag.*

**RM:** *But the current phoenix, that's got to go.*

**TK:** *I would simplify or stylize the phoenix. Depict a big, wide-winged bird coming out of flames. Emphasize those flames.*

**RM:** *So this San Francisco flag was designed by Frank Chimero based on Ted Kaye's suggestions. I don't know what he would do if he was completely unfettered and didn't follow those guidelines. Fans of my radio show and podcast, they've heard me complain about bad flags. They've sent me other suggested designs. This one's by Neil Mussett. Both are so much better. And I think if they were adopted, I would see them around the city.*

---

**Answers**

1 simple   2 (the) name   3 colours, Enlarge
4 writing, bigger, (the) middle   5 Simplify

---

### 6

- ▶ 5.12  Ask students to read the three statements. Check the meaning of *trademark symbol* (an indicator that shows that a name or design is owned by a company). Tell students that Pocatello is a small town in the American state of Idaho. Ask students to speculate about which statement(s) Mars would probably agree with. Make sure they're aware he may agree with more than one of them.

- Play Part 3 of the talk and ask students to tick the statement(s) that Mars would probably agree with. Ask students to compare their answers in pairs before checking answers in class.

**Transcript**

*Often when city leaders say, 'We have more important things to do than worry about a city flag', my response is, 'If you had a great city flag, you would have a banner for people to rally under to face those more important things.'*

*[...] So maybe all the city flags can be as inspiring as Hong Kong or Portland or Trondheim, and we can do away with all the bad flags like San Francisco, Milwaukee, Cedar Rapids, and finally, when we're all done, we can do something about Pocatello, Idaho, considered by the North American Vexillological Association as the worst city flag in North America. Yeah. That thing has a trademark symbol on it, people. That hurts me just to look at. Thank you so much for listening.*

---

**Answers**

a, b

---

## CRITICAL THINKING

### 7

- Tell students that in this activity the critical thinking skill they'll be using is the ability to test out an idea and evaluate its effectiveness.

- Students can choose any flag they know and which they can draw. They could draw the flag of their home town/city or country. Have students draw the flag in the rectangle and then take a look to see how clearly they can see it. They can use the small rectangle on the right to decide how good the flag's design is.

- **Optional step.** Put students into pairs to discuss how good the design of the flags they've chosen is, giving reasons for their answers. They may want to refer back to the five principles of flag design they completed in Exercise 5 to help them.

## VOCABULARY IN CONTEXT

### 8

- ▶ 5.13  Play the clips from the TED Talk. When each multiple-choice question appears, pause the clip so that students can choose the correct definition. Discourage the more confident students from always giving the answer by asking students to raise their hand if they think they know.

**Transcript and subtitles**

*1 My mission is to get people to engage with the design that they care about so they begin to **pay attention** to all forms of design.*

If you **pay attention** to something, you _____.

    a look at it carefully

    b give money to see it

    c stop doing it

*2 I'm kind of **obsessed with** flags.*

If you are **obsessed with** something, you probably _____.

    a think or talk about it a lot

    b are confused by its complexity

    c don't understand its symbolism

*3 Sometimes I **bring up** the topic of flags, and people are like, 'I don't care about flags'.*

What does **bring up** mean?

    a think about

    b mention

    c remember

*4 I don't know what he would do if he was completely unfettered and didn't follow those **guidelines**.*

What are **guidelines**?

    a numbers

    b advice or rules

    c famous speakers

*5 Fans of my radio show and podcast, they've heard me **complain** about bad flags.*

If you **complain**, you say _____ something.

    a that you like

    b that you are interested in

    c that you're not happy about

---

**Answers**

1 a  2 a  3 b  4 b  5 c

---

**9**

- Students are now going to use two of the terms they looked at in Exercise 8 – *to complain about something* and *to be obsessed with something* – to discuss their opinions about issues related to things they do in their free time.

- Put students into pairs and ask them to say their own answers to the questions, giving as much detail as they can. Circulate and monitor students' discussions and give them feedback when they've finished.

**PRESENTATION SKILLS** Numbering key points

**10**

- ▶ 5.14  Direct students to the Presentation skills box and ask them to read about why it's useful to number your points in a presentation and the words you can use to do that.

- Ask students to watch the clip about the basic principles of flag design and notice the words the narrator uses to number her points (*number 1*, *number 2*, *number 3*) and how this numbering makes it easier for the audience to follow what she wants to say.

- Ask students to share what they noticed in pairs or conduct whole-class feedback.

**11**

- ▶ 5.15  Remind students that they watched A. J. Jacobs' talk on genealogy in Unit 2. Ask them to read the two options in each pair and tell them that it would be correct to use either of them to number a presentation. Then, tell them to listen and circle the option that A. J. Jacobs uses for each of his four points.

- Check answers in class. Tell students that it may be a good idea to use the same format for every word you use to number your points, i.e. either *one*, *two*, *three*, *four*, or *first*, *second*, *third*, *fourth*, in the interests of consistency, but in reality many effective presenters will also mix these up, as A. J. Jacobs does.

---

**Answers**

1 First  2 Two  3 Three  4 Four

---

**12**

- Give students some time to think of three things they've learned in this unit. Encourage them to focus on things they've learned about design and flags, but they could also choose grammar or vocabulary. Depending on how much time is available and the amount of practice that students need with presenting, you could ask them to keep this presentation very brief, e.g. 30 seconds long, or to expand it into a longer presentation of about two minutes.

- Then, put students into groups of four or five and have them take it in turns to present the three things they've learned, using the options from Exercise 11 to number them. Monitor students and give them feedback when they've finished.

▶ Set Workbook page 42 for homework.

## 5.5 Keeping it simple

### COMMUNICATE Designing a new city flag

**1**

- Put students into groups of three or four and ask them to spend some time looking at the three flags closely. From left to right: the flags are those of the cities of Jacksonville, Florida, in the USA, Dallas, Texas, in the USA and Vancouver, Canada.

- Then, ask students to think about which flag they like the most and least, and discuss this in their groups, giving reasons.

**2**

- Put students into pairs. Students in each pair should both either live in, be from or at least be familiar with the same town or city, so they can design a flag for it. Tell them to decide which town or city they're going to design a flag for.

- Have students brainstorm four or five famous places, historical events, famous people or well-known natural or man-made features in or from their town/city which they could include in the flag design.

**3**   **21st CENTURY OUTCOMES**

*Create new and worthwhile ideas (both incremental and radical concepts)*

- Ask students to re-read Mars's flag design principles and use them to design a flag for their town/city which incorporates one or some of the ideas they brainstormed in Exercise 2. In order to fulfil the 21st CENTURY OUTCOMES, students need to be able to come up with a new and meaningful flag design.

- Tell students to draw their design on a piece of paper first and then make any changes they want to make so that it's as effective as possible. After that, they should draw their flag in the rectangle on this page so they can evaluate how good the design is, as they did in Exercise 7 in **5.4**.

**4**

- Ask students to draw the final version of their flag on an A4 or A3 piece of paper, making any changes they want to make in response to how the design looked in the small rectangle.

- Students then prepare a presentation of their flags for the rest of the group. Direct them to the Talking about meaning box and review the meaning of *mean* (to show an idea or fact), *represent* (to refer to something or show it in another form) and *symbolize* (to represent something through an image/images). Have students use these words in their explanations.

- **Optional step**. If possible, students could take a photo of their paper flags and then upload this photo to a PowerPoint slide, which could be shown in class while they're presenting.

- Students could either present their flag in class and then take questions about it afterwards, or have a conversation about the flag, with students asking and answering the questions from the Talking about meaning box.

- **Optional step**. Have students vote in class on which flag they think is the best.

- Give students feedback when they've finished.

### WRITING Describing your country's flag

**5**

- This activity may be more suitable as a self-study task. Ask students to read the example text about a flag. Then, have them do some research about the meaning of their country's flag online and prepare a description of its design, followed by an explanation of its meaning in a short text (60–80 words).

- Circulate and monitor while students are writing.

> **Answers**
> Students' own answers.

> **TEACHING TIP**
>
> **Displaying students' writing**
>
> Assuming that your students will have been working together now for some time, they will probably feel comfortable with displaying their written work for other students to read at the end of a lesson. You can use the walls or noticeboards in your classroom to display students' work and space the texts out around the room so that students have to move around to read them. Just remind students before they start writing that they will need to write clearly and make their writing large enough that other students will be able to read it when they're displayed. Or, if you know how to set up blogs, you could start a class blog and let your students post their writing there for other students to read.

▶ Set Workbook page 43 for homework.

# 6 Inspiring people

> **UNIT AT A GLANCE**
>
> **THEME:** Inspirational people
> **VOCABULARY:** Sources of inspiration
> **LISTENING:** My inspiration
> **SPEAKING:** Talking about an inspirational person, Getting advice
> **GRAMMAR:** Reported speech
> **PRONUNCIATION:** *that*, Giving emphasis
> **READING:** *Drawing your own success*
> **TED TALK:** *How a boy became an artist*. In this talk, Jarrett J. Krosoczka talks about the events that inspired his career as an author and illustrator.
> **PRESENTATION SKILLS:** Using your voice effectively
> **WRITING:** Describing an inspiring person

## WARM UP

- Books open. Draw students' attention to the unit title, the photo and the caption on page 61.
- Put students into pairs or small groups (three to four students) to discuss the questions.
- **Question 1**. Direct students to the photo of a group of Kenyan children sitting at a table with their teacher. Then, put students into pairs and have them tell each other what they think the children are learning and where and how they're learning it. Bring in students' own experiences by having them talk about the learning experience they had as children.
- **Question 2**. Ask students to think about teachers in general and encourage them to come up with a list of things that inspiring teachers do or don't do with their students, e.g. they don't tell students that they can't do something, they tell them to believe in themselves, etc.
- **Question 3**. Bring in students' own experiences and ask them to talk about teachers they've had, or still have, who they think are inspiring. They can describe these teachers and say what they do/did to inspire them.

## 6.1 They changed my life

### VOCABULARY Sources of inspiration

**1**

- ▶6.1 **Optional step.** Direct students to the title of this section and the photo of a father watching as his son launches a model rocket. Elicit the connection between the photo and the title, e.g. the father has changed his son's life by inspiring him to try new things like launching a model rocket.
- Check the meaning of *source* (a place or person that something comes from). Have students read the sentences and complete them with the correct verbs.
- Check answers in class.

> **Answers**
>
> 1 changed 2 inspired 3 was 4 showed
> 5 supported 6 gave

**2**

- Ask students to re-read the sentences and see if they could use either the first part of the sentence, e.g. *My biology teacher, Mrs Chang* ... (they could change the name of the subject and teacher) or the second part of the sentence ... *completely changed my life*, to make two or three sentences that are true for them.

> **Answers**
>
> Students' own answers.

> **TEACHING TIP**
>
> **Sensitivity when talking about who's inspired you**
>
> There will most likely be some variation within the group in terms of the relationships students had with the people around them when they were growing up and where they found inspiration, if they found it at all. As a result, it's important to make sure that students don't feel embarrassed or reluctant to communicate if they didn't grow up with inspiring family members or teachers. Tell students that they can just focus on famous people instead of people they know personally in Exercise 2. As always, make sure they're aware that the focus in these activities is on using the target language to communicate.

**3**

- Put students into pairs. Have them read the model conversation and elicit other possible responses and questions that students could use to react to their partners' sentences, e.g. Responses: *Really? That's interesting! I didn't know that*; Questions: *How did he/she do that? What's he/she like? What was the most useful advice he/she gave you?*

- Students then take it in turns to read their sentences to their partner and react and ask a follow-up question about each one. Encourage them to make this feel like a natural conversation.

## LISTENING My inspiration

### 4

- ▶ 6.2 Direct students to the Listening for expressions of uncertainty box and check the meaning of *uncertainty* (the feeling of being unsure about something). Tell students that we use expressions of uncertainty to show that we're not sure that something will happen, but there's a chance that it will. Tell students to listen out for these expressions in the recording.

- Tell students they're going to listen to a NASA astronaut called Franklin Chang Díaz, who they can see in the photo, talking about sources of inspiration. Ask them to read the three options and predict who his number one hero could be.

- Play the recording and ask students to circle the correct option. Check answers in class.

### Transcript

**Narrator:** *Franklin Chang Díaz is an engineer, and a former NASA astronaut. As an astronaut, he went on seven Space Shuttle missions and was the third Latin-American to go into space. But what inspired him in his career?*

**Franklin Chang Díaz:** *I was a child of the fifties. I was captivated by space because of the launch of Sputnik. Sputnik was something that probably lit the fire or lit the spark of space for many children. I have many heroes. Still do. The number one hero is my dad. My dad was the one person that I wanted to be like. He was not a scientist, he was not an engineer, but he was an adventurer. He was a guy that was not afraid of anything, and I wanted to be like him. Even today, when I'm faced with a difficult problem, I have to make a decision, I always ask myself, 'What would my father do in this same situation?' and it helps me a lot to arrive at a decision. Inspiration is in many ways a bit of a chain. I was inspired by others, and maybe I was, or I am, an inspiration to some. And that is part of the way it should be. I feel that this was not part of my plan, to be an inspiration, but it is a responsibility that I have acquired, and I have to be true to it. I hope those who come after me will inspire others as well, and so the chain will be unbroken.*

| Answer |
|---|
| c |

### 5

- ▶ 6.2 Tell students they're going to listen to the recording again and focus on some specific pieces of information Chang Díaz gives in the recording. Have students read the sentences before they listen and speculate about whether they're true or false, based on what they can remember from their first listening.

- Play the recording and ask students to decide if the sentences are true or false. Check answers in class. Note that sentence 4 is false because Chang Díaz doesn't say that he's 'certain' that he's an inspiration, he says 'maybe I am.'

| Answers |
|---|
| 1 F   2 T   3 F   4 F |

## Pronunciation *that*

### 6

- ▶ 6.3 Play the recording. Ask students to notice how the word *that* is pronounced in each sentence and identify the one sentence where it's pronounced differently. Then, put students into pairs to compare and say why the sound is different in it.

- Conduct whole-class feedback on the sentence with the different pronunciation of *that* and elicit the two different ways of pronouncing it. Then, elicit or explain that the sound is different in sentence 3 because in this sentence *that* is the subject (or main agent) and, therefore, an important, key content word, whereas in sentences 1 and 2 it's a linking word and, therefore, doesn't need to be stressed.

| Answer |
|---|
| 3 |

## SPEAKING Talking about an inspirational person

### 7

- ▶ 6.4 Ask students to read the conversation before they listen. Tell them to ignore the word choices on the right for the moment as they will focus on those in Exercise 8.

- Check the meaning of *advice* (something that you tell someone else in order to help them) and tell them to identify the music teacher's advice in the conversation. Play the recording and ask students to read and listen to the conversation at the same time.

- Check answers and elicit that when you 'follow your passion', you decide to do something that you love.

| Answer |
|---|
| follow your passion in life |

### 8

- Model the conversation that students have just listened to aloud with a student. Then, have students work in pairs to practise the conversation together. Make sure they alternate between A and B roles.

- Have students practise the conversation again using the words on the right instead of the words in bold in the conversation.

6  Inspiring people

## 9  21st CENTURY OUTCOMES

**Use communication for a range of purposes (e.g. to inform, instruct, motivate and persuade)**

• Put students into pairs and ask them to think of three inspiring people and the reason(s) why they're inspiring. Tell students to choose either family members, friends and people they know or famous people.

• Have students read the example sentences and use them as a model for what they say about each of the people they've chosen. They then take it in turns to tell their partner about the people who inspire them. In order to fulfil the 21st CENTURY OUTCOMES, students should also be able to effectively explain why these people inspire them.

• Circulate and monitor students while they're talking to each other and give them feedback when they've finished.

▶ Set Workbook pages 44 and 45 for homework.

▶ Photocopiable communicative activity 6.1. Go to page 173 for further practice of sources of inspiration vocabulary and talking about an inspirational person. The teaching notes are on page 192.

## 6.2  Inspiring words

### GRAMMAR  Reported speech

**1**

• ▶6.5  Elicit or explain that reported speech involves communicating what someone else said without using their exact words.

• Direct students to the infographic. Ask them to read the information about and the quotes from the three people. Note that the quotes in this unit are approximations of what people said and some have been adapted for level. Have students look up any words that they don't know, e.g. *weapon*, *movement* and *distinguish*. Then, have students make notes on anything else they know about each person.

• Put students into pairs to share and compare their notes about the three people. Conduct whole-class feedback.

#### Answers
Students' own answers.

### Extra activity

#### The most inspirational people in the world

Ask students whether they agree that the three people in the infographic are the world's most inspirational people. If they do, they could say what makes them more inspirational than other famous people. If they don't, they could say who they think the world's three most inspirational people are and why. They could choose any famous person: dead or alive.

**2**

• ▶6.6  Check the meaning of *admire* (to feel respect and appreciation for someone) and then ask students to listen and focus on identifying the names and the reasons the speaker gives and note them down.

• Play the recording. Then, check answers in class.

#### Transcript

*There are a lot of inspirational people in the world, but when I think about who I really admire, two people come to mind. The first is Leonardo da Vinci. We know him as a painter, of course, but he was much more than that. He was good at so many things – inventing, engineering, music, maths, astronomy, literature. He had such an incredible mind. Another person I admire is Mexican artist Frida Kahlo. I admire her because she was such a strong person. And her self-portraits are fascinating. There is one quote I remember. She once said, 'I paint myself because I am so often alone and because I am the subject I know best.'*

#### Answers

| Who does he admire? | Why does he admire them? |
| --- | --- |
| 1  Leonardo da Vinci | He was good at so many things. He had an incredible mind. |
| 2  Frida Kahlo | She was such a strong person. And her self-portraits are fascinating. |

**3**

• Ask students to read the example of direct speech and the example of reported speech and notice the differences between them. Elicit or explain that the *reported words* are the words that the speaker originally said and a *pronoun* is a word that refers to the people or things in a sentence, e.g. *I*, *he*, *she*, *it*, *we*, *they*.

• Students can check their answers and overall understanding of reported speech by turning to the Grammar summary on page 145.

• If you feel that students need more controlled practice before continuing, they could do the exercises in the Grammar summary. Otherwise, you could continue on to Exercise 4 in the unit and set the Grammar summary exercises for homework.

#### Answers

a  It changes from the present simple to the past simple.
b  *that*
c  It changes from *I* / the first person to *she* / the third person.

> **Answers to Grammar summary exercises**
>
> **1**
> 1 he found
> 2 (that) they studied
> 3 Bob Marley's music still sounded
> 4 a girl should be two things
> 5 (that) she wanted to live
> 6 (that) he was more convinced
>
> **2**
> 1 Safi and Adam said (that) they wanted to improve people's lives because there were many problems there
> 2 Liban said (that) he tried to treat people in the way he wanted people to treat him
> 3 The company Inspiraquote said (that) people came to their quotes website to get inspiration
> 4 Tom said (that) he'd like to buy this/that book about Mandela

**4**

- Find out what students know about Oscar Wilde.
- Have students change the examples of reported speech back into direct speech. Encourage students to refer back to the Grammar box if they need to.
- Check answers in class.
- **Optional step**. Check the meaning of some of the more challenging vocabulary items in the quotes: *resist* (to successfully fight against something), *temptation* (a strong feeling of wanting to do something) and *imitate* (copy).

> **Answers**
> 1 Oscar Wilde said, 'I can resist everything except temptation.'
> 2 Oscar Wilde said, 'Experience is simply the name we give our mistakes.'
> 3 Oscar Wilde said, 'Whenever people agree me, I always feel I must be wrong.'
> 4 Oscar Wilde said, 'Life imitates art far more than art imitates life.'

**5**

- Students are now going to practise changing direct speech into reported speech, using quotes which are well-known among native speakers of English.
- Have students rewrite the quotes as reported speech. Remind them to change the verbs forms in the original quotes. Weaker students can do this in pairs.
- Check answers in class

> **Answers**
> 1 Martin Luther King said (that) he had a dream.
> 2 Greta Garbo said (that) she wanted to be alone!
> 3 Neil Armstrong said (that) that was one small step for man, one giant leap for mankind.
> 4 Leonardo da Vinci said (that) learning never made the mind tired.

## Pronunciation  Giving emphasis

**6**

- ▶ 6.7  Check the meaning of *emphasis* (the stress you give words to show that they're important). Ask students to re-read the quotes they transformed in Exercise 5 and decide which words they think the speakers will emphasize.
- Then, play the recording so that students can listen and check their answers. You may need to stop the recording after each quote or play the recording more than once. Confirm the correct answers in class and then put students into pairs to practise saying the sentences with the same emphasis.

> **Answers**
> 1 I have a <u>dream</u>.
> 2 I want to be <u>alone</u>!
> 3 That's one <u>small</u> step for <u>man</u>, one <u>giant</u> leap for <u>mankind</u>.
> 4 <u>Learning</u> never makes the mind <u>tired</u>.

**TEACHING TIP**

**Using emphasis**

Following on from Exercise 6, elicit how speakers give emphasis to certain words (by saying them more loudly and making the sounds in them longer) and why they choose to emphasize them (to show they think these words are important). Then, put students into pairs and ask them to read the quotes in the infographic, the Grammar box and the direct quotes they wrote in Exercise 4 and decide which word(s) in them you would usually emphasize. They can then practise saying them with the emphasis they agreed on. If time is short, students could just choose one or a few of the quotes that they find interesting instead of doing all of them.

6  Inspiring people  **65**

## LANGUAGE FOCUS Reporting what people say

### 7

- ▶ 6.8 Ask students to read the Language focus box and notice how the words *said* and *told* are used to report what people say. Draw students' attention to the difference between the reported speech versions of direct speech with pronouns, e.g. *I admire ...*, and direct speech with imperatives, e.g. *Follow your dreams.*

- Students can check overall understanding of the language focus by turning to the Grammar summary on page 146.

- If you feel that students need more controlled practice before continuing, they could do the exercises in the Grammar summary. Otherwise, you could continue on to Exercise 8 in the unit and set the Grammar summary exercises for homework.

| Answers to Grammar summary exercises |
| --- |
| 1 |
| 2 told me to decide who I wanted to be |
| 3 She told me not to try to change other people |
| 4 She told me to respect the older generation |
| 5 She told me not to forget to say sorry when I did something wrong |
| 6 She told me (that) it was more important to be kind than to be right |
| 2 |
| 1 said   2 to love   3 told   4 said   5 not to worry   6 would |

### 8

- Students are now going to practise identifying when to use *told* and *said* in examples of reported speech. Tell them to refer back to the examples in the Language focus box if they need to.

- Have students compare their answers in pairs before checking answers in class. The most common mistake that students tend to make with *said* and *told* is putting a pronoun after *said*, e.g. *He said me to always do my best*, so draw their attention to this error and why this isn't correct (*said* can't be followed by a pronoun) if they make this mistake.

| Answers |
| --- |
| 1 told   2 said   3 told   4 told   5 told |

### 9

- Students are now going to practise writing sentences with reported speech and *said* or *told*. Elicit or explain that three of the examples of direct speech given here are statements with pronouns and two are with imperatives. Remind them that they will need to form the reported speech versions of these two different types of sentences differently, as they saw in the Language focus box.

- Ask students to compare their sentences in pairs before checking answers in class.

| Answers |
| --- |
| 1 to think carefully about my future |
| 2 (that) she wanted to lead our country some day |
| 3 not to make the same mistake twice |
| 4 she didn't want to stand in my way |
| 5 (that) he didn't worry about the little things |

### 10

- ▶ 6.9 Students are now going to read a text about Frida Kahlo, who they heard about in Exercise 2. Ask them to read the text and identify and correct four mistakes in the use of reported speech.

- Check answers in class.

| Answers |
| --- |
| She told a friend that she ~~wants~~ **wanted** to … |
| She once ~~told~~ **said** that … |
| He recognized her talent and ~~said~~ **told** her to … |
| However, Kahlo ~~told~~ **said** that her work … |

### Extra activity

#### Another inspirational person

Have students search online for the full list of the 100 inspirational people. Ask them to choose one person on the list and do some online research to find out more about him/her. Tell students to work individually and write a paragraph about the person. Tell them to include one quote from the person they've chosen and introduce it using reported speech. When students have finished writing, have them exchange their texts in pairs or small groups and then ask each other questions to clarify any details which are unclear or find out more information.

## SPEAKING Getting advice

### 11

- Ask students to think of two pieces of advice they've been given and write them down as examples of direct speech, e.g. *Follow your passion*.

- Put students into small groups (three or four students) and model an example exchange with one student, in which he/she says a piece of advice and you guess who gave the student this advice, e.g. *I think your mother told you to never give up. Is that right?* Then, have them take it in turns to read their pieces of advice out loud in their groups and guess who gave the other group members the advice. If students don't know each other very well, they may only be able to guess who gave the other group members the advice.

- Monitor students and give them feedback on their use of reported speech when they've finished.

▶ Set Workbook pages 46 and 47 for homework.

## 6.3 Inspiring lives

**READING** Drawing your own success

**1**

- **Optional step.** Draw students' attention to the title of the text and have them speculate, either in pairs or in class, about how someone could draw their own success.
- Direct students to the book cover on the right. Have them look carefully at the picture and the book's title and speculate about what the book is about. Ask students to discuss their ideas in pairs.
- Don't check or confirm answers at this stage.

> **Answers**
> Students' own answers.

**2**

- ▶ 6.10 Ask students to scan read the whole article for information about the story in the *Good Night, Monkey Boy* book and find out whether the answer they gave in Exercise 1 was correct. Check answers in class.

> **Answer**
> It's a story about a young energetic boy.

> **Background information**
>
> **The Lunch Lady graphic novels**
>
> One of Krosoczka's most popular series is about a woman who works in a school canteen. She is a superhero who serves food to children during the day and fights crime at night. There are nine Lunch Lady graphic novels that follow the adventures of this tough, funny and beloved character.

## Understanding main ideas

**3**

- Ask students to read paragraphs 3, 4 and 5 and focus on understanding what the main idea in each one is. They can then look back at the options and choose the best one.
- Point out the glossary at the bottom of the text and tell students to refer to it as they read or to look at the words and definitions before they start reading.

- Ask students to compare their answers in pairs before you check answers in class.

> **Answers**
> 1 a  2 b  3 a

## Understanding sequence

**4**

- Elicit or explain that a *sequence* is a series of events that happen one after the other. Point out that understanding sequence can help students understand the flow of a story.
- Check the meaning of *to publish* (to make printed works (usually books) available for public sale) and *to graduate* (to successfully complete a course of study at a high school (in the USA), university or college). Have students put the events in the correct order. They can do this from memory and then check their answers by re-reading the text or they can scan the text for the events given. Check answers in class.

> **Answers**
> a 4  b 2  c 3  d 5  e 1

## Understanding details

**5**

- Ask students to scan the text for the people or things listed on the left and then look for the things they did (or didn't do) which had an effect on Krosoczka's life and career. They can then match the people with the actions.
- Ask students to compare answers in pairs before checking answers in class. Clarify that when we say that someone 'was never around', we mean he/she was never in the place where he/she was needed.

> **Answers**
> 1 f  2 a  3 e  4 d  5 b  6 c

## Understanding vocabulary

**6**

- Ask students to read the sentences. They can then look back at the words in bold in the article and use them to choose the correct options to complete their definitions. If students are unsure about the meaning of any of the items in bold, they may find it helpful to look at how the words are used in context in the article.
- Check answers in class. Model and drill the pronunciation of *encourage* /ɪnˈkʌrɪdʒ/ as students may find this challenging.

> **Answers**
> 1 a  2 a  3 a  4 b

6 Inspiring people

**7**

- Put students into pairs. Ask them to imagine what being a children's author is like and what the good things about it could be. Encourage students to try to think of some positive things about this job, even if it isn't one they would want to do themselves.

- Have students discuss the best things about being a children's author in their pairs. Monitor students and give them feedback when they've finished.

▶ Set Workbook pages 48 and 49 for homework.

## 6.4 How a boy became an artist

### TEDTALKS

**1**

- Tell students they're now going to watch a TED Talk by Jarrett J. Krosoczka, the author and illustrator they read about in **6.3**. Have students read the summary of the talk and choose the correct options in their definitions. If students are unsure about which words to match with which items, encourage them to use deduction or simply have a guess.

- Students can compare their answers in pairs before you check answers in class.

| Answers |
|---|
| 1 draws the pictures |
| 2 nice |
| 3 very big |

**2**

- ▶ 6.11 Tell students that they're now going to watch Part 1 of Krosoczka's talk, in which he talks about his childhood and the effect that an author called Jack Gantos had on him.

- Ask students to read the questions and answer options. Then, play Part 1 and tell students to focus on understanding the gist of what Krosoczka says about Gantos and the start of his own career so they can answer the questions. Check answers in class.

**Transcript**

When I was in the third grade, a monumental event happened. An author visited our school, Jack Gantos. A published author of books came to talk to us about what he did for a living. And afterwards, we all went back to our classrooms and we drew our own renditions of his main character, Rotten Ralph.

And suddenly the author appeared in our doorway, and I remember him sort of sauntering down the aisles, going from kid to kid looking at the desks, not saying a word. But he stopped next to my desk, and he tapped on my desk, and he said, 'Nice cat'. And he wandered away. Two words that made a colossal difference in my life. When I was in the third grade, I wrote a book for the first time, The Owl Who Thought He Was The Best Flyer.

[...] So I loved writing so much that I'd come home from school, and I would take out pieces of paper, and I would staple them together, and I would fill those blank pages with words and pictures just because I loved using my imagination. And so these characters would become my friends. There was an egg, a tomato, a head of lettuce and a pumpkin, and they all lived in this refrigerator city, and in one of their adventures they went to a haunted house that was filled with so many dangers, like an evil blender who tried to chop them up, an evil toaster who tried to kidnap the bread couple, and an evil microwave who tried to melt their friend who was a stick of butter.

| Answers |
|---|
| 1 a   2 a   3 b |

**3**

- ▶ 6.12 **Optional step.** Ask students to speculate about who Mr Greenwood and Mr Lynch could be, based on their names and what they heard in Part 1 of the talk (they were Krosoczka's school teachers).

- Have students read the four statements. Then, play Part 2 of the talk and ask them to listen out for words or phrases which have the same meaning as those used in the statements, so they can identify which teacher did each of the four things. Make sure students are aware that they may have to tick both names for some statements.

- Check answers in class.

**Transcript**

So how did I make friends? I drew funny pictures of my teachers – and I passed them around. Well, in English class, in ninth grade, my friend John, who was sitting next to me, laughed a little bit too hard. Mr Greenwood was not pleased. He instantly saw that I was the cause of the commotion, and for the first time in my life, I was sent to the hall, and I thought, 'Oh no, I'm doomed. My grandfather's just going to kill me.' And he came out to the hallway and he said, 'Let me see the paper.' And I thought, 'Oh no. He thinks it's a note.' And so I took this picture, and I handed it to him. And we sat in silence for that brief moment, and he said to me, 'You're really talented. You're really good. You know, the school newspaper needs a new cartoonist, and you should be the cartoonist. Just stop drawing in my class.' So my parents never found out about it. I didn't get in trouble.

[...] I kept making comics, and at the Worcester Art Museum, I was given the greatest piece of advice by any educator I was ever given.

Mark Lynch, he's an amazing teacher and he's still a dear friend of mine, and I was fourteen or fifteen, and I walked into his comic book class halfway through the course, and I was so excited, I was beaming. I had this book that was how to draw comics in the Marvel way, and it taught me how to draw superheroes, how to draw a woman, how to draw muscles just the way they were supposed to be if I were to ever draw for X-Men or Spider-Man. And all the colour just drained from his face, and he looked at me, and he said, 'Forget everything you learned.' And I didn't understand. He said, 'You have a great style. Celebrate your own style. Don't draw the way you're being told to draw. Draw the way you're drawing and keep at it, because you're really good.'

### Answers
a Mr Greenwood, Mr Lynch
b Mr Greenwood
c Mr Greenwood
d Mr Lynch

**4**

- ▶ 6.13  Ask students to read the three things (a–c). Then, play Part 3 of the talk and tell them to listen out for them while they watch and make notes on why each one is important to Krosoczka.

- Students can then check answers in pairs before you check answers in class.

### Transcript

I graduated from RISD. My grandparents were very proud, and I moved to Boston, and I set up shop. I set up a studio and I tried to get published. I would send out my books. I would send out hundreds of postcards to editors and art directors, but they would go unanswered.

[…] Now, I used to work the weekends at the Hole in the Wall off-season programming to make some extra money as I was trying to get my feet off the ground, and this kid who was just this really hyper kid, I started calling him 'Monkey Boy', and I went home and wrote a book called Good Night, Monkey Boy. And I sent out one last batch of postcards. And I received an email from an editor at Random House with a subject line, 'Nice work!' Exclamation point. 'Dear Jarrett, I received your postcard. I liked your art, so I went to your website and I'm wondering if you ever tried writing any of your own stories, because I really like your art and it looks like there are some stories that go with them. Please let me know if you're ever in New York City.' And this was from an editor at Random House Children's Books. So the next week I 'happened' to be in New York. And I met with this editor, and I left New York for a contract for my first book, Good Night, Monkey Boy, which was published on June 12, 2001.

[…] And then something happened that changed my life. I got my first piece of significant fan mail, where this kid loved Monkey Boy so much that he wanted to have a Monkey Boy birthday cake. For a two-year-old, that is like a tattoo.

You know? You only get one birthday per year. And for him, it's only his second. And I got this picture, and I thought, 'This picture is going to live within his consciousness for his entire life. He will forever have this photo in his family photo albums.' So that photo, since that moment, is framed in front of me while I've worked on all of my books.

[…] And I get the most amazing fan mail, and I get the most amazing projects, and the biggest moment for me came last Halloween. The doorbell rang and it was a trick-or-treater dressed as my character. It was so cool.

### Answers
a It was the first reply he had received from a publishing company.
b It's the date his first book was published.
c It was his first piece of significant fan mail showing how much someone loved a character in his book.

### Extra activity

### Three things

Ask students to choose three things, dates, names or places that have been important to them, like the three things they looked at in Exercise 4 are important to Krosoczka. Put students into pairs and have them take it in turns to say the dates, names or places, or describe the things they've chosen. They then ask each other questions to find out why these items are important to their partner. With weaker students, elicit possible questions that students could ask, e.g. *What happened to you on 28th September 2016? Why do you still have that note? What did you do in Barcelona?*

## CRITICAL THINKING

**5**  **21st CENTURY OUTCOMES**

*Effectively analyse and evaluate evidence, arguments, claims and beliefs*

- Tell students that in this activity the critical thinking skill they'll be using is the ability to evaluate experiences in order to draw conclusions about the qualities that something needs to have.

- Put students into pairs. Ask them to think of some examples of compliments they've received or given, share them with their partner and discuss how good these compliments were. They can then decide what makes a good compliment.

- In order to fulfil the 21st CENTURY OUTCOMES, students should be able to show that they've analysed the words or the style of compliments to decide what makes a good one.

- Conduct whole-class feedback on students' conclusions.

## VOCABULARY IN CONTEXT

### 6

- ▶ 6.14 Play the clips from the TED Talk. When each multiple-choice question appears, pause the clip so that students can choose the correct definition. Discourage the more confident students from always giving the answer by asking students to raise their hand if they think they know.

**Transcript and subtitles**

1 So I loved writing so much that I'd come home from school, and I would take out pieces of paper and I would staple them together, and I would fill those **blank** pages with words and pictures just because I loved using my imagination.

If a page is **blank** it _____.
   a  is small
   b  has no writing on it
   c  is not interesting

2 So my parents never found out about it. I didn't get **in trouble**.

If you are **in trouble**, you are in a situation that someone is going to _____ about.
   a  get angry
   b  be pleased
   c  feel surprised

3 I graduated from RISD. My grandparents were very **proud** …

If you are **proud** of someone, you _____.
   a  are sad about something they do
   b  are confused about who they are
   c  feel very happy about their achievements

4 … and I moved to Boston, and I **set up** shop. I **set up** a studio and I tried to get published.

If you **set up** an organization or business, you _____ one.
   a  think about
   b  start
   c  want

5 'I liked your art, so I went to your website and I'm **wondering** if you ever tried writing any of your own stories, because I really like your art and it looks like there are some stories that go with them.'

If you are **wondering** something, you _____ about it.
   a  tell people
   b  do research
   c  want to know

**Answers**
1 b   2 a   3 c   4 b   5 c

### 7

- Students are now going to use two of the terms they looked at in Exercise 6 – *in trouble* and *proud* – to discuss their personal experiences.
- Put students into pairs and ask them to say their own answers to the questions, giving as much detail as they can. Circulate and monitor students' discussions and give them feedback when they've finished.

## PRESENTATION SKILLS Using your voice effectively

### 8

- ▶ 6.15 Direct students to the Presentation skills box and elicit or explain that when you *raise your voice*, you speak more loudly and when you *lower your voice*, you speak more quietly. Tell students that when speakers change their voice to indicate that they're quoting someone, they may use the accent that the person they're quoting has or speak in the style or tone they use.
- Play the clip of Krosoczka speaking softly and ask students to notice how he's using his voice. Then, put them into pairs to discuss why he does this.
- Conduct whole-class feedback on students' answers.

**Suggested answer**

To make the audience listen to him more carefully.

### 9

- ▶ 6.16 Ask students to read the two options for each speaker and check they understand them. Then, play the clips and ask students to listen and notice what each speaker does with his voice so they can choose the correct options.
- Check answers in class.
- **Optional step**. Ask students to discuss, either in pairs or in class, how effectively they think A. J. Jacobs and Roman Mars use their voices in the clips they've just watched and which speaker uses their voice more effectively.

**Answers**
1 a   2 b

### 10

- Ask students to read the text and have them underline the key words and circle the key moments in it. Then, put students into pairs and have them take it in turns to read the text in each of the three ways. They may need to have a practice run before they 'perform' it with their partner.
- Tell students to give each other feedback on how effectively they took on the three styles when they've finished. Monitor students and add your feedback.

> **TEACHING TIP**
>
> **Voice recordings**
>
> It's often difficult to perceive how your own voice sounds to other people and how effectively you're communicating. That's why making recordings of your voice, listening back to them and evaluating how you sound can be useful. Students often feel self-conscious about recording and listening to their own voices, but you may be able to help them overcome their inhibitions by recording yourself speaking and playing this recording for them. There are a wide range of apps that students can use to record their own voice and most of them are free. Students could record themselves saying the text in Exercise 10 in what they think is an effective way. You could then put them into small groups and have them play the recordings for each other and give each other feedback on how effectively they spoke and suggest what other group members could do to speak more effectively.

▶ Set Workbook page 50 for homework.

## 6.5 A world of inspiration

### COMMUNICATE A dinner party

**1**

- **Optional step.** Direct students to the title of this section and ask them if they've ever been to a dinner party. If they have, bring in students' own experiences and elicit what people talked about.

- Ask students to read the types of famous people in the box and look up any words that they don't know. Then, have them work alone to write a list of people in these categories who they think are inspirational. Tell them to think of one or two people for each category.

**2  21st CENTURY OUTCOMES**

*Elaborate, refine, analyse and evaluate their own ideas in order to improve and maximize creative efforts*

- Put students into pairs. Ask them to take it in turns to present the people they've chosen to their partner and find out whether their partner knows them, using the questions in the Finding out what someone knows box.

- Students then discuss which six people, out of the people they both chose, they want to invite to a dinner party and why. In order to fulfil the 21st CENTURY OUTCOMES, students should be able to decide which six suggestions are the best out of their own and their partner's ideas.

- **Optional step.** Encourage students to come up with and use a basic set of criteria for choosing the guests, e.g. Who would be the most interesting? Who would be the funniest?

**3**

- Ask students to look at the seating plan and think about which guests would enjoy talking to each other and which guest(s) they want to sit next to. They can then discuss their ideas for the seating plan in pairs and reach a consensus. Have them write the names of the guests on the seating plan.

**4**

- Put each pair together with another pair. Have the students in the two pairs present their seating plans to each other. Tell them to say the names of the people and ask the students in the other pair whether they know them, using the questions in the Finding out what someone knows box. If time allows, they could also describe the people to the other pair in as much detail as they can.

- Students then use what they discussed in Exercise 3 to explain why they chose these six people and why they've seated them in the way they have.

- Monitor students and give them feedback when they've finished.

### WRITING Describing an inspiring person

**5**

- Ask students to choose a person they think is inspirational. This could be either someone they know personally or a famous person. If students aren't sure who to choose, they could refer back to the personalized sentences they wrote in Exercise 2 in **6.1**.

- Then, ask students to read the example text about an inspiring person and use it as a model to write their own text.

- Circulate and monitor while students are writing.

| Answers |
|---|
| Students' own answers. |

▶ Set Workbook page 51 for homework.

▶ Photocopiable communicative activity 6.2. Go to page 174 for further practice of reported speech and vocabulary from Unit 6. The teaching notes are on page 192.

# Presentation 2 | UNITS 4–6

## MODEL PRESENTATION

**1**

- Tell students they're going to read the text of a presentation. The speaker's aim is to tell people about someone who's made a huge difference in their life.

- Ask students to read the text of the presentation all the way through and think about what the missing words could be as they do so. Then, ask them to look at the words in the box, read the text all the way through again and complete it with the correct words. Encourage students to look at what comes before and after the gaps to help them decide which words should go in them.

- Students can compare their answers in pairs, but don't confirm answers at this stage as they will find out what the correct answers are when they watch the presentation in Exercise 2.

> **Answers**
> 1 little   2 on   3 around   4 said   5 bright   6 relaxed
> 7 told   8 showed   9 gave   10 much

**2**

- ▶P.2 Play the recording of the presentation and ask students to listen closely for the words the presenter says in the gaps so they can check their answers from Exercise 1. Check answers in class.

- **Optional step.** Look in more detail at the adjectives and adverbs used in the presentation, for example by eliciting the words in the presentation which are synonyms for *very* (*so, extremely, a lot*) or eliciting the adverbs which describe how someone does something (*patiently* and *immediately*) and their meanings.

**3**

- ▶P.2 Ask students to read the list of presentation skills and think back to when they looked at providing background information (Unit 4), numbering key points (Unit 5) and using your voice effectively (Unit 6). Students can look back at the Presentation skills boxes from those units to refresh their memory of how presenters can do these things. Put students into pairs and ask them to discuss which of these skills they remember the speaker using in his presentation.

- Play the recording again so students can watch and check their answers.

- Elicit or explain that the speaker uses his voice effectively by stressing key content words and by using intonation and stressing words with a positive meaning to show enthusiasm.

> **Answers**
> He personalizes the presentation, closes the presentation effectively, provides background information and uses his voice effectively. He doesn't use questions to signpost or number his key points.

## YOUR TURN

**4**

- Ask students to think of a great teacher they had in the past and give them some time to prepare their presentations. Tell them to read the questions and make notes on their answers to all or most of them.

- **Optional step.** Remind students they will need to use the past simple, either *said* or *told*, as appropriate, to report what the teacher said to them, and also to use adjectives and adverbs to describe the teacher and their experiences with them, as in the example presentation where the speaker used: *kind, friendly, patiently, confident*, etc.

- Direct students to the list of presentation skills in Exercise 3 and tell them that the objective is to use all of them in their own presentations. They will, therefore, also need to think about how they can include these points in their presentations while they're preparing to speak.

**5**

- Direct students to the Useful phrases box. Ask them to read its contents and note down the phrases they want to use in their presentations. Tell students to use at least one phrase from each of the four categories in the box.

**6**

- Put students into pairs and tell them they're now going to take it in turns to give their presentations.

- Have students give their presentations and tick the skills their partner uses while they're listening to them. Make sure students are aware that when they're giving their partner feedback they're going to say two things they liked about it and one thing that could be improved, so they will also need to be thinking about this while they're listening.

**7**

- Ask students to read the example feedback in the speech bubble and use it as a model for giving their own feedback to their partner. Encourage them to start with a positive comment, as in the example, and then mention the good things that their partner did, using the ticks they made in their checklist, before saying something that their partner could improve.

- **Optional step.** When students have finished giving each other feedback, add your global feedback on students' presentations to their comments and highlight some areas for improvement for next time.

> **TEACHING TIP**
>
> **Talking about areas for improvement**
>
> Now that students have already had a go at giving their partner feedback on their presentations once (in Presentation 1: Units 1–3), they can work on giving more effective peer feedback. Review ways of saying how someone could improve, and write these up on the board before students watch each other's presentations this time, so they're ready to use them afterwards. Examples include: *You forgot to …, When you do …, you don't …, You could …, It's important to …*
>
> Encourage students to use sentence stress to emphasize the content words in their suggestions, e.g. *It's <u>important</u> to <u>close</u> your presentation <u>effectively</u>*, so they can get their points across more effectively. Also, encourage them to use the tone of their voice to show that even though they're saying something that their partner didn't do or didn't do well, they're doing this in order to help him/her. Model the example sentence given above in a friendly tone to show students how they can do this.

# 7 Ethical choices

## UNIT AT A GLANCE

**THEME:** Ethics
**VOCABULARY:** Ethical food choices
**LISTENING:** Sustainable chef
**SPEAKING:** Talking about ethical choices, Predicting future habits
**GRAMMAR:** *will* for predictions
**PRONUNCIATION:** Intonation in questions with options, *will*
**READING:** *Leather from a lab*
**TED TALK:** *Leather and meat without killing animals.* In this TED Talk, Andras Forgacs talks about how he uses to 3D printing technology to produce leather and meat.
**PRESENTATION SKILLS:** Creating effective slides
**WRITING:** Predicting the future of food

## WARM UP

- Books open. Draw students' attention to the unit title, the photo and the caption on page 73. In class, ask students to say how many cups of coffee they usually drink per day. Then, check the meaning of *ethical* (describing something which fits with our ideas about what the right thing to do is) and ask students to say if they think about whether the coffee they buy is ethical.

- Put students into pairs or small groups (three to four students) to discuss the questions.

- **Question 1.** Direct students to the photo of coffee beans drying in the sun, ask them to spend a minute looking closely at it while thinking about and saying what they think makes the production of this coffee 'ethical'. They can then think in more general terms about how coffee can be 'ethical'. If students are unsure, you could tell them that the ethics of a product is usually determined by its impact on the physical environment and on people and whether the steps in its production are legal and conform with corporate rules and regulations.

- **Question 2.** Tell students to think about the advantages and disadvantages of producing food ethically and what the effects of doing, or not doing, this are. They can then give their opinions on how important it is to produce food ethically and reasons for their views.

- **Question 3.** Bring in students' own experiences and ask them to talk about what influences their buying choices. Ask: *How important to them is the product's price, quality, reputation and whether or not it's ethically produced?* Have students think of some examples of ethical products that they buy or have bought and what stops them from buying more ethical products.

## 7.1 It's better for the environment

### VOCABULARY Ethical food choices

**1**

- ▶7.1 Ask students to read the words or expressions in the box and look up the meaning of any that they don't know. Then, have them read the sentences, identify the key words and use these to complete the sentences. Look at an example in class and elicit or explain that the key words in sentence 1 (*grown naturally ... without ... any special chemicals*) tell us that the missing word is *Organic*.

- Have students compare their answers in pairs before playing the recording so they can check them. Tell students that these are key words for the topic of ethical food choices, so they should note their meanings and/or translations for future use.

> **Answers**
> 1 Organic  2 free-range  3 Genetically modified
> 4 Fair-trade  5 locally-produced  6 Sustainable

### Pronunciation Intonation in questions with options

**2a**

- ▶7.2 Check the meaning of *intonation* (the rise and fall of your voice when you're speaking). Tell students it's important to use the right intonation when speaking English because it helps you to communicate your message clearly.

- Ask students to read the question and notice the direction that the arrows go in on the words *vegetarian* and *meat*. Then, play the recording and ask students to notice what the speaker does with their voice when they say these two words. Elicit that the intonation goes up on the word for the first option – *vegetarian* – and down on the word for the second option – *meat*.

## 2b

- ▶ 7.3 Ask students to read and listen to the speaker saying the questions and mark the intonation in the questions with up and down arrows.

- Check answers to ensure that students have marked the intonation correctly and then put them into pairs to practise asking the questions using the correct intonation and giving answers which are true for them. Monitor students and give them feedback on their intonation when they've finished.

> **Answers**
>
> 1 Do you usually buy organic ↗ or non-organic ↘ fruit?
>
> 2 Is it easy ↗ or difficult ↘ to find fair-trade foods where you live?
>
> 3 Is genetically modified food a good idea ↗ or a bad idea ↘?
>
> 4 Do you think it's important ↗ or not important ↘ to buy free-range eggs?

> **TEACHING TIP**
>
> **Intonation in questions with options**
>
> In questions with options, the intonation rises on the first option and then falls on the second, and this difference in intonation draws the listener's attention to the fact that two different options are being given. Ask students to think about and say whether the same intonation pattern is used in their first language. When they're doing Exercise 8, at the end of this section, students can again practise using intonation in questions with options by asking their partner about the things they buy more often, e.g. *Do you buy farmed fish or wild fish more often?*

## LISTENING Sustainable chef

### 3

- ▶ 7.4 Direct students to the title of this section and review the meaning of *sustainable* (describing something that you can continue to use, usually natural resources, for a long period of time). Then, direct them to the Identifying main ideas in fast speech box and tell them they're going to listen to an example of fast speech. Ask students to listen out for the key words that the speaker says more slowly so they can understand his main message.

- Tell students that they're going to listen to Barton Seaver, the 'sustainable chef', who's a chef and environmentalist, talking about his experiences.

- **Optional step**. Ask students to speculate about how someone could combine the roles of chef and environmentalist, and what the link between the two could be, e.g. cooking with ethically produced food which doesn't harm the environment.

- Play the recording and ask students to listen out for what Seaver did in Africa and tick the correct option. Check answers in class.

**Transcript**

*One of the things I really love about cooking is that it's such a universal experience. Food is how the vast majority of us interact with our resources.*

*I worked as a fisherman in Africa, off the coast of Essaouira, and the sardine fishermen were out there, and until this point, seafood had just been delivered as if by magic. But here, in this village, in this ages-old tradition, here is men and women who are casting nets into the sea in hopes of catching dinner – not dollars. Environmentalism, at its root, is a human concern.*

*Environmentalism is so often thought of as this distant idea – this whale that we need to save in some distant ocean far away. But dinner is full-contact environmentalism.*

> **Answer**
>
> b

### 4

- ▶ 7.4 Tell students they're going to listen out for the specific words that Seaver uses in three of the statements he makes.

- Ask students to read the sentences and speculate about what the missing word in each sentence could be before playing the recording. Then have students listen and complete the sentences. Students can then compare their answers in pairs before you check answers in class.

> **Answers**
>
> 1 Food   2 distant   3 dinner

### 5

- Students are now going to read the statements from Exercise 4 again and think about what exactly Seaver means by them or what they would mean in reality. Put students into pairs to explain their interpretations of the statements to each other, bringing in examples from everyday life, where appropriate.

- Conduct whole-class feedback on students' ideas.

## SPEAKING Talking about ethical choices

### 6

- ▶ 7.5 Ask students to read the conversation through once before they listen to it. Tell students to ignore the word choices on the right for the moment as they will focus on those in Exercise 7.

- Check answers and elicit that the woman didn't want to eat food that is grown using chemicals because she'd heard it's not very good for you. Check the meaning of *necessarily* (in negative sentences: in every case) in the conversation.

> **Answer**
>
> She didn't want to eat food that is grown using chemicals.

**7   Ethical choices   75**

### Extra activity

**Your views on organic food**

Either in pairs or in class, ask students to discuss:

a) whether they agree with the woman in the conversation in Exercise 6, who thinks you should eat organic food because other foods contain chemicals which are bad for you, and why / why not?

b) whether they agree that organic foods aren't always more expensive than non-organic foods, bringing in examples from their own shopping experiences.

**7**

- Model the conversation that students have just listened to aloud with a student. Elicit or explain that *fair enough* is an expression that native speakers of British English often use to show that they understand something or how someone feels. Then, have them work in pairs to practise the conversation together. Make sure they alternate between A and B roles.

- Have students practise the conversation again using the words on the right instead of the words in bold in the conversation.

> **TEACHING TIP**
>
> **Sensitivity when talking about buying choices**
>
> Keep in mind that the aim of this section, and the subsequent material that students will look at in this unit, isn't to tell students that they must make ethical buying choices. Instead, the aim is for them to learn and activate vocabulary for ethical choices because this issue is becoming more and more relevant in 21st-century life. Try to ensure that students don't judge each other because they don't eat organic food, for example, and remind them that their primary aim in this course is to improve their language skills.

**8**   **21st CENTURY OUTCOMES**

*Demonstrate knowledge and understanding of the environment and the circumstances and conditions affecting it, particularly as relates to air, climate, land, food, energy, water and ecosystems*

- Put students into pairs. Elicit adverbs of frequency that they can use in their discussions and write them up on the board, e.g. *always, often, sometimes, occasionally, rarely* and *never*.

- Have students discuss which type of food they buy more often and why. In order to fulfil the 21st CENTURY OUTCOMES, students should show that they're aware of the effect their buying choices have on the environment and make suggestions for how they could change their buying choices in order to reduce this impact.

- Circulate and monitor students while they're talking to each other and give them feedback when they've finished.

▶ Set Workbook pages 52 and 53 for homework.

▶ Photocopiable communicative activity 7.1. Go to page 175 for further practice of ethical food choices vocabulary and talking about ethical choices. The teaching notes are on page 193.

## 7.2 What does the future hold?

### GRAMMAR *will* for predictions

**1**

- ▶ 7.6 Check the meaning of *prediction* (a statement of what someone thinks will happen in the future) and tell students that *will* is the word that's most often used in predictions.

- Direct students to the infographic and check the meaning of *consumption* (the amount that someone eats) and ask them to look closely at the bar chart to identify the two countries with the biggest increase in meat consumption. Then, put students into pairs to compare their answers and say why they think meat consumption increased the most in these countries.

- Conduct whole-class feedback.

- **Optional step**. If students' home country isn't included in the infographic, ask them to discuss how much of an increase in meat consumption they would expect there to be in their country and why.

> **Answers**
>
> China and South Korea
>
> Possible answer: People in these countries have recently become richer and, therefore, can afford to buy more meat.

**2**

- ▶ 7.7 Ask students to read the sentences before they listen and check the meaning of *to decrease* (to go down or become less / the opposite of *increase*) and *population* (the number of people living in one place). You could also elicit or explain that the words *increase* and *decrease* can be used as both verbs (as in sentence 2) and nouns (as in sentences 1 and 3).

- Play the recording. Ask students to listen out for what the speaker says about demand for meat and population size and circle the correct options. Then, ask students to compare answers in pairs before checking answers in class.

- **Optional step**. Ask students if they found any of the information in the infographic or the recording surprising or interesting and, if so, what information that was. Students could share this either in pairs or in class.

## Transcript

**Interviewer:** Thank you for talking to us. So, we know that today, people around the world are eating more meat than ever before. Do you think this trend will continue in the future?

**Expert:** Yes, I do. We can be pretty sure about this. First of all, the world's population is increasing. Every day, there are around 228,000 more people on the planet. So, by 2050, we think that the population of the world will increase by about 35 per cent. And, of course, the demand for meat will increase as the population increases. But also, in developing countries, people are becoming richer. By 2050, many more people will be able to buy meat regularly. We think there will be a 100 per cent increase in demand for meat from developing countries.

So when you take the two together – the global population growth and the increased demand from developing countries – it means that, in the next 30 years, there will be a huge rise in the number of people demanding meat. The big question is, however, will we be able to produce enough meat for the increased demand? In my opinion, it won't be easy.

### Answers
1 35%  2 increasing  3 100%

## 3

• Students are now going to look at some examples of predictions with *will* or *won't* and also see how to use verbs and prepositions for describing trends. First, have students complete the first two sentences with the information from Exercise 2 and check answers in class. They can then re-read the sentences they've completed and write the answers to the questions. Check the meaning of *contracted form* (short form / a form where two words become one) and remind students that native speakers of English usually use these when they're speaking and also in informal written communication. Model and drill the pronunciation of *won't* /wəʊnt/ as students may find this challenging.

• Students can check their answers and overall understanding of *will* for predictions by turning to the Grammar summary on page 146.

• If you feel that students need more controlled practice before continuing, they could do the exercises in the Grammar summary. Otherwise, you could continue on to Exercise 4 in the unit and set the Grammar summary exercises for homework.

### Answers
1 35  2 increase, 100

a things you imagine happening in the future
b the infinitive without *to*
c won't

## Answers to Grammar summary exercises

### 1
1 will produce  2 will destroy  3 won't change
4 will change  5 won't be  6 'll see

### 2
2 I imagine I'll meet some nice new people in the village
3 I'm not going to work so much
4 I fear I won't have any grandchildren for many years
5 I'm going to learn to grow my own vegetables
6 I hope I'll stay healthy

## 4

• ▶ 7.7 Ask students to read the sentences and identify whether they're statements about what's happening now or predictions about the future. They can then use this information to choose the correct option in each sentence.

• Students can compare their answers in pairs before you check answers in class.

### Answers
1 are eating  2 will continue  3 are  4 will be able to
5 will be  6 won't be

## 5

• Elicit the sentences from Exercise 4 which students identified as being predictions about the future. Then, elicit that these sentences all contain either *will* or *won't*.

### Answers
4, 5, 6

## LANGUAGE FOCUS Discussing the future

## 6

• ▶ 7.8 Ask students to read the Language focus box and notice how and where the adverbs *definitely* and *probably* are used in the example sentences. Also, draw their attention to the use of *by* and *in* to say when you predict that something will happen in the future and also the difference in how you use them: *by* means *up until this point in the future* and is followed by a date or year and *in* means *after this period of time has passed* and is followed by a time period.

• Students can check overall understanding of the language focus by turning to the Grammar summary on page 147.

• If you feel that students need more controlled practice before continuing, they could do the exercises in the Grammar summary. Otherwise, you could continue on to Exercise 7 in the unit and set the Grammar summary exercises for homework.

### Answers to Grammar summary exercises

**1**

2 will people live

3 Will food be cheaper

4 How will we travel / How will transport change / How will the way we travel change

5 Will people be healthier / How will people's health change

6 Will people live longer / Will we live longer

**2**

1 We will definitely find cures for some diseases.

2 People will probably live on other planets.

3 Robots probably won't organize our lives.

4 Driverless cars will probably be normal.

5 Phones definitely won't look like they do now.

6 There will definitely be technology that we can't predict!

**7**

- Students are now going to practise forming predictions. Tell students to focus on getting the correct word order in the sentences and refer them back to the examples in the Language focus box to help them if they need to.

- Have students compare their answers in pairs before checking answers in class.

**Answers**

1 The UN says we will need to double our food production.

2 People definitely won't be able to eat meat so frequently.

3 We will probably start to use more insects in cooking.

4 Restaurants will definitely offer more and better vegetarian options.

5 Being a vegan probably won't be an unusual life choice.

6 New technology might allow us to grow food in the desert.

**8**

- ▶7.9 Ask students to read the text, which contains predictions about climate change, identify the three mistakes with the use of *will* and *won't* and correct them. Students can refer back to the examples in the Language focus box if they need to.

- Play the recording again so they can listen and check their answers.

**Answers**

First paragraph: others ~~won't~~ probably **won't** do so well

Second paragraph: They **will** probably decline by up to two per cent

Third paragraph: Other crops that will ~~be~~ definitely **be** under threat

### Pronunciation *will*

**9a**

- ▶7.10 Play the recording and ask students to listen and notice the different ways that *will* is pronounced. You could make this easier by telling students that they will hear *will* being pronounced in two different ways.

- Conduct whole-class feedback.

**Transcript**

*1 It'll be hotter and drier in some places.*

*2 We'll need to save water.*

*3 Wet places will get wetter.*

*4 Some plants will grow well.*

*5 Will the weather change?*

*6 Yes, I'm sure it will.*

**Answer**

*Will* is pronounced more strongly in sentences 5 and 6 than in sentences 1–4.

**9b**

- ▶7.10 Direct students to the audioscript of the recording they've just listened to. Tell them to read the sentences and notice the difference between sentences 5 and 6 and the first four sentences. They can then think about how this difference influences how strongly *will* would be pronounced. Conduct feedback and establish that *will* is pronounced more strongly in questions and short answers to show either that you're questioning something or to stress that the response is positive or negative.

- Then, play the recording again and have students listen and repeat the sentences with the stronger emphasis on *will* in sentences 5 and 6.

### SPEAKING Predicting future habits

**10** 21st CENTURY OUTCOMES

Demonstrate knowledge and understanding of society's impact on the natural world (e.g. population growth, population development, resource consumption rate, etc.)

- Put students into pairs. Check the meaning of *habit* (something that people do regularly). Ask them to think of five things that could change or stay the same in people's eating habits in the future and then write questions with *will* or *won't* for each one to ask their partner if he/she thinks these things will happen. In order to fulfil the 21st CENTURY OUTCOMES, they should be able to demonstrate their understanding of society's current impact on the natural world and its possible future consequences.

- Monitor students as they're writing their questions, offering assistance or feedback as appropriate.

**Answers**

Students' own answers.

## 11

- Students take it in turns to ask and answer the questions they wrote in Exercise 10. Tell students to use *definitely*, *probably* or *might* to say how likely they think the things they're being asked about are. Clarify that we use *might* to say we think something is possible, but there's only a small chance that it will happen.

- Give students feedback on how successfully they asked and answered the questions about predictions.

▶ Set Workbook pages 54 and 55 for homework.

▶ Photocopiable communicative activity 7.2. Go to page 176 for further practice of *will* for future predictions and ethical food choices vocabulary. The teaching notes are on page 193.

## 7.3 A kinder way

### READING Leather from a lab

**1**

- Put students into pairs to discuss which leather products they own.

- **Optional step**. Students show each other any leather products they have on or with them and say what they're called in English, e.g. *wallet*, *boots*, *belt*, etc.

**2**

- **Optional step**. Before students start to read the first paragraph of the article, ask them to work in pairs and use *will* to predict what they think the problem with leather is.

- Ask students to read the first paragraph and focus on identifying the problem with leather. Check answers in class.

- **Optional step**. Ask students whether they're surprised that so many animals are killed to make leather products and whether knowing this fact will influence their buying habits in future.

> **Answer**
> Over a billion animals are killed every year to make leather products.

### Understanding details

**3**

- ▶ 7.11 Tell students that they're now going to read the whole article and focus on understanding some of the details. Have them read the sentences and elicit what the meaning of *biofabrication* could be. Tell students that *bio* is short for *biological* and *fabrication* is the process of making something.

- Students then read the whole article and find information about the issues mentioned in the sentences and decide whether they're true, false or if the information is not given. Point out the glossary at the bottom of the text and tell students to refer to it as they read or to look at the words and definitions before they start reading.

- Ask students to compare their answers in pairs before you check answers in class.

> **Answers**
> 1 T  2 NG  3 T  4 F  5 T

### Understanding process

**4**

- Tell students that they're now going to look at the steps in the process of creating biofabricated leather in more detail. Ask students to read the eight steps and number them in the order that they happen. Students could either number the steps from memory, use the diagram to help them or re-read the first paragraph of the text.

- Students can check their answers in pairs before checking answers in class.

> **Answers**
> a 2  b 6  c 5  d 3  e 1  f 4  g 7  h 8

### Extra activity

**Describing processes**

Here are some activities which students could do to give them some more practice with describing processes:

1. Have students rewrite the process they looked at in Exercise 4 as a paragraph, adding in any extra details they can remember from reading the article. Remind students to use the present simple and words to introduce the steps of a process, e.g. *first, then, after that, finally*, and ask students to use them.

2. Put students into pairs. Ask them to choose a process they know well from their work, studies or everyday life, but which they think their partner will also know something about. Have them write five sentences describing five different steps in the process on strips of paper or cards – one sentence on each. Students then mix up their strips of paper or cards and give them to a partner who has to read the sentences and put the steps back in the correct order.

3. Put students into pairs. Ask them to choose a process they know well from their work, studies or everyday life, but which they think their partner will not be familiar with, and draw a diagram or picture showing the different steps in that process. Students then take it in turns to use their diagram or picture to describe the process. Encourage students to ask their partner questions about the process.

## Understanding vocabulary

**5**

- Ask students to read the sentences. They can then look back at the words in bold in the article and use these to complete them. If students are unsure about the meaning of any of the items in bold, they may find it helpful to look at how the words are used in context in the article.

- Check answers in class. Elicit and explain that *lab* is a common short form of *laboratory*. Model and drill the pronunciation of *layer* /ˈleɪə(r)/ and *efficient* /ɪˈfɪʃ(ə)nt/ as students may find these challenging.

> **Answers**
> 1 d   2 c   3 a   4 e   5 b

**6**

- Put students into pairs to discuss the questions. Tell them to use the contracted form *I'd* when giving their answers and also to give reasons for their answers.

- Conduct whole-class feedback on students' opinions and the reasons for them.

▶ Set Workbook pages 56 and 57 for homework.

## 7.4 Leather and meat without killing animals

### TEDTALKS

**1**

- Tell students that they're now going to watch a TED Talk by Andras Forgacs, whose support for the biofabrication of leather they read about in **7.3**.

- Have students read the summary of the talk and match the words in bold with their synonyms. If students are unsure about which words to match with which items, encourage them to use deduction or simply have a guess.

- Students can compare their answers in pairs before you check answers in class. Draw students' attention to the pronunciation of *tissues* /ˈtɪʃuːz/, *slaughter* /ˈslɔːtə(r)/ and *humane* /hjuːˈmeɪn/ as they may find these challenging.

> **Answers**
> 1 living things   2 brain   3 kill   4 kind and gentle

**2**

- Check the meaning of *slide* (a 'page' of a presentation) and ask students to look carefully at the slide from Forgacs' presentation and think about what he uses it to say. Ask students to use the language for predictions about future trends that they learned in **7.2** to write or, in pairs, say the sentence they think Forgacs will say while showing this slide.

> **Suggested answer**
> In 2012, there were 7 billion people and 60 billion land animals. In 2050, it is predicted that there will be 10 billion people and 100 billion land animals.

**3**

- ▶ 7.12 Tell students that they're now going to watch Part 1 of Forgacs' talk, in which he explains why he's concerned about having so many animals on the planet. Check the meaning of *concerned* (worried / having a bad feeling about something) and ask students to read the four options.

- Play the recording and ask students to listen out for the key words in the options and tick the ones they hear. Make sure students are aware that Forgacs mentions more than one option.

- Check answers in class.

**Transcript**

*I'm convinced that in 30 years, when we look back on today and on how we raise and slaughter billions of animals to make our hamburgers and our handbags, we'll see this as being wasteful and indeed crazy. Did you know that today we maintain a global herd of 60 billion animals to provide our meat, dairy, eggs and leather goods? And over the next few decades, as the world's population expands to ten billion, this will need to nearly double to 100 billion animals.*

*But maintaining this herd takes a major toll on our planet. Animals are not just raw materials. They're living beings, and already our livestock is one of the largest users of land, fresh water, and one of the biggest producers of greenhouse gases, which drive climate change. On top of this, when you get so many animals so close together, it creates a breeding ground for disease and opportunities for harm and abuse. Clearly, we cannot continue on this path which puts the environment, public health and food security at risk. There is another way, ...*

> **Answers**
> a, b, d

**4**

- ▶ 7.13 Students are now going to watch Part 2 of the talk, in which he talks about why biofabricating leather is a good idea. Ask students to read the options and predict the ones that Forgacs will mention.

- Then, play Part 2 of the talk and ask students to listen for the reasons Forgacs gives for leather being a good place to begin for biofabrication.

- Students can compare their answers in pairs before checking answers in class.

### Transcript

*There is another way, because essentially, animal products are just collections of tissues, and right now we breed and raise highly complex animals only to create products that are made of relatively simple tissues. What if, instead of starting with a complex and sentient animal, we started with what the tissues are made of, the basic unit of life, the cell? This is biofabrication, where cells themselves can be used to grow biological products like tissues and organs.*

*[…] And we should begin by reimagining leather. I emphasize leather because it is so widely used. It is beautiful, and it has long been a part of our history. Growing leather is also technically simpler than growing other animal products like meat. It mainly uses one cell type, and it is largely two-dimensional.*

### Answers
a, b, d, e

**5**

- ▶7.14 Tell students they're now going to watch Part 3 of the talk, in which Forgacs talks about the benefits of biofabricated leather. Ask students to read the first and second halves of the notes before they watch, and check the meaning of *scar* (a mark left on the skin where it's been cut or burnt).
- Play the recording and ask students to listen out for Forgacs saying the ideas in the first half of the sentences and match them with the second half.
- Students can check their answers in pairs before you check answers in class.

### Transcript

*And so I'm very excited to show you, for the first time, the first batch of our cultured leather, fresh from the lab. This is real, genuine leather, without the animal sacrifice. It can have all the characteristics of leather because it is made of the same cells, and better yet, there is no hair to remove, no scars or insect's bites, and no waste. This leather can be grown in the shape of a wallet, a handbag or a car seat. It is not limited to the irregular shape of a cow or an alligator.*

*And because we make this material, we grow this leather from the ground up, we can control its properties in very interesting ways. This piece of leather is a mere seven tissue layers thick, and as you can see, it is nearly transparent. And this leather is 21 layers thick and quite opaque. You don't have that kind of fine control with conventional leather.*

*[…] We can design new materials, new products and new facilities. We need to move past just killing animals as a resource to something more civilized and evolved. Perhaps we are ready for something literally and figuratively more cultured. Thank you.*

### Answers
1 c   2 e   3 d   4 a   5 b

> **TEACHING TIP**
>
> **Paraphrasing**
>
> Draw students' attention to the fact that the notes they matched in Exercise 5 *paraphrase* (to say the same thing in different words) what Forgacs said, rather than using his exact words, and this is a good strategy to use when you're summarizing what someone has said or written. Ask students to compare the notes from Exercise 5 with the words in the transcript of Part 3 of the talk which they paraphrase, so they can see how different and simpler words are used to say the same thing. For example, the first note says: *It's just like normal leather because it is made from the same cells* and this paraphrases Forgacs, who said: *It can have all the characteristics of leather because it is made of the same cells*. The simpler and shorter *It's just like* replaces *It can have all the characteristics of*. Ask students to either read the transcript of Part 1 or 2 of the talk and make notes which paraphrase its contents or, for an extra challenge, re-watch Part 1 or 2 and make notes that paraphrase what they hear.

## CRITICAL THINKING

**6**

- Tell students that the critical thinking skill they'll be using in this activity is the ability to use what they know about certain groups of people to deduce what their opinions about a specific topic would be.
- Give students some time to think about whether the three groups would support biofabrication and why or why not, and then put them into pairs to discuss their views. Conduct whole-class feedback.

## VOCABULARY IN CONTEXT

**7**

- ▶7.15 Play the clips from the TED Talk. When each multiple-choice question appears, pause the clip so that students can choose the correct definition. Discourage the more confident students from always giving the answer by asking students to raise their hand if they think they know.

**Transcript and subtitles**

*1 I'm **convinced** that in 30 years, when we look back on today and on how we raise and slaughter billions of animals to make our hamburgers and our handbags, we'll see this as being wasteful and indeed crazy*

If you are **convinced** about something, you feel _____ about it.
  a  happy
  b  sure
  c  sad

*2 Did you know that today we maintain a global herd of 60 billion animals to provide our meat, dairy, eggs and leather **goods**?*

What are **goods**?
  a  objects we make to sell
  b  interesting objects
  c  high quality objects

*3 Animals are not just **raw materials**. They're living beings …*

Which is an example of a **raw material**?
  a  wood
  b  leather
  c  a handbag

*4 **On top of this**, when you get so many animals so close together, it creates a breeding ground for disease…*

What does **on top of this** mean?
  a  in addition
  b  however
  c  in other words

*5 We can design new materials, new products and new **facilities**.*

Which is an example of **facilities**?
  a  some easy exercises
  b  your legs and arms
  c  modern buildings with good equipment

**Answers**

1 b  2 a  3 a  4 a  5 c

**8**

- Students are now going to use two of the terms they looked at in Exercise 7 – *convinced* and *facilities* – to talk about what they think will happen in the future and about the place where they work or study.

- Put students into pairs and ask them to say their own answers to the questions, giving as much detail as they can. Remind students to use language for making predictions and saying how likely they think it is that something will happen in the future, e.g. *definitely*, *probably*, *might*, from **7.2** when answering question 1. Circulate and monitor students' discussions and give them feedback when they've finished.

## PRESENTATION SKILLS  Creating effective slides

**9**

- ▶ 7.16  Ask students to read the information about how to create effective slides and check the meaning of *plain* (simple or basic). Tell students that although presentations are more than just slides, they're the messages you communicate when you use them; having effective slides makes it easier for the audience to understand those messages and can make them more interested in the subject that's being presented.

- Tell students that the slide they will see in the clip is the one they looked at and discussed in Exercise 2. Then, play the recording and ask students to notice whether Forgacs has done the things in the box when creating the slide they can see here.

- Students compare their ideas about how effective the slide is in pairs before you conduct whole-class feedback.

- **Optional step**. Play the first ten seconds of the clip and ask students to notice what Forgacs says to get the audience's attention and think about why this is effective. Then, elicit that he starts by asking *Did you know … ?* and then saying a fact that people may not know. This gets the audience's attention because he's directly engaging with them by asking them a question and he's giving them some information which he expects to be new to them.

**Answers**

Students' own answers.

**10**

- ▶ 7.17  Students are now going to see another one of Forgacs' slides and use what they've learned about what makes an effective slide. Play the clip and ask students to make notes on how effective the different elements mentioned in the Presentation skills box are, i.e. background, text, colours and graphics or images.

- **Optional step**. For an extra challenge, students could do this without referring back to the Presentation skills box and see how much they can remember.

- Students can discuss and compare their ideas in pairs again before you conduct whole-class feedback.

**Answers**

Students' own answers.

▶ Set Workbook page 58 for homework.

## 7.5 Looking ahead

### COMMUNICATE Arguing for and against

**1** **21st CENTURY OUTCOMES**

*Use a wide range of idea-creation techniques (such as brainstorming)*

- Put students into groups of four or five and ask them to read the information and instructions. Check the meaning of *perception* (a way of seeing something). Ask students to read the ideas in the box and then work together to brainstorm as many arguments for and against opening a biofabrication lab in their town/city as they can. They should think of at least five for each side. In order to fulfil the 21st CENTURY OUTCOMES, students should be able to use brainstorming to generate as many ideas for arguments as they can think of.

- Tell students to make notes rather than writing complete sentences and encourage them to consider any factors that are specific to the place where they live, e.g. what they think the public perception of a biofabrication lab would be there.

- Monitor students while they're brainstorming and offer assistance or feedback where appropriate.

**2**

- Divide each of the groups from Exercise 1 into two pairs or a pair and a group of three and have them decide which pair/group will be for and which will be against the biofabrication lab. Have each pair or group decide which three or four arguments from Exercise 1 are the strongest and then work together to prepare a slide for each argument that they can present in Exercise 3.

- If students have access to computers during their lesson, they could use them to create the slides. Otherwise, they could create the slides as a self-study task or, if this isn't possible either, draw what they want to have on their slides on pieces of paper. Encourage students to refer back to the advice on creating effective slides in the Presentation skills box on page 81 to help them.

**3**

- The pairs or groups (A and B) take it in turns to present their arguments to each other, using the slides they've created. As in a typical debate, one side will present one argument and then the other pair/group will present one of theirs. Direct students to the Acknowledging a point box and tell them to make notes on the key points the other pair/group make and then use one of the phrases in the box to *acknowledge* (say that you've listened to it) each point and then make one of their own.

- Monitor students' debates and give them feedback on how clearly and accurately they presented their arguments when they've finished.

- **Optional step**. When both sides have presented all of their arguments, ask them to discuss which side they think won the debate.

### Extra activity

### Peer feedback on slides

After students have finished their debate, ask them to look more closely at the slides that the other pair/group created. They can then give each other feedback on how effective their slides are, referring back to the points in the Presentation skills box and giving reasons for their opinions. They can also make suggestions for how the slides could be improved.

### WRITING Predicting the future of food

**4**

- Check the meaning of *optimistic* (a feeling that good things will happen in the future) and *pessimistic* (a feeling that bad things will happen in the future) and ask students to consider what their opinion on the future of food is.

- Ask students to read the example text and then write their own with at least three predictions about the future of food which support their optimistic/pessimistic view of it.

- **Optional step**. Stronger students can also expand their texts by giving reasons to support their predictions.

- Circulate and monitor while students are writing, offering assistance and feedback where appropriate.

> **Answers**
> Students' own answers.

▶ Set Workbook page 59 for homework.

**7 Ethical choices   83**

# 8 Better cities

**UNIT AT A GLANCE**

**THEME:** Cities
**VOCABULARY:** Features of a city
**LISTENING:** Living abroad
**SPEAKING:** Talking about where you live, Talking about places to go
**GRAMMAR:** Phrasal verbs
**PRONUNCIATION:** Showing enthusiasm, Stress in phrasal verbs

**READING:** Having a say about your city
**TED TALK:** *It's our city. Let's fix it.* In this TED Talk, Alessandra Orofino talks about how we can use technology and 'people power' to fix big problems in the world's cities.
**PRESENTATION SKILLS:** Using anecdotes
**WRITING:** Describing a change for the better

## WARM UP

- Books open. Draw students' attention to the unit title, the photo and the caption on page 83.
- Put students into pairs or small groups (three to four students) to discuss the questions.
- **Question 1.** Direct students to the photo, which gives you an aerial view of the High Line (the green and grey strip about three quarters down the photo). This is a public park built on a disused railway track in New York City. Students say whether they've been to the High Line and give their opinion on it, either based on their experience of visiting it or what they can see in the photo. They could also go online to find out more information and see some more photos of it.
- **Question 2.** Tell students that the High Line is an example of positive change in a city because its developers changed something that nobody was using into something attractive that people can now use and enjoy. Ask students to tell each other about any other examples of positive change in cities they know: either their home town/city or any other places they've visited. If students have access to the Internet, they could search for images of the examples of positive change they're talking about and show these to the other members of their group.
- **Question 3.** Ask students to think about areas, structures of buildings in their town or city which aren't being used anymore, aren't in a good condition or aren't being used as well as they could be. Students can then make suggestions about how these places could be improved. With weaker students, you may need to elicit or model the language they can use to do this, e.g. *We could …, We should …, One option would be to …*

## 8.1 What makes a great city?

**VOCABULARY** Features of a city

**1**

- Check the meaning of *feature* (a part or aspect of something) and then ask students to read and categorize the words in the box. Looking up the meaning of the words in the box and the examples already in the table, if they need to, and identifying whether the words in the box are nouns or adjectives, should help them do this.
- Check students' answers in class and model and drill the pronunciation of *lively* /ˈlaɪvli/ and *ancient* /ˈeɪnʃ(ə)nt/ as students may find these challenging.
- **Optional step.** Elicit which of these areas and things to enjoy exist in the town or city where they live and which of the words to describe a city could also be used to describe their town/city.

| Answers | | |
|---|---|---|
| Areas of a city | Things to enjoy | Words to describe a city |
| historic centre | amusement parks | ancient |
| industrial estate | concert halls | lively |
| suburbs | galleries | multicultural |

**2**

- Put students into pairs. Ask them to add two more words to each column of the table. Encourage students to think of their own town/city to help them come up with ideas and refer to a dictionary if they need to.
- Conduct whole-class feedback on students' words and write them up on the board. Also, model and drill the pronunciation of the words if students can't say them correctly.

> **Answers**
>
> Students' own answers.

## 3

- Put students into pairs. Direct them to the model conversation and ask them to also say what they like and why, and then say whether they agree or disagree and why. Encourage students to be positive about their towns/cities and ask them to each think of four or five good things about them.

- Conduct whole-class feedback on what students like about their towns/cities and why.

## LISTENING  Living abroad

## 4

- ▶ 8.1  Direct students to the Listening for time expressions box and tell them to listen out for time expressions in the recording to help them identify which periods of time the speaker is talking about. Students may also find it helpful to note down these time expressions for future reference.

- Tell students they're going to listen to Claire Street, who they can see in the photo, talking about the different places she's lived in. Ask them to read the sentences and check the meaning of *to grow up* (to become an adult). Then, play the recording and ask students to write in the correct countries.

- Check answers in class.

### Transcript

*I grew up in a place called Whitworth. It's a very small town in the north of England. Only about 8,000 people live there, so it's a very quiet place. You can go walking in the countryside, which is lovely, but other than that, there's not much to do.*

*When I was 21, I moved to Singapore, which was a huge change. Singapore is a bustling, modern, multicultural city – the exact opposite of Whitworth! Singapore was a great place to live. I met people from so many different backgrounds and I had a really great time. I lived in Singapore for nine years, and then in 2009, I moved to Sydney, Australia, which is where I live now. Sydney is a wonderful place. I feel like I have the best of both worlds here. I live in the suburbs in a quiet neighbourhood not too far from the city. There are a lot of parks near where I live, and it's a pretty peaceful place. But if I want a bit more excitement, I'm only a short drive from the city centre. There's so much to do in Sydney, I never get bored. I've got no plans to move again in the future. I'm really happy where I am now.*

> **Answers**
>
> 1 (the north of) England   2 Singapore   3 Australia

## 5

- ▶ 8.1  Tell students they're going to listen to the recording again and focus on the specific information Claire gives about each of the three places she talks about. Play the recording and ask students to note down the key words and phrases Claire uses when talking about each place.

- In pairs, have students discuss what they noted down and say which place they think is Claire's favourite. Check answers in class.

> **Answers**
>
> Whitworth: a small town, very quiet, lovely, not much to do
>
> Singapore: bustling, modern, multicultural, a great place
>
> Sydney: wonderful, the best of both worlds, a quiet neighbourhood, a peaceful place
>
> Favourite place: Sydney

### Extra activity

### Whitworth, Singapore, Sydney?

Put students into pairs. Ask them to discuss what they think of the three places Claire talked about. They can also say:

- whether they've ever been to any of these places and, if they have, what they did there or, if they haven't, whether they'd like to go to any of them

- which place they'd most like to go to on holiday or live in and why.

## Pronunciation  Showing enthusiasm

### 6a

- ▶ 8.2  Check the meaning of *enthusiasm* (an intense feeling of enjoyment and interest). Tell students that showing enthusiasm when you speak is important because a) it shows how you feel about something and b) it's likely to make other people feel enthusiastic about the thing(s) you're talking about too.

- Elicit any ideas students have about how you can show enthusiasm with your voice. Then, play the recording and have students listen to the sentences while they read them and notice what the speaker does to show their enthusiasm.

- Have students compare their ideas in pairs before conducting whole-class feedback.

> **Answer**
>
> The speaker emphasizes the words with positive meanings: *great*, *wonderful*, *so much*.

### 6b

- Ask students to change the place names in the sentences from Exercise 6a to the names of places they know. If necessary, they can also change some of the other words in the sentences so that they're true for these places, as long as the sentences still say something positive.

- Put students into pairs and ask them to take it in turns to say the sentences with enthusiasm by emphasizing the positive words. Monitor and give students feedback on how effectively they did this.

## SPEAKING Talking about where you live

**7**

- ▶ 8.3 Ask students to read the conversation through once before they listen to it. Tell students to ignore the word choices on the right for the moment as they will focus on those in Exercise 8.

- Check answers and elicit that Speaker A really likes the area of Brisbane called South Bank Parklands and the nice restaurants there.

- **Optional step.** Draw students' attention to the phrasal verb *check something out* in the last line of the conversation and elicit or explain that, in this context, it means to look at or visit a place in order to find out what it's like. Tell students that they'll look at more phrasal verbs like this one in **8.2**.

- **Optional step.** If students have access to the Internet, ask them to go online and find images of Brisbane and South Bank Parklands so they can see for themselves and discuss whether they look like the kinds of places they'd like to live in.

> **Answers**
> It's a busy place; the South Bank Parklands; nice restaurants; a great place to hang out with friends

**8**

- Model the conversation that students have just listened to aloud with a student. Then, have students work in pairs to practise the conversation together. Make sure they alternate between A and B roles.

- Have students practise the conversation again using the words on the right instead of the words in bold in the conversation.

**9**

- **Optional step.** Draw students' attention to the use of *I'd like* /ˌaɪd ˈlaɪk/ to say a wish for something in the future. Model and drill its pronunciation if you think students may struggle with saying it correctly.

- Put students into pairs and ask them to think of a few cities that they'd like to live in. These don't have to be places they've visited. Some students may be against the idea of moving to a different city, but tell them that the objective of this exercise is to use vocabulary for cities and language for saying where they'd like to live and why.

- Then, have students read the example conversation and use it as a model for some exchanges about the cities they thought of. Remind students to also say as much as they can about why they'd like to live in that place.

- Circulate and monitor students while they're talking to each other and give them feedback when they've finished.

▶ Set Workbook pages 60 and 61 for homework.

▶ Photocopiable communicative activity 8.1. Go to page 177 for further practice of features of a city vocabulary. The teaching notes are on page 194.

## 8.2 Happy cities

### GRAMMAR Phrasal verbs

**1**

- ▶ 8.4 Elicit or explain that a *phrasal verb* is a verb + preposition combination which has a particular meaning.

- Direct students to the infographic. Ask them to read the information about the four cities and then have them choose the city or cities they'd like to live in.

- **Optional step.** Put students into pairs to discuss which cities they'd like to live in and why, and why they don't want to live in the city/cities they haven't chosen.

> **Answers**
> Students' own answers.

**2**

- ▶ 8.5 Tell students they're now going to listen to two people talking about the city of Monterrey in Mexico.

- **Optional step.** Find out what students already know about Monterrey, what they think of it and whether they've ever been there.

- Ask students to read the sentences and then play the recording so they can listen and circle the correct option in each one.

- Have students compare answers in pairs before you check answers in class. Draw students' attention to the three examples of phrasal verbs in the sentences – *grow up*, *hang out with* and *get around* – and check the meaning of *hang out with someone* (spend time relaxing with someone) and *get around* (travel; usually within a town or city). Students encountered *grow up* in Exercise 4 on page 85.

**Transcript**

**A:** Hey, this in interesting. It says Monterrey, Mexico, is one of the happiest cities in the world. You grew up there, right?

**B:** Yeah, that's right.

**A:** So, what do you think? Was it a happy city?

**B:** Well, I loved living there. I used to love hanging out with my friends on the riverfront. I didn't have a car in those days, but it was so easy to get around by bus. I was always happy.

**A:** Cool. I should visit there one day.

**B:** Yeah. If you go, make sure you check out the Santa Lucia Riverwalk. It's really cool.

**A:** OK, thanks for the advice.

86   8   Better cities

> **Answers**
>
> 1 Monterrey   2 riverfront   3 bus

## 3

- ▶ 8.6 Ask students to read the examples of sentences with separable and inseparable phrasal verbs. Elicit or explain that separable phrasal verbs are called separable because you can put another word between the different parts of the phrasal verb, but you can't put other words between the different parts of phrasal verbs that are inseparable.

- Students can check their answers and overall understanding of how to use phrasal verbs by turning to the Grammar summary on page 147.

- If you feel that students need more controlled practice before continuing, they could do the exercises in the Grammar summary. Otherwise, you could continue on to Exercise 4 in the unit and set the Grammar summary exercises for homework.

> **Answers**
>
> a sometimes have three   b inseparable   c pronoun
> d inseparable   e separable

> **Answers to Grammar summary exercises**
>
> **1**
>
> 1 ate out   2 moving out   3 set off   4 tried on
> 5 looked after   6 meet up with
>
> **2**
>
> 2 mother took it up last year
> 3 Luckily, I didn't throw them away
> 4 I finally figured it out
> 5 We looked them up
> 6 I showed him around my university
>
> **EXTRA INFORMATION**
>
> **1**
>
> 1 back   2 up   3 after   4 for   5 around   6 out
> 7 forward   8 around
>
> Intransitive verbs: 1, 6, 8
>
> **2**
>
> A: I can't wait for the weekend.
> B: Yes, I'm really looking forward ~~it~~ to **it**.
> A: Do you want to check out the new *Star Wars* film?
> B: Good idea. We can meet up with Dave, too.
> A: Yeah, it's a while since I hung out **with** him.
> B: OK, I'll probably drive, so I can pick ~~up~~ you **up**.

> **Learning and using phrasal verbs**
>
> Phrasal verbs are frequently used by native speakers of English, so learning and using them will make it easier for students to understand them and make their own English sound more natural. One of the most common mistakes that students make with phrasal verbs is putting a pronoun (words like *him*, *it*, *us*) after the verb and particle instead of between the verb and particle, for example: *He put away them [the books]*. This example is incorrect because the pronoun (*them*) should come between the verb and the particle: *He put them away*. Another point students need to be aware of is that one phrasal verb can have several meanings: *put away*, for instance, has six different meanings, and changing the particle you use after a verb can completely change the meaning of the phrasal verb too.
>
> Encourage students to note down whether a phrasal verb is separable or inseparable when they record it and also to write an example sentence or short phrase which includes the phrasal verb. You can also encourage students to use the phrasal verbs they see in this section as much as they can, where appropriate, in subsequent speaking activities because activating the language in this way should help them remember how to use it.

*TEACHING TIP*

## 4

- Students are now going to check their understanding of the meaning of four commonly used phrasal verbs. They've already looked at the meaning of *get around*, *grow up* and *hang out with*, and *look for* should also be known to them.

- Have students read the questions and choose the correct phrasal verb to complete each one. Students don't need to change the form of the verbs. Check answers in class.

> **Answers**
>
> 1 grow up   2 get around   3 hang out with   4 look for

## Pronunciation Stress in phrasal verbs

### 5a

- ▶ 8.7 Ask students to read the instructions and elicit or explain that, in this context, the *particle* is the preposition(s) that follows the verb in a phrasal verb. Play the recording and ask students to listen very closely to the pronunciation of the phrasal verb in each question so they can identify whether the speaker says the verb or the particle more strongly, and which sentence has a different stress pattern to the other three. You will probably need to play the recording two or three times.

8   Better cities

- Have students discuss and compare their answers in pairs before conducting whole-class feedback. The most important thing that students need to take away from this exercise is the fact that it's more common to have the main stress on the particle than on the verb. They can also remember that in many phrasal verbs, both the verb and the particle are stressed, but one is stressed more than the other, and this word then has what is called the main stress.

> **Answer**
>
> In sentences 1, 2 and 3 the main stress is on the particle. Sentence 4 is different because only the verb is stressed.

## 5b

- Put students into pairs and give less confident students a little time to prepare their answers to the questions from Exercise 4. Then, have them take it in turns to ask the questions and give their answers, ensuring that they stress the right words in the phrasal verbs.
- Monitor and give students feedback on their use of stress in phrasal verbs.

## 6

- ▶ 8.8 Students are now going to practise identifying the preposition that should be used in some other examples of phrasal verbs. Ask students to read the text about San Sebastián in Spain all the way through first, and then go back and choose the correct preposition options. Tell students to use a dictionary to help them find the correct verb + preposition combinations if they need to.
- Play the recording of the text so students can listen and check their answers.

> **Answers**
>
> 1 out   2 out   3 to   4 up   5 on   6 out   7 in

## 7

- Ask students to read the conversation and use the phrasal verbs from Exercise 6 to complete it. Tell them they will need to change the tense of some of the verbs so that they fit with the rest of the sentence.
- Have students compare their answers in pairs before playing the recording so students can check them.
- **Optional step.** Put students into pairs and have them read the conversation out loud, using the correct stress when they say the phrasal verbs. They may need to read the conversation silently first so they can identify and underline the stressed words before they do this.

> **Answers**
>
> 1 chilled out   2 going on   3 headed to   4 check out
> 5 end up   6 ate out   7 took in

## SPEAKING  Talking about places to go

## 8

- Ask students to read the different question options and check the meaning of *on a budget* (cheaply). Put students into pairs to tell each other their answers to the questions, giving information about the town/city where they live and noting down the answers they give.
- **Optional step.** Have students add more questions of their own about the town/city where they live using other phrasal verbs from this section, e.g. *What's the best way to get around?*

## 9

- Put each pair together with another pair to tell each other their answers to the questions from Exercise 8 and say whether they agree or disagree with each other's answers and why. Ask students to try to reach a consensus on the best places in their town/city to do these things in their groups of four.
- Conduct whole-class feedback on the places each group decided on and establish which place in each category is the most popular in the class. Give students feedback on how clearly and accurately they communicated during their discussions.

### Extra activity

### Future cities

Ask students to either tell their partner or write a paragraph about what they think their town or city will be like in ten years' time. Tell them to use the phrasal verbs they've learned in this section, and *will* and *won't* for predictions from Unit 7. They can think about what changes there will be in: the size of the town/city and the importance/size of its different areas, free-time activities, public transport, green spaces, shops, etc.

▶ Set Workbook pages 62 and 63 for homework.

# 8.3 Connecting citizens

## READING  Having a say about your city

## 1

- Check the meaning of *citizen* (a person who lives in a particular town, city or country) and *to have a say* (to have some input into and control over something). Put students into pairs to discuss whether they think people who live in cities are happier than people who don't. Tell students to bring in their own experiences of living in a city, if they have them, and/or the experiences of living in a city that people they know have had.

- **Optional step.** Ask students to make a list of the pros and cons of living in a city, and then use it to help them decide whether living in a city makes you happier.
- Conduct whole-class feedback on students' opinions and the reasons for them.

## 2

- ▶ 8.9 Ask students to scan read the whole article for any mention of the connection between living in cities and happiness, and find out whether the article's writer agrees with the opinion students gave in Exercise 1.
- Check answers in class.

> **Answer**
> She thinks people who live in cities aren't so happy.

### Extra activity

#### How happy is Rio?

In pairs, ask students to scan read the whole article again and identify pieces of information about the city of Rio de Janeiro which tell you how happy/unhappy its population is. They can then use the notes they've made on how happy Rio is to compare it with the four happiest cities in the infographic in 8.2 and say how happy they think Rio is and why. Students can then follow this up by using their comparison to make suggestions (*I think Rio should/could … / Rio needs …*) for how Rio could become a happier city in their pairs.

## Understanding purpose

### 3

- Review the meaning of *purpose* (the reason why we do something) and check the meaning of *to highlight* (to draw attention to). Then, have students read the article all the way through again and focus on identifying what message the author wanted to communicate to the reader, so they can circle the correct option.
- Students can compare their answers in pairs before you check answers in class.

> **Answer**
> b

## Understanding main ideas

### 4

- Have students go through the article again and identify the main message in each paragraph. They can then compare their ideas with the options given and choose the correct option for each paragraph.
- Point out the glossary at the bottom of the text and tell students to refer to it as they read or to look at the words and definitions before they start reading.

- Students can compare their answers in pairs before you check answers in class.

> **Answers**
> 1 c  2 d  3 a  4 b  5 f  6 e

## Understanding details

### 5

- Tell students they're now going to focus on understanding some of the details given in the article. Have students read the sentences, then go through the whole article to find information about the issues mentioned and decide whether they're true, false or not given.
- Ask students to compare their answers in pairs before you check answers in class.

> **Answers**
> 1 NG  2 T  3 F  4 T  5 NG  6 T  7 T

## Understanding vocabulary

### 6

- Ask students to read the paragraph and think about what the missing words could be, based on the context of the sentences and the words that come before and after the gaps. Stronger students could complete the sentences without looking back at the article, while weaker students can look back at the article and use the words in bold as their word pool. Weaker students may also find it helpful to look at how the words in bold are used in context.
- Check answers in class.

> **Answers**
> 1 election  2 citizens  3 vote  4 required
> 5 pay a fine

### 7  21st CENTURY OUTCOMES

*Participating effectively in civic life through knowing how to stay informed and understanding governmental processes*

- Put students into pairs and ask them to think about and discuss what problems exist in the town/city where they live, and what similarities there are between these and the problems in Rio they've just read about. In order to fulfil the 21st CENTURY OUTCOMES, students should show their understanding of the effects that local government has on their town/city by identifying any problems that their town/city shares with Rio and suggesting what their local government body could do to fix them.
- Conduct whole-class feedback on students' ideas.

▶ Set Workbook pages 64 and 65 for homework.

## 8.4 It's your city. Let's fix it.

### TEDTALKS

**1**

- Tell students they're now going to watch a TED Talk by Alessandra Orofino, a political mobilization activist who they read about in **8.3**.

- Have students read the summary of the talk and complete the definitions with the words in bold. Students can compare their answers in pairs before you check answers in class.

**Answers**
1 invention   2 developing   3 slums   4 fix

**2**

- ▶ 8.10 Tell students they're now going to watch the first part of Orofino's talk, in which she introduces the challenges facing cities today and introduces the organization that she founded. Ask them to read the sentences, and use their general knowledge and what they can remember from the article in **8.3** to speculate about the correct percentages for each statistic.

- Then, play Part 1 of the talk and ask students to listen out for the statistics and match the sentences with the correct percentages. Students can then check answers in pairs before you check answers in class.

- **Optional step.** Ask students whether they found any of the statistics surprising or interesting and why.

**Transcript**

*Fifty-four per cent of the world's population lives in our cities. In developing countries, one third of that population is living in slums. Seventy-five per cent of global energy consumption occurs in our cities, and 80 per cent of gas emissions that cause global warming come from our cities. So things that you and I might think about as global problems, like climate change, the energy crisis or poverty, are really, in many ways, city problems. They will not be solved unless people who live in cities, like most of us, actually start doing a better job, because right now, we are not doing a very good one.*

*[…] Three years ago, I co-founded an organization called Meu Rio, and we make it easier for people in the city of Rio to organize around causes and places that they care about in their own city, and have an impact on those causes and places every day. In these past three years, Meu Rio grew to a network of 160,000 citizens of Rio. About 40 per cent of those members are young people aged 20 to 29. That is one in every fifteen young people of that age in Rio today.*

**Answers**
1 c   2 b   3 a   4 d

**3**

- ▶ 8.11 Tell students they're now going to watch Part 2 of Orofino's talk, in which she talks about three people in Rio and how they're having a positive effect on their community. Students are going to focus on some of the specific information, mainly numbers, given in this part of the talk.

- Ask students to read the notes and then play the recording so they can watch and complete them. With weaker students, you could stop the recording when Orofino finishes talking about each of the three people and elicit their answers before continuing.

- Students can compare their completed notes in pairs before you check answers in class. Draw students' attention to the fact that Orofino speaks American English and that's why she uses the term *parking lot*, but the British equivalent would be *car park*.

**Transcript**

*Amongst our members is this adorable little girl, Bia, to your right, and Bia was just eleven years old when she started a campaign using one of our tools to save her model public school from demolition. Her school actually ranks amongst the best public schools in the country, and it was going to be demolished by the Rio de Janeiro state government to build, I kid you not, a parking lot for the World Cup right before the event happened. Bia started a campaign, and we even watched her school 24/7 through webcam monitoring, and many months afterwards, the government changed their minds. Bia's school stayed in place.*

*There's also Jovita. She's an amazing woman whose daughter went missing about ten years ago, and since then, she has been looking for her daughter. In that process, she found out that first, she was not alone. In the last year alone, 2013, 6,000 people disappeared in the state of Rio. But she also found out that in spite of that, Rio had no centralized intelligence system for solving missing persons cases. In other Brazilian cities, those systems have helped solve up to 80 per cent of missing persons cases. She started a campaign, and after the secretary of security got 16,000 emails from people asking him to do this, he responded, and started to build a police unit specializing in those cases. It was open to the public at the end of last month, and Jovita was there giving interviews and being very fancy.*

*And then, there is Leandro. Leandro is an amazing guy in a slum in Rio, and he created a recycling project in the slum. At the end of last year, December 16, he received an eviction order by the Rio de Janeiro state government giving him two weeks to leave the space that he had been using for two years. The plan was to hand it over to a developer, who planned to turn it into a construction site. Leandro started a campaign using one of our tools, the Pressure Cooker, the same one that Bia and Jovita used, and the state government changed their minds before Christmas Eve.*

### Answers

Bia: eleven, school
Jovita: daughter, ten, 16,000
Leandro: recycling, leave

## 4

- ▶8.12 Students are now going to watch Part 3 of the talk, in which Orofino sums up what she's talked about and issues a call to action to the audience.

- Have students read the sentences, which summarize what Orofino says, and predict the correct options. Then, play the recording and ask students to concentrate on understanding the gist of what she says and choose the correct endings for the sentences.

- Check answers in class.

### Transcript

*These stories make me happy, but not just because they have happy endings. They make me happy because they are happy beginnings. The teacher and parent community at Bia's school is looking for other ways they could improve that space even further. Leandro has ambitious plans to take his model to other low-income communities in Rio, and Jovita is volunteering at the police unit that she helped create.*

*[…] With the Our Cities network, the Meu Rio team hopes to share what we have learned with other people who want to create similar initiatives in their own cities. We have already started doing it in São Paulo with incredible results, and want to take it to cities around the world through a network of citizen-centric, citizen-led organizations that can inspire us, challenge us, and remind us to demand real participation in our city lives.*

*It is up to us to decide whether we want schools or parking lots, community-driven recycling projects or construction sites, loneliness or solidarity, cars or buses, and it is our responsibility to do that now, for ourselves, for our families, for the people who make our lives worth living, and for the incredible creativity, beauty, and wonder that make our cities, in spite of all of their problems, the greatest invention of our time. Obrigado. Thank you.*

### Answers
1 a  2 a

## CRITICAL THINKING

### 5  21st CENTURY OUTCOMES

*Effectively analyse and evaluate evidence, arguments, claims and beliefs*

- Tell students that in this activity the critical thinking skill they'll be using is the ability to take a model they've learned about, namely 'people power', imagine what would happen if it was applied to their own context and evaluate its potential effectiveness.

- Give students some time to think about whether the 'people power' solutions Orofino described would work in their town/city and why / why not. In order to fulfil the 21st CENTURY OUTCOMES, students should be able to analyse and evaluate the evidence they have about how interested the people in their town/city are in taking control of what happens there to draw conclusions about whether these solutions would work there. They may want to refer back to the transcripts of Part 2 and Part 3 of the talk so they can look at these solutions again. Then, put students into pairs to discuss their opinions, bringing in examples from things that happen in their community, and the opinions and attitudes of the people who live there.

- Conduct whole-class feedback.

## VOCABULARY IN CONTEXT

## 6

- ▶8.13 Play the clips from the TED Talk. When each multiple-choice question appears, pause the clip so that students can choose the correct definition. Discourage the more confident students from always giving the answer by asking students to raise their hand if they think they know.

### Transcript and subtitles

*1 Three years ago, I co-founded an organization called Meu Rio, and we make it easier for people in the city of Rio to organize around causes and places that they **care about** in their own city, and have an impact on those causes and places every day.*
If you **care about** something, you feel that _____.
    **a** it's important
    **b** it's difficult
    **c** it is strange

*2 In these past three years, Meu Rio grew to a **network** of 160,000 citizens of Rio.*
What does **network** mean?
    **a** a small city
    **b** a large institution
    **c** a group of people who are connected

*3 Bia started a campaign, and we even watched her school **24/7** through webcam monitoring …*
What does **24/7** mean?
    **a** 24 minutes every day
    **b** all the time
    **c** easily

*4 There's also Jovita. She's an amazing woman whose daughter **went missing** about ten years ago, and since then, she has been looking for her daughter.*
If someone **goes missing**, it means other people _____.
    **a** feel sad they are not here
    **b** don't know where they are

*5 The plan was to **hand** it **over** to a developer, who planned to turn it into a construction site.*
If you **hand** something **over to someone**, you _____.
    **a** give it to them
    **b** take it from them

8 Better cities

| Answers |
|---|
| 1 a  2 c  3 b  4 b  5 a |

**7**

• Students are now going to use two of the terms they looked at in Exercise 8 – *to care about something* and *24/7* – to talk about whether their friends and family care about the environment, and give their own opinions about communication today.

• Put students into pairs and ask them to say their own answers to the questions, giving as much detail as they can. Tell students to bring in their own experiences of being able to communicate with other people all the time, e.g. using social media sites or apps and messaging services on their smartphones, and the positive and negative consequences of this that they've experienced.

• Circulate and monitor students' discussions and give them feedback when they've finished.

## PRESENTATION SKILLS Using anecdotes

**8**

• ▶ 8.14 Direct students to the Presentation skills box and check the meaning of *anecdote* (an interesting or funny short story about something that really happened). Elicit whether students tell anecdotes in their first language and, if so, what situations they use them in and why.

• Play the clip from Part 2 of the talk and ask students to make notes on how effective the anecdote is and then discuss and compare their ideas in pairs. Conduct whole-class feedback on students' opinions.

| Answers |
|---|
| Students' own answers. |

> **TEACHING TIP**
>
> **What makes a good anecdote?**
>
> This may be the first time that students have told an anecdote in English, but anecdote-telling is an important component of presentations and informal conversation. Here are some tips for telling anecdotes:
>
> 1. Think about the purpose of your anecdote.
> 2. Consider your audience and what they'll find interesting or funny.
> 3. Humour helps, but remember that it doesn't always translate.
> 4. Start the anecdote in an interesting way.
> 5. Use pace and timing effectively.
> 6. Make sure your anecdote has a beginning, a middle and an end.
> 7. Include relevant details.
> 8. Have a memorable 'punch-line' at the end, i.e. a statement of what happened at the end of the story which shows the audience the point you wanted to make with your anecdote.

**9**

• ▶ 8.15 Tell students that most TED speakers use at least one anecdote in their talks. Ask students to read the names of the speakers they've previously watched – Ann Morgan (Unit 3), Daria van den Bercken (Unit 4) and Jarrett J. Krosoczka (Unit 6) – and the summaries of the anecdotes they used. Then, have them match the speakers with the anecdotes, based on what they can remember from their TED Talks. Play the clips so students can listen and check their answers. Tell students that they'll just see excerpts from the anecdotes in order to give them a flavour of them. If time allows, students can re-watch the TED Talks so they can hear the whole anecdotes.

• **Optional step.** Ask students to also think about and make notes on how effective they think each anecdote is and discuss this in their pairs.

• Confirm the correct answers in class.

| Answers |
|---|
| 1 c  2 b  3 a |

**10**

• Students are now going to use what they've learned about what makes a good anecdote to have a go at telling one themselves. Put them into small groups (three to four students) and ask them to each choose one of the topics in the box to tell an anecdote about. Give students some time to prepare their anecdotes.

• Students then take it in turns to tell their anecdotes.

• Monitor and then ask students to give each other peer feedback on how effective they were, before adding your own global feedback.

▶ Set Workbook page 66 for homework.

## 8.5 Creative solutions

### COMMUNICATE Let's fix this!

**1**

• Put students into groups of four or five and ask them to read the information and instructions. Then, have them work together to brainstorm some possible ways in which an app could help you find lost pets. Tell students to bring in their own experiences of looking after pets, finding lost pets and using apps.

• Direct students to the model exchange and encourage them to use the same format while they're brainstorming, i.e. one student says an idea and other students say whether they think it's a good idea and why.

• Monitor students while they're brainstorming and offer assistance or feedback where appropriate.

## 2   21st CENTURY OUTCOMES

*Exercise flexibility and willingness to be helpful in making necessary compromises to accomplish a common goal*

- Have students discuss which app idea or ideas (two or three) they think is/are the best. In order to fulfil the 21st CENTURY OUTCOMES, students should show the flexibility and willingness to reach compromises so they can reach a consensus in their groups, where necessary. They can then write notes on the idea or ideas they've chosen in the box.

- **Optional step.** When students are making notes on how the app works, they should find the structure *by* + verb + *-ing* useful, e.g. *It works by sending you a notification when your dog is within 500 metres of where you are.*

- Direct students to the Giving examples box and tell them to use these phrases when they're giving examples of what the app can do or how it works in their notes.

- **Optional step.** Elicit or explain that all of the phrases in the Giving examples box have the same function, but *for example* is more informal and *for instance* and *such as* are more formal.

## 3

- Put each group together with another group and have them present their app ideas to each other, using their notes from Exercise 2.

- When all the ideas have been presented, ask students to discuss which one would provide the best solution to the problem of finding lost pets.

- Conduct whole-class feedback and ask each group to present the idea they've chosen in class.

## WRITING   Describing a change for the better

## 4

- Ask students to think about the town/city where they live and what changes could be made to improve it. Then, have them choose one change to write about.

- Tell students to read the example text and then use it as a model for their own texts. They need to describe the change they'd like to make and why they'd like to make it. They could also add what effect(s) this change would have on their town/city.

- Circulate and monitor while students are writing, offering assistance and feedback where appropriate.

> **Answers**
> Students' own answers.

▶ Set Workbook page 67 for homework.

▶ Photocopiable communicative activity 8.2. Go to page 178 for further practice of features of a city vocabulary and phrasal verbs. The teaching notes are on page 194.

# 9 Giving

> **UNIT AT A GLANCE**
>
> **THEME:** Giving money to charity
> **VOCABULARY:** Fundraising
> **LISTENING:** My fundraising adventure
> **SPEAKING:** Talking about good causes, Planning an event
> **GRAMMAR:** *will* for offers and first conditionals
> **PRONUNCIATION:** Linking with /w/ and /j/, Intonation with conditional sentences
>
> **READING:** *Giving on the go*
> **TED TALK:** *Should you donate differently?* In this talk, Joy Sun tells us why she thinks it's better to give money directly to people instead of investing it in aid programmes.
> **PRESENTATION SKILLS:** Using supporting evidence
> **WRITING:** Describing a charity

## WARM UP

- Books open. Draw students' attention to the unit title, the photo and the caption on page 93.
- Put students into pairs or small groups (three to four students) to discuss the questions.
- **Question 1**. Direct students to the photo of a hairdresser giving a homeless man a free haircut in New York and ask them if they've seen similar photos before or seen something like this themselves in real life. Ask students to say what their reaction to the photo is / how it makes them feel. Then, have them say what they think is being 'given' in this photo and why they think the hairdresser is giving it.
- **Question 2**. Ask students to think of some other examples of people giving their time for free – these could be general things or specific examples of things that they do / have done, or people who they know do / have done.
- **Question 3**. If students already do some kind of voluntary work, they can say what skills they use when they're doing this work and how they use them. If students don't do any kind of voluntary work at the moment, they could think about voluntary work they've done in the past and/or what skills they have now which they could use to help people.

## 9.1 It's for a good cause

### VOCABULARY Fundraising

#### Extra activity

**It's for a good cause**
Direct students to the title of this section (*It's for a good cause*) and elicit or explain that people say 'It's for a cause' when they want other people to give them money which will help other people, animals or places, e.g. a rainforest.

Elicit or explain that giving money to a good cause is called *donating money*, and organizing the donation of money is called *fundraising*. Have students brainstorm examples of good causes that they know of and say who, what or how each one helps. Students can then use these example charities later in Exercise 2.

**1**

- Have students read the verbs on the left and look up the meanings of any words they don't already know. Tell students that here the word *raise* means to collect or encourage people to donate money. Then, ask them to read the noun in each line and circle the one that doesn't come after the verbs. Students may find that saying verb-noun combinations out loud helps them to notice which ones are possible and which aren't.
- Ask students to compare their answers in pairs before you check answers in class. Tell students to record any words or collocations from this exercise that were new for them.

> **Answers**
> 1 social work   2 volunteers   3 a cause   4 a charity
> 5 money   6 money

**2**

- Put students into pairs. Ask them to look at the table and check the meaning of *animal welfare* (the condition in which animals live as it affects their health, well-being and chances of survival). Have students brainstorm charities they know which help in the three different areas given in the table.
- Tell students to write in at least one charity in each category, but encourage them to think of as many as they can and, if possible, to choose charities they're familiar with. You could give them a time limit for doing this, e.g. think of as many charities as you can in two minutes. If students are struggling to think of charities and they have access to the Internet, they could go online to get some ideas.
- Conduct whole-class feedback on the charities students have chosen.

> **Answers**
>
> Students' own answers.

## 3

- Direct students to the model conversation and ask them to use the first sentence as a model for explaining what a charity from their table in Exercise 2 does. Tell students to re-use the verb-noun collocations from Exercise 1, where relevant, to help them do this. As in the second sentence in the model conversation, the student's partner can then say whether they know what the charity does too and add any extra information they know about it.

- In the same pairs from Exercise 2, have students choose some of the charities they thought of and talk about them in this way.

- **Optional step**. Conduct whole-class feedback and have each student in each pair explain what one of the charities they thought of does.

> **Answers**
>
> Students' own answers.

## LISTENING  My fundraising adventure

## 4

- ▶9.1 Direct students to the Understanding directions box and elicit or explain that *directions* are the instructions you give someone so they know how to get from one place to another. Ask students to listen out for the words for directions in the recording they're going to listen to.

- Tell students that they're going to listen to Neil Glover, who they can see in the photo, talking about a journey he made to raise money for charity.

- **Optional step**. Based on what they can see in the photo of Neil, and without looking at the three options in this exercise, have students speculate about what kind of journey he made and where. They can do this either in pairs or in class.

- Have students read the three options which summarize Neil's journey. Then, play the recording and ask students to circle the correct sentence. Check answers in class.

### Transcript

*In 2016, I and a group of friends took part in an event called the Dumball Rally in India. The event was to raise money for a charity called the Teenage Cancer Trust. The rally involved about 30 teams. Each team had a car, which they drove around the southern part of India. The journey took eight days. We started in Chennai, we drove south along the east coast, and then north up the west coast, and finished in our final destination, in Goa. We used social media to ask our friends and family for donations. Using Facebook and a website called JustGiving.com, it was really easy to contact everyone to receive their donations online.*

*Our team raised around $4,000, and in total, the event raised around $170,000. And of course, the journey itself was lots of fun, too. We drove for about twelve hours every day, and saw some incredible scenery along the way. We also got a chance to talk to some of the local people, and we even managed to have a game of cricket! It was an experience I will never forget, and hopefully the money we raised will go some way to making people's lives better.*

> **Answer**
>
> c

## 5

- ▶9.1 Tell students they're going to listen to the recording again and focus on some of the specific information that Neil gives about his journey.

- Play the recording and ask students to listen out for the information in the sentences and decide whether the sentences are true or false.

- Students then compare their answers in pairs before you check answers in class.

> **Answers**
>
> 1 F   2 T   3 T   4 F

## Pronunciation  Linking with /w/ and /j/

### 6a

- ▶9.2 Students are now going to listen to an extract from the recording by Neil Glover that they've just listened to and notice how an extra /w/ or /j/ sound is added between two words when they're linked together. Ask students to read the sentence before they listen to it and notice where the extra /w/ or /j/ sounds are. Then, play the recording and have them listen carefully to these two extra sounds.

### 6b

- ▶9.3 Ask students to read the sentences and refer back to the sentence in Exercise 6a to help them identify and mark where they think the /w/ or /j/ sounds will be. Students should find it helpful to practise saying the sentences out loud to see if they naturally add the sounds.

- Play the recording and have students mark where the words are linked in the sentences, and which sounds are added where. Check answers in class and then put students into pairs to practise saying the sentences with the linking sounds.

> **Answers**
>
> 1 The /j/ event raised a lot of money.
> 2 They wanted to /w/ ask us questions.
> 3 They /j/ all encouraged us.
> 4 We met a man who /w/ asked us to play cricket.

9  Giving   95

## TEACHING TIP

### Linking

What students are learning about in Exercises 6a and 6b is how linking works. Linking involves inserting additional sounds in between two words that are said together in connected speech. The insertion of the /w/ and /j/ sounds between two adjacent words is a typical example of linking. As with other aspects of connected speech, the most important thing for students at this level is being able to recognize it in other people's speech. They shouldn't be aiming to use it themselves. Encourage students to listen out for other examples of linking when they're doing subsequent listening and video-watching activities.

## SPEAKING Talking about good causes

**7**

- ▶9.4 Ask students to read the conversation through once before they listen to it. Tell students to ignore the word choices on the right for the moment as they will focus on those in Exercise 8.

- Check answers and elicit that the two people both agree to donate £20 to a charity that helps save the rainforest.

- **Optional step.** Ask students whether they would also donate, or have also donated, money to a charity that helps save the rainforest. Ask: *Do you think this is a good cause worth giving money to and why / why not?*

| Answer |
| --- |
| donating money |

**8**

- Model the conversation that students have just listened to aloud with a student. Then, have students work in pairs to practise the conversation together. Make sure they alternate between A and B roles.

- Have students practise the conversation again using the words on the right instead of the words in bold in the conversation.

**9** **21st CENTURY OUTCOMES**

*Exercising the rights and obligations of citizenship at local, state, national and global levels*

- Direct students to the model sentence and then give them some time to think about a time they helped a charity, e.g. by donating money or volunteering, or did something to help someone, e.g. going food shopping for an elderly relative or a neighbour. Even if students initially think that they haven't done anything to help, everyone will have done something, however big or small, to help other people at some point. They may even have helped their fellow students in the English lesson, for example.

- Put students into pairs to tell each other about the time they helped someone. Remind them to use a time expression to say when they did it. Encourage students to respond to what their partner says by expressing interest and asking a question to find out more information. In order to fulfil the 21st CENTURY OUTCOMES, students should be able to show that they understand the effects their actions have on their local community and why helping other people is important in that community.

- Circulate and monitor students while they're talking to each other and give them feedback when they've finished.

▶ Set Workbook pages 68 and 69 for homework.

▶ Photocopiable communicative activity 9.1. Go to page 179 for further practice of fundraising vocabulary. The teaching notes are on page 195.

## 9.2 I'll help!

### GRAMMAR *will* for offers and first conditionals

**1**

- ▶9.5 **Optional step.** Engage students with the topic of online fundraising by asking them if they've ever used it to donate or raise money. If they have, ask them to say which website or social media site was used, what the good cause was and how successful the fundraising effort was.

- Direct students to the infographic. Ask them to look at the graphs, and identify and make notes on the benefits of online fundraising and the most effective way of doing it.

- Check answers in class.

| Suggested answers |
| --- |
| It generates more money and has lower costs; Twitter |

**2**

- ▶9.6 Tell students they're now going to listen to two people talking about fundraising for a charity marathon run. Ask students to read the sentences and then play the recording so they can listen and complete them with the words they hear.

- Ask students to compare answers in pairs before checking answers in class.

## Transcript

**A:** I heard you're planning to run a marathon for charity.

**B:** Yeah, that's right. I'm raising money for a local children's charity.

**A:** That's great. Can I make a donation?

**B:** Of course. I have a Facebook page where you can donate online.

**A:** OK, cool. I'll do it later today. How much have you raised so far?

**B:** Well, so far it's $950. So, if you donate $50, I'll reach my target of $1,000.

**A:** Oh, well done! OK, $50 is no problem.

**B:** Great! Thanks.

### Answers

1 children's   2 (a) Facebook (page)   3 50

## 3

- Direct students to the title of the Grammar box and elicit or explain that a first conditional sentence is a sentence with the word *if* in it that tells you what you will do or what will happen in the future if a likely condition is fulfilled. Ask students to read the example sentences, identify which sentence is an offer and which is a first conditional sentence, and identify the verb forms used in the *if* clause and main clause (the part of the sentence that doesn't have *if* in it) in the first conditional sentence.

- Students can check their answers and overall understanding of *will* for offers and first conditionals by turning to the Grammar summary on page 149.

- If you feel that students need more controlled practice before continuing, they could do the exercises in the Grammar summary. Otherwise, you could continue on to Exercise 4 in the unit and set the Grammar summary exercises for homework.

### Answers

a 1   b 2   c present simple, *will*   d possible future

### Answers to Grammar summary exercises

**1**

1 c   2 d   3 e   4 a   5 b

**2**

Suggested answers:

2 I'll book the venue

3 I'll contact some sponsors

4 I'll organize the food

5 I'll print some tickets

6 I'll clean up afterwards

## 4

- Tell students they're now going to focus on how to form first conditionals by looking at some more examples and identifying where the word *will* isn't needed. Using *will* where it isn't needed is one of the most common mistakes that learners at this level make with the form of first conditionals.

- Have students compare their answers in pairs, but don't check answers at this stage.

### Answers

1 If I ~~will~~ win the lottery, I'll give half of it to charity.

2 I'll support you for your sponsored run if you ~~will~~ remind me.

3 If you~~'ll~~ come on Saturday, I'll help you with your French.

4 I'll visit Granny in hospital if I~~'ll~~ have time.

5 If they ~~will~~ decide to support our charity, it will make a big difference.

## Pronunciation Intonation with conditional sentences

## 5

- ▶ 9.7 Play the recording of the sentences from Exercise 4, and tell students to check their answers and also notice how the speaker's voice goes up in the *if* clause of the sentences that start with *if* (1, 3 and 5) and then goes down in the main clause that follows it. Alternatively, play the recording twice: once for students to check their answers and again for them to notice the intonation.

- Confirm the correct answers and check that students noticed the intonation.

## LANGUAGE FOCUS Making offers and describing possible future events

## 6

- ▶ 9.8 Ask students to read the Language focus box and to notice how *I'll* + infinitive without *to* is used to make spontaneous offers of help and how first conditionals can be used to say what would have to happen for you to be able to help in the future. In the sentence *I'll help if I have enough time*, for example, having enough time in the future will make it possible for the speaker to help.

- Students can check overall understanding of the language focus by turning to the Grammar summary on page 149.

- If you feel that students need more controlled practice before continuing, they could do the exercises in the Grammar summary. Otherwise, you could continue on to Exercise 7 in the unit and set the Grammar summary exercises for homework.

> **Answers to Grammar summary exercises**
>
> **1**
>
> 1 help   2 will   3 make   4 call   5 will you   6 I'll do
> 7 have   8 don't   9 won't   10 get   11 will you
> 12 I will
>
> **2**
>
> 1 We'll get good publicity if we invite a few famous people.
> 2 We'll help to raise awareness if we set up a website.
> 3 If people can pay online, they will find it easier.
> 4 Will enough people come if we don't use social media?
> 5 They won't donate if we don't explain what the charity does.
> 6 If you need to drive, I'll bring my car.
> 7 Will we raise more money if we hold the event on a Saturday?
> 8 If I design the tickets, will you print them?

**7**

- Students are now going to look at some more examples of offers with *will* and match the sentences with the offers that could follow them.

- Have students match the sentences with the offers and then check answers in class.

> **Answers**
> 1 d   2 a   3 e   4 b   5 c

### Extra activity

### Helping each other out

Put students into pairs and ask each student to make a list of five or six real problems they currently have which someone else could help them with. Give them a couple of examples to show them what you mean, e.g. *I haven't got any paper left*, *Your head is blocking my view of the teacher*. Students then read the things on their lists to their partner, who either offers help using a sentence with *will*, e.g. *I'll give you some of mine*, *I'll move to the left*, if they can help, or, if they can't help, says: *Sorry I can't help you because …* and gives a reason why they can't. Model an example exchange with one student before everyone starts.

**8**

- ▶ 9.9 Students are now going to practise identifying the verb forms that should be used in different clauses of first conditional sentences. Ask students to read the text about a fundraising app all the way through first, so they understand its gist, and then go back and choose the correct verb forms. Tell them to refer back to the example first conditional sentences in the Grammar summary and Language focus boxes if they need to.

- Play the recording of the text so that students can listen and check their answers.

> **Answers**
> 1 decide   2 will send   3 add   4 will send   5 are

### Extra activity

### Reviewing One Today

In Exercise 8, students read about the One Today app. Put students into pairs and ask them to go online (either in class or, if this isn't possible, as a self-study task) and look at the featured projects on the One Today app website to give them a better idea of how the app works. Then, ask students to download the app, which is free, test it out and either write a review of it or tell a partner what they think about it in class.

**9**

- Ask students to read the first line and the start of the second line in each mini-conversation and write possible endings to the second line. Ask them to look at the verb form (*will* + infinitive without *to* or the present simple) that's used in the first part of the sentence they have to complete and use this to help them decide what verb form should be used in the second part.

- Put students into pairs to compare their sentences.

- **Optional step**. Have students read the mini-conversations out loud with a partner, using the rising and falling intonation in the *if* sentences that they looked at in Exercise 5.

> **Answers**
> Students' own answers

## SPEAKING Planning an event

**10**  **21st CENTURY OUTCOMES**

*Exercise flexibility and willingness to be helpful in making necessary compromises to accomplish a common goal*

- Put students into groups of four or five. Ask students to choose a charity that they all think is a good cause, and then discuss and decide the details of a fundraising event for that charity, using the questions to guide their discussion. In order to fulfil the 21st CENTURY OUTCOMES, students should be able to acknowledge the value of other students' ideas and show willingness to make compromises if other students' ideas differ from their own.

- In the final question, 'each person' refers to each student in a group, so make sure students are aware of this and remind them to use *I'll* to offer to do things.

### Extra activity

#### Too loud or too quiet

Often when students are taking part in discussion and decision-making tasks, some of them want to talk a lot and others stay quiet and say very little. The results are big variations in terms of how much the students use English and contribute to the task in hand, which can cause the quieter students' motivation levels to drop. Here are some tips for dealing with this kind of imbalance:

1. Group more dominant students together and quieter students together. This will push the dominant students to assert themselves and use their voices even more and it will also push the quieter students to contribute because they won't feel inhibited by the stronger students. Also, if they don't say or do something the task won't get done.

2. Assign the role of 'team leader' or 'discussion leader' to one student in each group so that you have someone there to monitor and control students' contributions. If you think they'll be able to handle it, ask quieter students to take on this role – it should boost their confidence.

3. Circulate and monitor so you can pick up any imbalances in participation and try to deal with them by asking quieter students questions.

### 11

- Check the meaning of *backup plan* (a second option that you have if the first one doesn't work). Ask students to read the three problems in the box and the example sentences and then work together in their groups – or individually for an extra challenge – to write first conditional sentences about the backup plan they have for each situation. Encourage them to personalize these sentences to the specific details of their event.

- Give students feedback on how successfully they've used first conditional sentences to describe their backup plans when they've finished.

▶ Set Workbook pages 70 and 71 for homework.

▶ Photocopiable communicative activity 9.2. Go to page 180 for further practice of *will* for offers and first conditionals and fundraising vocabulary. The teaching notes are on page 195.

## 9.3 Donation revolution

### READING Giving on the go

### 1

- Direct students to the title of the article they're going to read – *Giving on the go* – and tell them to think about what its two parts (*giving* and *on the go*) could refer to, and use this to deduce what the article is mainly about. Put them into pairs to discuss their ideas. If students are unsure, you could give them the hint that the main idea in the article is connected to what they read about in the infographic in **9.2**.

> **Answers**
> Students' own answers.

### 2

- ▶9.10 Ask students to scan read the article to find out what the article is mainly about and check whether their answer from Exercise 1 was correct. Check answers in class, and elicit or explain what an *earthquake* is (a sudden shaking of the earth which causes a lot of damage).

### Understanding purpose

### 3

- Ask students to read the article again more slowly. After reading each paragraph, ask them to think about what its main purpose was, i.e. what the author wanted to do in it or why they wrote it. They can then compare their ideas with the two options given and choose the correct one in each case.

- Students can compare their answers in pairs before you check answers in class.

> **Answers**
> Paragraph 1: a
> Paragraph 2: b
> Paragraph 3: a
> Paragraph 4: b

### Understanding details

### 4

- Tell students to read the sentences, and then read the whole article again and find information about the issues mentioned in them. They can then decide whether they're true, false or not given, and circle the correct options.

- Point out the glossary at the bottom of the text and tell students to refer to it as they read or to look at the words and definitions before they start reading.

- Check answers in class.

> **Answers**
> 1 NG  2 T  3 T  4 NG  5 T  6 F

### Understanding vocabulary

### 5

- Ask students to read the sentences and consider what the missing words could be. Stronger students could complete the sentences without looking back at the article, while weaker students can look back at the article and use the words in bold in it as their word pool. Weaker students may also find it helpful to look at how the words in bold are used in context.

- Check answers in class.

> **Answers**
>
> 1 advances   2 innovative   3 disaster   4 impact
> 5 damage

**6**

- Ask students to read paragraph 4 again and make notes on what each of the apps – Charity Miles and SnapDonate – does. Then, put them into pairs to discuss which one they think would be more effective at raising money and why, referring back to their notes.
- Conduct whole-class feedback on students' opinions about the two apps and establish which one the majority of students finds more effective.

▶ Set Workbook pages 72 and 73 for homework.

## 9.4 Should you donate differently?

### TEDTALKS

**1**

- Tell students that they're now going to watch a TED Talk by Joy Sun, who's an aid worker. Check the meaning of *aid worker* (someone who works for a not-for-profit organization, such as a charity, that helps people in need, e.g. by bringing them food and other supplies or providing technical or logistical assistance), and then have students read the summary of the talk and match the words in bold with their definitions. If students are unsure about which words to match with which items, encourage them to use deduction or simply have a guess.
- Students can compare their answers in pairs before you check answers in class. Draw students' attention to the pronunciation of *recipient* /rɪˈsɪpiənt/ as they may find this challenging.

> **Answers**
>
> 1 recipients   2 dedicated   3 veteran   4 investing

**2**

- ▶ 9.11 Tell students that they're now going to watch Part 1 of Sun's talk, in which she talks about her old beliefs about the best way to help the poor and what she believes now. Ask them to read the three options.
- Then, play Part 1 of the talk and ask students to focus on understanding what Sun believes now, so they can tick the correct statements. Encourage them to listen out for the tense Sun uses – present simple or past simple – to help them identify whether she's talking about the past or the present. Students can then check answers in pairs before you check answers in class.

**Transcript**

I suspect that every aid worker in Africa comes to a time in her career when she wants to take all the money for her project – maybe it's a school or a training programme – pack it in a suitcase, get on a plane flying over the poorest villages in the country, and start throwing that money out the window. Because to a veteran aid worker, the idea of putting cold, hard cash into the hands of the poorest people on Earth doesn't sound crazy, it sounds really satisfying.

[…] Well, why did I spend a decade doing other stuff for the poor? Honestly, I believed that I could do more good with money for the poor than the poor could do for themselves. I held two assumptions: one, that poor people are poor in part because they're uneducated and don't make good choices; two is that we then need people like me to figure out what they need and get it to them. It turns out, the evidence says otherwise.

> **Answer**
>
> a

**3**

- ▶ 9.12 Tell students that they're now going to listen to Part 2 of Sun's talk, in which she talks about what happens when you give poor people cash, and complete the notes about what happened in three countries where aid workers did this.
- **Optional step.** Ask students to speculate about whether Sun will say that giving cash to poor people was a good or a bad idea, giving reasons for their answers.
- Ask students to read the notes and draw their attention to the definition of *assets* below the table. Then, play the recording so they can listen and complete the notes.
- Students can compare their completed notes in pairs before you check answers in class.

**Transcript**

In recent years, researchers have been studying what happens when we give poor people cash. Dozens of studies show across the board that people use cash transfers to improve their own lives. Pregnant women in Uruguay buy better food and give birth to healthier babies. Sri Lankan men invest in their businesses. Researchers who studied our work in Kenya found that people invested in a range of assets, from livestock to equipment to home improvements, and they saw increases in income from business and farming one year after the cash was sent.

> **Answers**
>
> Uruguay: food
> Sri Lanka: businesses
> Kenya: increased

## 4

- ▶9.13 Students are now going to watch Part 3 of the talk, in which Sun talks about a study of an aid programme that was done with the poor in India. Check the meaning of *study* (here: a detailed analysis of a subject) and *livestock* (farm animals that are seen as assets). Put students into pairs, and ask them to look at the graph and use the information in it to decide and discuss whether they think it shows that this aid programme was successful or unsuccessful.

- Then, play Part 3 of the talk and ask students to listen to understand the gist of whether the programme was successful or not, so they can check the answers they gave in their discussions.

- In class, confirm that this aid programme was unsuccessful and elicit that we know this because the people who received the livestock sold them for cash rather than using them to build up their farms, which was the programme's aim. Elicit that this study supports Sun's argument that the poor want cash and not material things.

### Transcript

*One very telling study looked at a programme in India that gives livestock to the so-called ultra-poor, and they found that 30 per cent of recipients had turned around and sold the livestock they had been given for cash. The real irony is, for every 100 dollars' worth of assets this programme gave someone, they spent another 99 dollars to do it. What if, instead, we use technology to put cash, whether from aid agencies or from any one of us directly into a poor person's hands?*

#### Answer
The graph shows an unsuccessful aid programme.

## 5

- ▶9.14 Students are now going to watch Part 4 of the talk in which Sun talks about an organization she's started called GiveDirectly.

- **Optional step.** Ask students to speculate about what GiveDirectly does, based on its name and what they already know about Sun's beliefs. They can either do this in pairs or in class.

- Play the recording and ask students to concentrate on listening out for the correct options so they can circle them.

- Have students compare their answers in pairs before checking answers in class.

### Transcript

*Today, three in four Kenyans use mobile money, which is basically a bank account that can run on any cell phone. A sender can pay a 1.6 per cent fee and with the click of a button send money directly to a recipient's account with no intermediaries.*

*[…] That's what we've started to do at GiveDirectly. We're the first organization dedicated to providing cash transfers to the poor. We've sent cash to 35,000 people across rural Kenya and Uganda in one-time payments of 1,000 dollars per family. So far, we've looked for the poorest people in the poorest villages, and in this part of the world, they're the ones living in homes made of mud and thatch, not cement and iron.*

*[…] Something that five years ago would have seemed impossible we can now do efficiently and free of corruption. The more cash we give to the poor, and the more evidence we have that it works, the more we have to reconsider everything else we give. Today, the logic behind aid is too often, well, we do at least some good.*

*[…] What if the logic was, will we do better than cash given directly? Organizations would have to prove that they're doing more good for the poor than the poor can do for themselves. Of course, giving cash won't create public goods like eradicating disease or building strong institutions, but it could set a higher bar for how we help individual families improve their lives.*

#### Answers
1 money   2 35,000   3 one-time   4 poorest

## CRITICAL THINKING

### 6   21st CENTURY OUTCOMES

***Analyse and evaluate major alternative points of view***

- Tell students that in this activity the critical thinking skill they'll be using is the ability to evaluate the effect that listening to another person talking about their experiences and beliefs has on their opinions about the subject the person talked about.

- Put students into pairs to discuss what they thought about giving to charity before watching Sun's talk, whether this is different now, and how and why it's changed. Encourage students to refer back to the transcript of Sun's talk so they can bring specific points or examples that Sun uses into their discussions. If students say that the talk hasn't had any effect on their own views, ask them to say why this is, e.g. because they had the same view as Sun before they watched or because her arguments didn't convince them to agree with her. In order to fulfil the 21st CENTURY OUTCOMES, students should be able to show that they've thought about and evaluated the point of view that Sun put forward in her talk.

- Conduct whole-class feedback on students' views.

## VOCABULARY IN CONTEXT

## 7

- ▶9.15 Play the clips from the TED Talk. When each multiple-choice question appears, pause the clip so that students can choose the correct definition. Discourage the more confident students from always giving the answer by asking students to raise their hand if they think they know.

## Transcript and subtitles

**1** I suspect that every aid worker in Africa comes to a time in her career when she wants to take all the money for her project – maybe it's a school or a **training programme** – pack it in a suitcase, get on a plane flying over the poorest villages in the country and start throwing that money out the window.

What is a training **programme**?
    a  a TV show to learn a new skill
    b  a plan to improve the education system
    c  several classes to teach people how to do something

**2** I held two assumptions: one, that poor people are poor in part because they're uneducated and don't make good choices; two is that we then need people like me to **figure out** what they need and get it to them.

If you **figure** something **out**, you _____.
    a  know it well
    b  try to understand it
    c  get something wrong

**3 Dozens** of studies show across the board that people use cash transfers to improve their own lives.

If there are **dozens** of something, it means there are _____ of them.
    a  lots
    b  a few
    c  too many

**4** Today, three in four Kenyans use mobile money, which is basically a bank account that can run on any cell phone. A sender can pay a 1.6 per cent **fee** and with the click of a button send money directly to a recipient's account

If you pay a **fee**, you give some money _____.
    a  to buy something in a shop
    b  to go on public transport
    c  to use a service

**5** Organizations would have to **prove** that they're doing more good for the poor than the poor can do for themselves.

If you **prove** something you, _____.
    a  tell people that it is good
    b  show that it's definitely true
    c  try it for the first time

| Answers |
| --- |
| 1 c  2 b  3 a  4 c  5 b |

**8**

- Students are now going to use two of the terms they looked at in Exercise 7 – *training programme* and *fee* – to talk about their interests and opinions.

- Put students into pairs and ask them to say their own answers to the questions, giving as much detail as they can.

- Circulate and monitor students' discussions and give them feedback when they've finished.

## PRESENTATION SKILLS Using supporting evidence

**9**

- ▶9.16 Direct students to the Presentation skills box and check the meaning of *supporting evidence* (facts that we give to show that something we say is true).

- Ask students to watch the clip from Sun's talk and notice the language Sun uses to give supporting evidence. Then, elicit that these are: *Researchers have been studying what happens ...*; *Dozens of studies show across the board ...*

- **Optional step**. Ask students which of the two phrases Sun uses to introduce supporting evidence they think are more likely to make the audience believe that what she says is true. [Suggested answer: *Dozens of studies show across the board ...* because it uses evidence from many studies and *across the board* means *in all cases*.]

| Answers |
| --- |
| Students' own answers |

**10**

- ▶9.17 Review the meaning of *anecdote* and *to quote*. Then, play the clips from three TED Talks that students watched in previous units and have them match the speaker with the type of supporting evidence they use.

- Ask students to compare their answers in pairs before you check answers in pairs.

- **Optional step**. In pairs, ask students to discuss which use of supporting evidence from the three clips they think is the most effective and why. Conduct whole-class feedback.

| Answers |
| --- |
| 1 b  2 a  3 c |

**11**

- Put students into groups of three or four and ask them to each choose a different topic from the box. Give students some time to prepare their talks on the topic they've chosen. In their talk, students should a) introduce what they're talking about and b) give some supporting evidence which shows why it's good or better than something else.

- Encourage students to use what they already know about what they're talking about to come up with an example of supporting evidence, but if they have access to the Internet, students could also go online to find relevant information, such as research findings.

- Students then take it in turns to give their talks. Monitor students while they're speaking and give them feedback when they've finished.

▶ Set Workbook page 75 for homework.

## 9.5 Make a difference

### COMMUNICATE  Choosing a charity

**1**

• Ask students to turn to page 157 and read the information about six different charities there. Tell them to look up any unknown words in a dictionary and make brief notes on the key points about each charity.

**2**

• Put students into groups of four or five, and ask them to read the information and instructions. Then have them discuss how to donate the money, giving their opinions about which charity/charities they should donate the money to and why, and reacting and responding to other group members' opinions. Direct students to the model exchange and encourage them to use some of the language, e.g. *I think we should …*, *Maybe we should …* (to give an opinion) and *It will help …* (to give reasons for an opinion). Stop students after about five minutes and ask them to reach a decision about what to do with the money.

• Monitor students' discussions and offer assistance or feedback where appropriate.

**3**

• Put each group together with another group. Have them present what they've decided to do with the money to each other and use the phrases in the Explaining reasons box to say why they've decided this. Encourage students to react to what the other group tells them by asking them questions or commenting on their choices.

• **Optional step**. Conduct whole-class feedback and ask each group to present their choice and the reason(s) for it.

### WRITING  Describing a charity

**4**

• Ask students to think of a cause or charity that they either actively support or think is good. Tell them this could be anything from a major international charity, such as UNICEF, to a small local group working in the community where they live. They will just need to be able to think of a reason why it is a good cause. Then, have students read the questions and make notes on their answers for the cause/charity they've chosen.

**5**

• Ask students to read the example text, and then use this model and the notes they made in Exercise 4 to write their own text about the cause/charity they've chosen.

• **Optional step**. Stronger students could extend their texts by giving examples of specific activities or projects that the charity does or has done.

• Circulate and monitor while students are writing, offering assistance and feedback where appropriate.

> **Answers**
> Students' own answers.

> **TEACHING TIP**
>
> **Workshopping your writing**
>
> Sometimes we prioritize speaking practice in class over writing practice because writing is usually seen as something that you can do at home and then get feedback on later. However, you can also explore the advantages of writing in class with students by giving writing activities more of a workshop feel. You can:
>
> 1. Have students write texts collaboratively in pairs or groups, discussing and giving each other feedback on their ideas as they write.
>
> 2. Have students write individually, but get feedback from other students on their writing and then incorporate this into a new draft of the text.
>
> 3. Circulate and read students' texts as they're writing them, ask them questions about what they've written and what they're going to write to get them thinking, and give them feedback on what they've written so far, which they can then incorporate in the rest of their texts.

▶ Set Workbook page 76 for homework.

# Presentation 3 | UNITS 7–9

## MODEL PRESENTATION

### 1

- Tell students they're going to read the text of a presentation. The aim of the presentation is to tell people about a city the speaker visited and liked.

- Ask students to read the text of the presentation all the way through and think about what the missing words could be as they do so. Then, ask them to look at the words in the box, read the text all the way through again and complete it with the correct words. Encourage students to look at what comes before and after the gaps to help them decide which words should go in them.

- Students can compare their answers in pairs, but don't confirm answers at this stage as they will find out what the correct answers are when they watch the presentation in Exercise 2.

> **Answers**
> 1 to   2 largest   3 grew up   4 suburbs   5 museums
> 6 ate out   7 check out   8 locally   9 In   10 definitely

### 2

- 🔊 P.3 Play the recording of the presentation and ask students to listen closely for the words the presenter says in the gaps so they can check their answers from Exercise 1. Check answers in class.

- **Optional step.** Elicit the phrasal verbs the speaker uses and review their meanings (*grow up*: go through the process of becoming an adult; *eat out*: eat food in a restaurant; *check out*: find out what something is like by experiencing it for the first time).

### 3

- 🔊 P.3 Ask students to read the list of presentation skills and think back to when they looked at creating effective slides (Unit 7), using anecdotes (Unit 8) and using supporting evidence (Unit 9). Students can look back at the Presentation skills boxes from those units to refresh their memory of how presenters can do these things. Put students into pairs and ask them to discuss which of these skills they remember the speaker using in her presentation.

- Play the recording again so students can watch and check their answers. Elicit or explain that the speaker's slide isn't effective because it only contains text, which makes it not very interesting to look at, and it contains a lot of big numbers which the audience will try to read, thus distracting them from the presentation, when most of this information isn't relevant to its content anyway.

- **Optional step**. Put students into pairs to discuss what is or isn't in the text of the presentation, what the speaker does or what they could see during the presentation, i.e. in the slide, which told them which skills the speaker uses or doesn't use. Look at an example in class, e.g. *She personalizes the presentation by saying: I stayed for a week with my friend Josh, who grew up in Toronto, I visited the downtown area almost every day*, etc. Stop students after a few minutes and conduct whole-class feedback.

> **Answers**
> The speaker personalizes the presentation, closes the presentation effectively, provides background information, uses their voice effectively, tells an anecdote, uses supporting evidence. She doesn't use questions to signpost, number key points or use an effective slide.

## YOUR TURN

### 4

- Ask students to think of a city they've either visited or would like to visit. Students should be familiar with the city they choose or, if they're not, be prepared to do some online research to find out the answers to the questions about it.

- Give students some time to prepare their presentations. Tell them to read the questions and make notes on their answers to all or most of them.

- Direct students to the list of presentation skills in Exercise 3 and tell them that the objective is to use all of them in their own presentations. They will, therefore, also need to think about how they can include these points in their presentations while they're preparing to speak.

- In order to fulfil the objective of using an effective slide, students will, of course, have to create a slide. If time allows, they could also extend their presentation to make it longer than the example presentation they read and create several slides to accompany it. You can set the creation of the slides as a self-study task if time is short, particularly if students don't have access to computers in class. Students could also draw/write their slide(s) on a piece of paper instead of using a computer.

### 5

- Direct students to the Useful phrases box. Ask them to read its contents and note down the words and phrases they want to use in their presentations. Tell students to use at least one word or phrase from each of the four categories in the box.

**6**

- Put students into pairs and tell them they're now going to take it in turns to give their presentations.

- Have students give their presentations and tick the skills their partner uses while they're listening to them. Make sure students are aware that when they're giving their partner feedback they're going to say two things they liked about it and one thing that could be improved, so they will also need to be thinking about this while they're listening.

**7**

- Ask students to read the example feedback in the speech bubble and use it as a model for giving their own feedback to their partner. Encourage them to start with a positive comment, as in the example, and then mention the good things that their partner did, using the ticks they made in their checklist, before saying something that their partner could improve.

- **Optional step**. When students have finished giving each other feedback, add your global feedback on students' presentations to their comments and highlight some areas for improvement for next time.

> **TEACHING TIP**
>
> **Giving feedback**
>
> Students may have a tendency to be critical of each other when they're giving feedback on each other's presentations – possibly because they believe the point of feedback is to tell people what they did wrong. However, make sure they're aware that the purpose of feedback is to show someone what they're already doing well, so they can do it well again, and to suggest areas for improvement so they can do it even better next time.

# 10 Mind and machine

## UNIT AT A GLANCE

**THEME:** The human brain
**VOCABULARY:** Brain functions
**LISTENING:** The power of visualization
**SPEAKING:** Talking about a game, A logic puzzle
**GRAMMAR:** Adverbs and adverbial phrases
**PRONUNCIATION:** Word stress with three-syllable words, Pausing with adverbs of attitude
**READING:** *The power of the mind*
**TED TALK:** *A headset that reads your brainwaves.* In this talk, Tan Le talks about the life-changing applications of new technology that 'reads our minds'.
**PRESENTATION SKILLS:** Dealing with the unexpected
**WRITING:** Writing a proposal

## WARM UP

- Books open. Draw students' attention to the unit title, the photo and the caption on page 105.
- Put students into pairs or small groups (three to four students) to discuss the questions.
- **Question 1**. Direct students to the photo and check the meaning of *attach* (securely join or connect one thing to another thing). Bring in students' own experiences and ask them if they've ever had any kind of technology attached to their heads and, if they have, what it was, what it did and how they felt while it was attached. If students don't have any experience of this, ask them to imagine how they think they would feel and tell each other about that, e.g. *I think I'd find it …*
- **Question 2**. Direct students to the caption, so they can see that Neil Harbisson is 'hearing' the colours around him. Ask students to speculate about how technology can help people to do this or say anything they already know about how this works.
- **Question 3**. Check the meaning of *senses* (five abilities that you can use to find out what is happening in the world around you) and elicit or explain that the English words for the five senses are: *sight*, *hearing*, *smell*, *taste* and *touch*. Ask students to choose a sense they would like technology to help improve because they would like one of their senses to be even better than it is. Students then tell each other which sense they've chosen and why, and what they expect the effects of this improvement to be.

## 10.1 The brain

### VOCABULARY Brain functions

**1**

- ▶ 10.1 Direct students to the diagram of the brain. Ask them to look closely at it and read the names of the different parts of the brain in the key.

- Ask students to read the names of the brain parts and their functions in Exercise 1, and speculate about which parts match with which functions. Then, play the recording, and ask students to listen out for the different parts of the brain and the function of each one so they can match them.

- Have students compare their answers in pairs before checking answers in class.

### Transcript

*The human brain is the most complex organ in the human body. There are five main parts.*

*The frontal lobe is the part of our brain that helps us concentrate. We use it when we are trying to solve problems. But it's also responsible for our emotions, and so it influences our personality quite a lot. The occipital lobe is at the back of the brain. It helps us understand things that we see, such as colour, shape and distance. It's also the part of our brain that makes us dream. The temporal lobe is the part responsible for our long-term memory. It helps us organize information and understand language. The cerebellum helps us balance and control our muscles. It's important for hand-eye coordination.*

*The parietal lobe is the part that is responsible for our pain and touch sensations. It also enables us to understand time, numbers, and to be able to spell words. The brain is a truly amazing thing, and there's still so much that we don't know about it.*

**Answers**

1 c   2 d   3 a   4 e   5 b

**2**

- Students are now going to check their understanding of some of the key words they heard in the recording by completing their definitions. If students aren't sure about the meaning of any of the words in bold, they can either look them up in a dictionary or, alternatively, read the transcript for track **10.1**, identify the words in bold, see how they're used in context and deduce their meanings.

- Check answers in class. Ask students to note down any words which were new for them with their definition or an example.

> **Answers**
>
> 1 walk   2 think hard   3 asleep   4 love   5 remember
> 6 physical feeling

### 3

- Put students into pairs. Ask them to read the activities in the box. Check the meaning of *solve* (find an answer to a problem) and *sunset* (the time in the evening when the sun goes down).

- Ask them to refer back to the information about the different parts of the brain in Exercise 1 and think about which part you would use to do each of the activities. Direct students to the model conversation and ask them to use the language in it – *I think ..., I agree.* (or *I disagree*) – to tell each other which part of the brain you would use for each activity, agree or disagree with each other's opinions and add any extra relevant information.

- Conduct whole-class feedback on students' choices and ask them to explain them.

> **Suggested answers**
>
> solving a maths problem: frontal lobe
>
> looking at a pretty sunset: frontal lobe, occipital lobe
>
> playing tennis: occipital lobe, cerebellum
>
> writing an essay: frontal lobe
>
> cooking dinner: parietal lobe
>
> remembering your fifth birthday: temporal lobe

## LISTENING   The power of visualization

### 4

- ▶10.2   Direct students to the Listening for instructions box and review the meaning of *instructions*. Draw their attention to the fact that we use what's called the imperative – the infinitive form of the verb without *to* in positive sentences and *don't* + the infinitive form of the verb without *to*. Tell students they'll hear instructions in the recording of psychology professor Brian Scholl describing a brain experiment that they're going to listen to.

- Check the meaning of *aim* (something that someone wants to do) and then play the recording and ask students to identify the reason for the experiment and make a note of it.

- Students can then compare their answers in pairs before you check answers in class.

### Transcript

*How good would you say that your hand-eye coordination is? Good? Really good? Do you wish you could improve it? Many athletes believe that simply visualizing an action can improve their coordination. But does it work? Let's find out.*

*Let's run our experiment on the greatest sport ever invented. Set up a waste basket, crumple up some pieces of paper, and try to make some baskets. Sometimes you miss your shot. Sometimes you make it. Here's our question: can visualizing your throw before you take it improve your shooting?*

*This time, before shooting, try visualizing what it'll feel like for your arm to take the shot, and also the path that the paper will take on its way to the basket. Get set up. Do you see it? OK, then take the shot. If you're playing along at home, try taking a bunch of shots. On half of them, try visualizing first. On the other half, just go ahead and shoot. Keep track of your performance. Does it really help to visualize?*

*There's some evidence that mental practice of this sort can actually improve some types of athletic performance. Now some of these improvements might just be due to getting yourself into a relaxed and focused state of mind. But some of them might be because visualizing actions turns out to activate some of the same brain regions produced in making the motions themselves.*

> **Answer**
>
> to see if visualization can improve hand-eye coordination

### 5

- ▶10.2   Ask students to read the steps in the experiment that they've just heard and check the meaning of *crumple* (to press something, usually paper, into a small compact mass). Tell students to have a go at ordering the steps, based on what they can remember from their first listening and what they think is a logical order.

- Play the recording and ask students to check that they have the correct answers. Confirm the correct order in class.

> **Answers**
>
> a 3   b 2   c 4   d 1

---

**TEACHING TIP**

**Easy listening?**

Have you ever tried giving students the answers to a listening exercise before they listen? Giving students the answers can help them to focus on the content they're listening to and on noticing what you want them to notice, in this case the order of the steps, because they don't have to worry about matching options, circling letters and writing numbers. You obviously can't do this with every listening exercise because students do also need to complete comprehension tasks if they're going to improve their listening skills, but doing it occasionally will help students to concentrate on 'just' listening and maybe even help them to enjoy listening activities more.

## Pronunciation Word stress with three-syllable words

### 6a

- ▶ 10.3  Review the meaning of *word stress* (saying some sounds in a word more strongly than others). Tell students that three-syllable words usually have one of two possible stress patterns: **Ooo** or **oOo**. Play the recording and ask students to listen and read the two words, and notice which syllable is stressed in each.

### 6b

- ▶ 10.4  Ask students to read the words in the box and also try saying them out loud to see if they can hear which syllable is stressed in each word. Tell students to decide which stress pattern each word has and add them to the table.

- Play the recording so students can listen to the word stress in each word and check their answers. Then, play the recording again, and have students listen again and repeat.

**Answers**

| Ooo | oOo |
|---|---|
| **con**centrate | e**mo**tion |
| **me**mory | re**mem**ber |
| **phy**sical | sen**sa**tion |

### Extra activity

#### Adding more examples of word stress

Ask students to look at the transcripts of tracks **10.1** and **10.2**, find some more examples of three- and four-syllable words, and identify their word stress patterns. Students can then either write them in the correct column in the table in Exercise 6a or in a table in their notebooks. Tell students to add an extra column to their tables for four- or five-syllable words, like *coordination*, and draw their stress pattern; for example, *coordination* has the following stress pattern: **oOoOo**. Monitor students as they do this to check that they're categorizing the words correctly.

## SPEAKING Talking about a game

### 7

- ▶ 10.5  Ask students to read the conversation through once before they listen to it. Tell students to ignore the word choices on the right for the moment as they will focus on those in Exercise 8.

- Check answers.

**Answer**

a brain game

### Extra activity

#### Are you a brain gamer?

Ask students if they play or have ever played games designed to exercise their brain. If they have, ask them to describe what they do while playing these games and how the games exercise their brain. They can discuss this in pairs. Students could also tell their partner whether they would recommend the game(s) to others and why or why not.

### 8

- Model the conversation that students have just listened to aloud with a student. Then have students work in pairs to practise the conversation together. Make sure they alternate between A and B roles.

- Have students practise the conversation again using the words on the right instead of the words in bold in the conversation.

### 9

- Put students into pairs. Ask them to look at the words and say what colour each one is without actually reading them. Tell students to do this as quickly as they can without thinking about it too much. See **Background information: The Stroop Effect** for some information on how this type of exercise works and what it shows.

**Background information**

**The Stroop Effect**

The Stroop Effect describes what happens when people are given the task of saying words for colours, some of which are the colour of the word and some of which are different colours. It's named after John Ridley Stroop, who published his research findings in 1935. Stroop noticed that people found the naming of colour words easier and could do it more quickly if the words had the colour that they denoted, but they were more likely to make errors and did the task more slowly if the words didn't have the colour they denoted. This tells us that the brain finds it easier to perceive words than colours, and the Stroop Effect task is now regularly used to test the brain's ability to process external stimuli.

### 10

- Ask students to tell their partner how easy or difficult they found the experiment they did in Exercise 9. If they found it difficult, ask them to think about and say what made it difficult. Conduct whole-class feedback on how students' found the experiment.

- Tell students to turn to page 158 and try the two brain games they'll find there.

- **Optional step**. When students have tried the two brain games on page 158, ask them to tell their partner how easy/ difficult they found them and what brain functions they thought they were using while they were doing them.

▶ Set Workbook pages 76 and 77 for homework.

▶ Photocopiable communicative activity 10.1. Go to page 181 for further practice of brain functions vocabulary. The teaching notes are on page 196.

## 10.2 That's amazing!

**GRAMMAR** Adverbs and adverbial phrases

**1**

- ▶10.6 Check the meaning of *fibre* (a thin, thread-like structure that you can find in the body) and *estimated* (describing what you believe something to be when you don't know what it is exactly). Then, direct students to the infographic, ask them to read the facts about the brain and think about which one they find the most incredible.

- Put students into pairs to tell each other which fact they find the most incredible and why.

**Answers**

Students' own answers.

**2**

- ▶10.7 Tell students they're now going to listen to an expert saying some more facts about the brain. Ask them to read the sentences before they listen and decide whether they think they're true or false.

- Then play the recording and ask students to listen out for the information in the sentences so they can confirm whether they're true or false. Check answers in class and ask students which fact they found the most surprising.

**Transcript**

*The brain is incredible, and scientists are learning more and more about it every day. Did you know, for example, that your brain is able to generate power? Experts believe that it can generate enough electricity to power a light bulb.*

*There are also some common myths about the brain. You may have heard that we only use ten per cent of our brains. Well, most scientists now agree that that's not true. We use different parts of our brains for different purposes at different times. So the percentage is generally higher.*

*And do men have bigger brains than women? It appears so, although not by much. Men's brains are on average about ten per cent larger than women's. When you think about it, it makes sense. Men's bodies are generally bigger than women's.*

**Answers**

1 T  2 F  3 F

**3**

- ▶10.8 Tell students that adverbs and adverbial phrases are words and phrases that we use to say how someone does something (time and manner) or how we feel about something that someone does (attitude). Ask students to read the example sentences and identify the one type of adverb or adverbial phrase that answers each question.

- Students can check their answers and overall understanding of how to use adverbs and adverbial phrases by turning to the Grammar summary on page 150.

- If you feel that students need more controlled practice before continuing, they could do the exercises in the Grammar summary. Otherwise, you could continue on to Exercise 4 in the unit and set the Grammar summary exercises for homework.

**Answers**

a time  b manner  c attitude  d attitude

**Answers to Grammar summary exercises**

**1**

1 **Apparently**, a baby's brain is almost the same size as an adult's

2 If we read **slowly**, we retain more information

3 We have to write dreams down **immediately** if we want to remember them

4 Studies show that people who eat seafood **once a week** have lower rates of dementia

5 **Not surprisingly**, reading aloud and talking to a child promotes brain development

**2**

1 At  2 Next  3 for a month  4 in both days
5 When  6 in  7 a fortnight  8 After,

**EXTRA INFORMATION**

**1**

1 hard  2 late  3 fast  4 daily  5 well

**2**

**1**

a Pat spent the whole day **happily** doing brain games.

b **Happily**, he didn't find the brain games difficult.

**2**

a After a whole day of studying I couldn't see **clearly**!

b I **clearly** need to take more breaks when I'm studying./ **Clearly**, I need to take more breaks when I'm studying.

**3**

a There are some interesting lectures which you can access **free** online.

b Research shows that there is most activity in the brain when our thoughts wander **freely**.

**4**

- Tell students that they're now going to use what they've learned about the position of adverbs and adverbial phrases in sentences by forming sentences with the words given. Tell students to refer back to the examples in the Grammar box and the position of the adverbs and adverbial phrases in those sentences if they need to, and to add a comma where necessary.

- Have students compare their answers in pairs before checking answers in class.

**Answers**

1 Randy studied science for a long time.
2 Carrie learned three languages before the age of ten.
3 Bianca can solve word problems easily.
4 Unfortunately, Matt didn't pass the exam.

**5**

- Students are now going to practise identifying when to use adjectives and when to use adverbs – something that many students find challenging, especially if the same word can have both an adjectival and adverbial function in their first language. Tell students to read the sentences and notice whether the word describes a) a noun, in which case it needs to be an adjective, or b) a verb or an attitude, in which case it needs to be an adverb.

- Have students choose the correct options and then check answers in class.

**Answers**

1 very hard   2 obvious   3 Amazingly   4 correctly
5 good   6 lucky

**6**

- Ask students to read the sentences and choose the two time adverbials which are a possible fit with the contents of the sentence. Look at an example in class and elicit or explain that *during the summer* and *in the university holidays* are the only two adverbials that would fit in sentence 1 because these are the only two time periods in which you could do a course for a week.

- Have students compare their answers in pairs before checking answers in class.

**Answers**

1 during the summer, in the university holidays
2 next week, the day after tomorrow
3 in a couple of hours, soon
4 in the morning, at night
5 all day, until I went to bed

**Pronunciation** Pausing with adverbs of attitude

**7a**

- ▶ 10.9  Review the meaning of *emphasize*. Then, ask students to listen to the sentences while reading them and notice how the adverbs at the start of each sentence are emphasized and a pause is added after them.

- **Optional step**. In pairs, ask students to practise saying the sentences out loud with the emphasis on the adverbs and a pause after them.

**7b**

- Tell students to choose three adverbs of attitude, either the ones in the sentences in Exercise 7a, any others they know, or a combination of the two, and then use these to write short sentences that are true for them.

- Put students into pairs and have them read their sentences out loud to each other, emphasizing the adverb and adding a pause, as they heard in the recording in Exercise 7a. Monitor students and give them feedback on how successfully they emphasized the adverbs.

**Answers**

Students' own answers.

**8**

- ▶ 10.10  Students are now going to practise using prepositions and adverbs in the context of a text about an autistic savant called Daniel Tammet. Explain that an autistic savant is a person who has extraordinary abilities, especially in the areas of mathematics, memory skills, and artistic and musical abilities. *Savant* is a person who knows a lot.

- Ask students to read the text all the way through first and think about what the missing words could be, before going back to the beginning and choosing the correct word for every gap. Tell students to look at the words that come before and after the gaps, and also to notice whether there's a comma after the gap. They can then use this information to help them choose the right words.

- Play the recording of the text so that students can listen and check their answers.

**Answers**

1 Amazingly   2 in   3 easily   4 constantly
5 well   6 at

## SPEAKING  A logic puzzle

**9**

- **Optional step**. Elicit or explain that a *logic puzzle* is a game where you have to take what you see or what you're given, and use it to work something out. Ask students whether they've done logic puzzles before. If so, they could briefly describe what these involved.

- Put students into pairs and tell them to turn to page 158 and do the logic puzzle.

- **Optional step**. Conduct whole-class feedback on how easy/difficult students found the logic puzzle and whether they'd like to do more puzzles like this.

▶ Set Workbook pages 78 and 79 for homework.

▶ Photocopiable communicative activity 10.2. Go to page 182 for further practice of adverbs and adverbial phrases. The teaching notes are on page 196.

## 10.3  Look, no hands!

### READING  The power of the mind

**1**

- Ask students to look carefully at the title and then scan read the article with the aim of identifying what it's mainly about. Give them ten seconds to do this, so they have to scan the article. They can then look at the two options given and decide which one best describes the main idea in the article.

- Students can compare their answers in pairs, but don't confirm the correct answer at this stage.

> **Answer**
> b

**2**

- ▶10.11 Ask students to read the article more slowly this time and make sure that they've understood all of it, so they can check whether they chose the correct option in Exercise 1.

- Point out the glossary at the bottom of the text and tell students to refer to it as they read or to look at the words and definitions before they start reading.

- Confirm that students have chosen the correct option in class.

### Understanding main ideas

**3**

- Ask students to re-read the paragraphs about the three types of mind-control application and focus on understanding the main thing that each application does or allows you to do. They can compare their ideas with the options given and match the applications with the sentences that describe them.

- Students can compare their answers in pairs before you check answers in class.

> **Answers**
> 1 c  2 a  3 b

### Understanding details

**4**

- Tell students that they're now going to focus on understanding some of the details about each of the three types of mind-control applications described in the article. Ask students to read the six options given, and then re-read the three paragraphs and find these details or words that have the same meaning in them.

- They can then write the letters of the options in the right place on the Venn diagram. Explain that if an option is only true of one of three applications, they should write its letter in the part of the circle which is only for that type, but if an option is true for more than one type, they should write its letter in the part of the Venn diagram where the circles for these types overlap.

- Ask students to compare their Venn diagrams in pairs before checking answers in class.

**Answers**

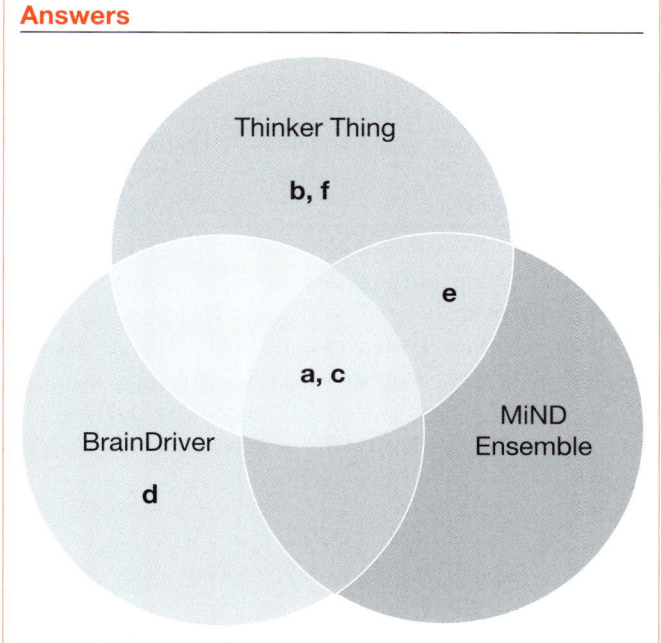

**10  Mind and machine   111**

> **TEACHING TIP**
>
> **Using Venn diagrams**
>
> Venn diagrams, like the one students completed in Exercise 4, are a useful way of presenting the similarities and differences between different sets of information or concepts, and of organizing and categorizing information and ideas more generally. Here are two suggestions for how you can use Venn diagrams with your students:
>
> 1. As a warm-up activity. Give students two topics or areas, e.g. sport and business, and ask them to write key words for things which are specific to them in the outer circles of the diagram and things that they have in common in the overlapping area.
>
> 2. When students have been learning about several different things or types of things, such as the applications in this section, ask them to use a Venn diagram to organize their notes on the similarities and differences between these things so that they can clearly see them. They can then use the diagram to help them prepare a text or presentation in which they compare and contrast the things they're focusing on.

## Understanding vocabulary

**5**

- Ask students to read the sentences and circle the correct option. If students are unsure about the meaning of any of the words in bold, they could look them up in a dictionary or look at how the words are used in context in the article.

- Check answers in class and model and drill the pronunciation of *breakthrough* /ˈbreɪkθruː/ and *autonomous* /ɔːˈtɒnəməs/ as students may find these challenging.

> **Answers**
>
> 1 discovery   2 changes   3 no one   4 meaning
> 5 information

**6**  `21st CENTURY OUTCOMES`

**Effectively analyse and evaluate evidence, arguments, claims and beliefs**

- Put students into pairs to make their lists of the advantages and disadvantages of each application – ask them to think of two or three advantages and disadvantages for each type. They can then discuss and decide which one they think will be the most common in the future and why.

- Tell students to divide the work between them in their pairs. One student could focus on one application, the other student could focus on the second and then they could work together to list the advantages and disadvantages of the third, before sharing their lists with each other. In order to fulfil the 21st CENTURY OUTCOMES, students should show that they've evaluated the evidence they were given about the applications in the article and then used this to identify each one's advantages and disadvantages, and decide which one will be the most common in the future.

- Conduct whole-class feedback.

▶ Set Workbook pages 80 and 81 for homework.

## 10.4 A headset that reads your brainwaves

### TEDTALKS

**1**

- **Optional step**. Direct students to the title of the TED Talk they're going to watch – *A headset that reads your brainwaves* – and put them into pairs to tell each other how they think a headset could read your brainwaves and how this kind of technology could be used in real life. Conduct whole-class feedback.

- Tell students they're now going to watch a TED Talk by Tan Le, who's a telecommunications entrepreneur. Check the meaning of *entrepreneur* (someone who starts their own company) and then have students read the summary of the talk and match the words in bold with their definitions. If students are unsure about which words to use with which items, encourage them to use deduction or simply have a guess.

- Students can compare their answers in pairs before you check answers in class.

> **Answers**
>
> 1 virtual   2 applications   3 visualizing   4 interface

**2**

- ▶10.12  Tell students that they're now going to watch Part 1 of Le's talk, in which she talks about different types of communication and what her goal is. Ask them to read the summary of this part and complete the gapped sentences with the words in the box that logically fit.

- Then, play Part 1 of the talk and ask students to listen out for the two types of communication Le mentions and what her goal is, so they can check their answers. Confirm the correct answers in class.

112   10   Mind and machine

## Transcript

Up until now, our communication with machines has always been limited to conscious and direct forms. Whether it's something simple like turning on the lights with a switch, or even as complex as programming robotics, we have always had to give a command to a machine, or even a series of commands, in order for it to do something for us. Communication between people, on the other hand, is far more complex and a lot more interesting because we take into account so much more than what is explicitly expressed. We observe facial expressions, body language, and we can intuit feelings and emotions from our dialogue with one another. This actually forms a large part of our decision-making process. Our vision is to introduce this whole new realm of human interaction into human-computer interaction so that computers can understand not only what you direct it to do, but it can also respond to your facial expressions and emotional experiences. And what better way to do this than by interpreting the signals naturally produced by our brain, our centre for control and experience.

### Answers

1 machine   2 light   3 human   4 body language
5 emotions   6 brain

## 3

- ▶10.13   Tell students that they're now going to listen to Part 2 of Le's talk in which she gives a demonstration of how people can control technology with their minds. In this section, Le uses instructions like the ones students looked at in the Listening for instructions box in **10.1**.

- Ask students to read the steps in the demonstration before they watch and speculate about the correct order. Then, play the clip, and ask students to listen carefully to what Le tells Evan to do and number the steps accordingly.

- Have students compare their answers in pairs before checking answers in class.

## Transcript

So with that, I'd like to invite onstage Evan Grant, who was one of last year's speakers, who's kindly agreed to help me to demonstrate what we've been able to develop.

[…] So Evan, choose something that you can visualize clearly in your mind.

Evan Grant: Let's do 'pull'.

Tan Le: OK, so let's choose 'pull'. So the idea here now is that Evan needs to imagine the object coming forward into the screen, and there's a progress bar that will scroll across the screen while he's doing that. The first time, nothing will happen, because the system has no idea how he thinks about 'pull'. But maintain that thought for the entire duration of the eight seconds. So: one, two, three, go. OK. So once we accept this, the cube is live. So let's see if Evan can actually try and imagine pulling. Ah, good job! That's really amazing.

### Answers

a 4   b 3   c 1   d 2   e 5

## 4

- ▶10.14   Students are now going to watch Part 3 of the talk, in which Le talks about how this technology could be used in everyday life. Ask students to read the options.

- Then, play Part 3 of the talk and ask students to listen out for the specific applications of the technology that Le mentions.

- Check answers in class.

- **Optional step**. Ask students whether they found any of the applications surprising or unsurprising and why. For example, it seems unsurprising that you can use this technology for playing games and controlling things in your house, but it may be surprising that it could also be used to help people with disabilities.

## Transcript

So I'd like to show you a few examples, because there are many possible applications for this new interface. In games and virtual worlds, for example, your facial expressions can naturally and intuitively be used to control an avatar or virtual character. Obviously, you can experience the fantasy of magic and control the world with your mind. And also, colours, lighting, sound and effects can dynamically respond to your emotional state to heighten the experience that you're having, in real time. And moving on to some applications developed by developers and researchers around the world, with robots and simple machines, for example – in this case, flying a toy helicopter simply by thinking 'lift' with your mind.

The technology can also be applied to real world applications – in this example, a smart home. You know, from the user interface of the control system to opening curtains or closing curtains. And of course, also to the lighting – turning them on or off. And finally, to real life-changing applications, such as being able to control an electric wheelchair. In this example, facial expressions are mapped to the movement commands.

[Video] Man: Now blink right to go right. Now blink left to turn back left. Now smile to go straight.

TL: We really – thank you. We are really only scratching the surface of what is possible today, and with the community's input, and also with the involvement of developers and researchers from around the world, we hope that you can help us to shape where the technology goes from here. Thank you so much.

### Answers

a, b, e, f

## CRITICAL THINKING

**5**

- Tell students that in this activity the critical thinking skill they'll be using is the ability to apply something that they've learned about to the practicalities of everyday life and evaluate how effective it would be in that context.

- Put students into pairs to share their lists of everyday tasks with each other, explain what they think it would be like to do these tasks if they could use their minds and say whether they think there would be any disadvantages.

- Conduct whole-class feedback on students' ideas and opinions.

## VOCABULARY IN CONTEXT

**6**

- ▶10.15 Play the clips from the TED Talk. When each multiple-choice question appears, pause the clip so that students can choose the correct definition. Discourage the more confident students from always giving the answer by asking students to raise their hand if they think they know.

### Transcript and subtitles

*1 … we have always had to give a command to a machine, or even **a series of** commands, in order for it to do something for us.*
**A series of** things means _____.
  a several things, one after the other
  b several things at different times
  c two different things

*2 Communication between people, **on the other hand**, is far more complex and a lot more interesting because we take into account so much more than what is explicitly expressed.*
We use **on the other hand**, to introduce _____.
  a an example
  b a different opinion
  c an additional idea

*3 Our **vision** is to introduce this whole new realm of human interaction into human-computer interaction …*
Someone's **vision** is their _____.
  a way of communicating
  b difficulty in doing something
  c hope or dream for the future

*4 The technology can also be applied to real world applications – in this example, a **smart** home. You know, from the user interface of the control system to opening curtains or closing curtains.*
In this context, a **smart** home is a house that _____.
  a is very tidy
  b uses computer technology
  c costs a lot of money

*5 We are really only **scratching the surface** of what is possible today …*
When you **scratch the surface** of something, you deal with _____ it.
  a only a small part of
  b every part of
  c only the positive aspects of

> **Answers**
> 1 a  2 b  3 c  4 b  5 a

**7**

- Students are now going to use two of the terms they looked at in Exercise 6 – *on the other hand* and *vision* – to give an alternative view of controlling technology with their mind and talk about their future career plans.

- Put students into pairs and ask them to say their own sentences, giving as much detail as they can.

- Circulate and monitor students' discussions and give them feedback when they've finished.

## PRESENTATION SKILLS  Dealing with the unexpected

**8**

- ▶10.16 Direct students to the Presentation skills box and check the meaning of *the unexpected* (things that are surprising because you didn't think they would happen).

- Ask students to read the three options and speculate about what the problem in the clip will be, based on what they can remember from their first viewing. Then, play the recording and ask them to choose the correct option.

- Check answers in class.

> **Answer**
> c

**9**

- ▶10.16 Play the clip again and ask students to watch and notice Le's reaction to the demo not working very well.

- Check answers in class and elicit that Le did what is usually the best thing you can do when unexpected things happen.

> **Answer**
> She remained calm and kept talking until Evan completed the task.

**10**

- Put students into small groups (three to four students) and have them work together to brainstorm other unexpected things that could happen in a presentation. Direct students to the model conversation and tell them to use the structure *You/Someone could ….*

- Tell students to bring in examples of unexpected things that have happened in presentations. These could either be presentations they've watched – live or in videos, such as the TED Talk videos – or ones they've given themselves. If students haven't watched or given many presentations, they could think of unexpected things that have happened in their English lessons, for example.

- Conduct whole-class feedback on students' ideas.

▶ Set Workbook page 82 for homework.

## 10.5 It'll make your life easier

### COMMUNICATE Creating a new product

**1**

- Put students into groups of four or five. Ask them to think back to what the technology Le described in the talk could do.

- Have students brainstorm some possible applications of the technology in the areas given in the box. Stop them after about five minutes, so they can go on to the next step.

**2**

- Have students decide what they think is the best application for the technology out of the ideas they thought of in Exercise 1. They then think about and discuss what this product would be, why it would be useful and who would buy it, using the prompts in the box. Tell students to use the phrases in the Explaining the uses of something box, and any other useful expressions they know, to write notes, which they can then use to present it in Exercise 3.

**3** **21st CENTURY OUTCOMES**

*Develop, implement and communicate new ideas to others effectively*

- Ask students to think of an idea for a TV advertisement for the product they've chosen.

- **Optional step.** If students have access to the Internet, have them go to a video-sharing website and look at some examples of TV advertisements for products that are similar to their product to give them some ideas for their advertisement.

- Students then work together to write the script for their advertisement. Tell them to make sure there's a part in the advertisement for every member of the group and have them refer to the example lines from an advertisement that are given. Draw students' attention to the rhetorical question in the first line and elicit that using questions is an effective way of getting the audience's attention.

- Circulate and monitor while students are writing the script for their advertisement, offering assistance and feedback where appropriate.

- Give students some time for a practice run of their advertisement and then have the groups take it in turns to act them out in class. When they've finished, have them reflect on their own performances and how effective their advertisements were. Students from different groups can then give each other feedback before you add yours. In order to fulfil the 21st CENTURY OUTCOMES, students should be able to effectively communicate information about their product idea to other students through their advertisement.

> **TEACHING TIP**
>
> **Into the Dragons' den**
>
> The BBC (British Broadcasting Corporation) produces a TV show called *Dragons' Den*, which is still on television in the UK and has been syndicated to other television networks around the world, under different names. The show's concept is that inventors who've designed and developed a new product – which could be anything from a new type of vacuum cleaner to a sauce mix – pitch and demonstrate their product to a group of four business people (the dragons of the title) in the hope of convincing them to invest some of their own money in the product. At any point during the pitch, the dragons can say 'I'm out!' to indicate that they're not interested in investing in the product. The dragons also often make deals with the contestants they're interested in investing in, using first conditional sentences, e.g. *I'll invest £75,000 if you give me a 20 per cent stake in your company*.
>
> Explain the concept of *Dragons' Den* to students and then ask them to go online, either in class or as a self-study task, and find a clip from the BBC version of the show so they can see how it works in practice. Then, set up a *Dragons' Den* scenario as either a replacement for or an extension of Exercise 3. Four students – each one from a different group – play the role of the dragons while another group of students pitches their product idea and says how much money they need from the dragons to be able to develop, mass-produce and sell it. Each group has £250,000 to invest in a product idea or ideas when a member of their group is playing the role of a dragon. Rotate the dragons after each pitch. The dragons decide whether they want to invest in the product as they're listening, and either say 'I'm out!' or make the group that's pitching an offer of money or a deal.

## WRITING Writing a proposal

**4** `21st CENTURY OUTCOMES`

***Articulate thoughts and ideas effectively using oral, written and nonverbal communication skills in a variety of forms and contexts***

- Tell students to choose one of the products they heard students from another group present in Exercise 3. Then, ask students to read the opening of an email in the example text and then use this model to start their own emails and continue with information about what their product is, how it works and why Tan Le should be interested in it or want to invest in it. In order to fulfil, the 21st CENTURY OUTOMES, students should be able to show that they understand the norms of email communication and that they can use it to effectively communicate their product idea.
- Circulate and monitor students' writing and give them feedback when they've finished.

> **Answers**
> Students' own answers.

### Extra activity

#### An email from Tan Le

Ask students to send the emails they write in Exercise 4 to another student. They can do by this either by really sending their text as an email to the other student's email address or by giving the other student the email in paper form. Students read the email they've received and decide whether they think the product idea described in the email is a good one, and whether Tan Le would want her technology to be used in it. Then, have them write an email back to their partner in which they tell them what their decision is and the reasons for it.

▶ Set Workbook page 83 for homework.

# 11 Nature

## UNIT AT A GLANCE

**THEME:** Nature
**VOCABULARY:** Nature
**LISTENING:** My experiences in nature
**SPEAKING:** Talking about nature, Experiences in nature
**GRAMMAR:** Present perfect
**PRONUNCIATION:** /ðə/ and /ði:/, Weak forms (2): *have*

**READING:** *The miracle of pollen*
**TED TALK:** *The hidden beauty of pollination*. In this TED Talk, Louie Schwartzberg tells us that we should all be appreciating nature more and this will motivate us to protect it.
**PRESENTATION SKILLS:** Calling others to action
**WRITING:** Writing a journal entry

## WARM UP

• Books open. Draw students' attention to the unit title, the photo and the caption on page 115. Put students into pairs or small groups (three to four students) to discuss the questions.

• **Question 1**. Direct students to the photo of monarch butterflies and ask them to read the caption. Find out what students already know about the extraordinary journey that the monarch butterflies make (millions of monarch butterflies migrate to one small forest in Mexico every winter). Then, ask students to think of other examples of extraordinary journeys in nature that they've heard of. If students can't think of any other examples, they could go online and search for some there. Students may also be interested in finding out more about the monarch butterfly migration online.

• **Question 2**. Check the meaning of *memorable sight* (something that you clearly remember seeing). Then, ask students to think of and describe one or two examples of memorable sights they've seen in the natural world. If possible, they should think of sights they've seen themselves, or choose sights they've seen in photographs. These could be sights of animals, birds or insects, like the migration of the monarch butterflies, or examples from the physical environment, such as canyons or waterfalls.

• **Question 3**. Bring in students' own experiences of spending time in nature and ask them to describe what they like to do when they go out into the natural world and why they like doing it. Students could talk about anything from weekend walks near their homes to holidays where they've enjoyed spending time in the natural world.

## 11.1 Nature at its best

### VOCABULARY Nature

**1**

• Ask students to read the natural features in the box and decide which preposition comes in front of each one. Encourage students to try saying the preposition + noun combinations they think are correct out loud to see if they can hear whether they sound correct. You might want to draw their attention to the fact that different prepositions are used with *the mountains* and *top of a mountain*.

• Have students compare their answers in pairs and then check answers in class. Once you know that students have added the natural features in the correct column, have them add one more natural feature to each one.

• Conduct whole-class feedback on students' extra words. Write them up on the board and check that students have put them in the correct column.

### Answers

| on | in |
| --- | --- |
| the coast | the desert |
| an island | a forest |
| top of a mountain | the mountains |
| | the woods |

**2**

• Students are now going to combine the verbs with the nouns to make collocations for activities you can do in the natural world.

• Once they've matched all of the items, check answers in class and elicit or explain that when *go* is followed directly by another verb in collocations, this verb is always in the *-ing* form, and *go* + preposition combinations, e.g. *go for a* or *go on*, are often followed by a noun. Then, ask students to think of one more verb or noun that works in each set. Conduct feedback on the new words students have added.

### Answers
1 b   2 a   3 c

**3**

• Make sure students are aware that by *neutral* words, we mean words that could have both a negative or positive meaning, or don't have either a positive or a negative meaning. Ask students to read the list of adjectives and look up any words they don't know in a dictionary.

- Check answers in class and model and drill the pronunciation of *breathtaking* /ˈbreθˌteɪkɪŋ/ and *gorgeous* /ˈɡɔː(r)dʒəs/ as students may find these challenging. Then, put students into pairs and have them use the adjectives to describe places in the natural world that they've been to.

- **Optional step.** Ask students to describe some of the places they've just talked about in their pairs in class.

| Answers |
|---|
| 1 N   2 P   3 N   4 P   5 P   6 N |

## 4

- Put students into pairs. Direct them to the model conversation and elicit the phrases for saying how often you do something: *every week* and *once a month*. Ask students to use these or any other frequency expressions they know to say how often they spend time in the countryside and words and collocations with *go* to say what they do there.

- Give students a few minutes to tell each other their answers to the questions.

- **Optional step.** If students have photos of the places they go to in the countryside or the activities they do there on their mobile phones, they could show these to each other as they talk about them. If they don't, but they do have access to the Internet, they could go online and find any images they want to show their partner there.

- Monitor students' conversations and then give them feedback on their use of vocabulary and collocations in class. Draw students' attention to any new or interesting vocabulary that's used.

## LISTENING  My experiences in nature

## 5

- ▶11.1 Direct students to the Noticing auxiliary verbs box and check the meaning of *auxiliary verb* (a verb that gives grammatical information not given by the main verb, e.g. what tense the main verb is in, whether the main verb is active or passive or whether it has a positive or a negative meaning). Tell students they're going to practise listening out for the contracted (or short) forms of these auxiliary verbs because understanding these will help them to understand what period of time a speaker is talking about.

- Tell students they're going to listen to Tony Gainsford, who they can see in the photo, talking about his love of nature. Ask them to read the four natural places in the box.

- Play the recording and ask students to circle the options Gainsford says he can enjoy near his home. Check answers in class.

### Transcript

*I love nature. I've always been a fan of nature. I'm now lucky enough that I live in a part of the world where I'm near a beach, and near a lovely park where I enjoy cycling. I sometimes see large monitor lizards and exotic birds, and I really enjoy it.*

*I've been on a couple of nature holidays. My last one was in Greece. It was a Greek island called Zakynthos, which is famous for turtles. We went in June, and we were lucky enough to see the baby turtles on the beach, and we took some wonderful photographs. I've also been to Cairns, which is in Australia, and we went snorkelling at the Great Barrier Reef, which was amazing. We saw nurse sharks, we saw jellyfish, we saw other colourful fish, and I even saw an octopus. I would really like to visit South Africa to go on safari, to see animals in the wild, in their natural habitat. I would love to take some photographs of the lions and the giraffes. I think that would be an amazing adventure.*

| Answers |
|---|
| a beach, a park |

## 6

- ▶11.1 Students are now going to listen to the recording again and focus specifically on the things Gainsford has done / hasn't done in the three different places he mentions. Ask students to read the sentence parts and predict the correct answers, based on what they can remember from their first listening.

- Play the recording so that students can check or complete their answers. Then, check answers in class.

| Answers |
|---|
| 1 b   2 c   3 a |

> **TEACHING TIP**
>
> **Turn the volume down**
>
> Auxiliary verbs are an example of words that people usually pronounce as weak forms or don't stress, but which do convey useful information to the listener. In order to make it easier for students to hear words like these, you can turn the volume down a little the next time you're playing students an audio or video recording. This will make it more difficult for them to differentiate the content words, which are usually stressed, from the other words, such as auxiliary verbs, thus increasing the likelihood that they will notice these other words. Students will find this activity challenging, but it should make them more well-rounded listeners who try to hear and understand every word in a sentence and not just the stressed content words.

## 7

- Put students into pairs and ask them to discuss whether they've ever been on a holiday like the ones Gainsford described, and had similar experiences with nature.
- **Optional step.** If they have, they can tell each other about one of these holidays, including information about where they went, what they did and what nature they saw. If they haven't, they can tell each other what kind of nature they would like to see on a holiday and/or where they would like to go on a nature holiday.
- **Optional step.** If they have them, students can show each other photos on their mobile phones from the nature holidays they decide to talk about.

## Pronunciation /ðə/ and /ði:/

### 8a

- ▶ 11.2 Tell students there are two different ways you can say the word *the* and these are represented by the phonemic symbols /ðə/ and /ði:/. The first one is used when the first letter of the next word is a consonant and the other one is used when the first letter of that word is a vowel.
- Play the recording and ask students to read the sentences while listening to them and notice the difference in how the word *the* is pronounced. You'll probably need to play the recording a few times before students can clearly hear the difference. The /ðə/ sound is used in *the coast* and the /ði:/ is used in *the island*. We could say that when *the* comes before a vowel, the sound of the word is a little stronger or more emphasized than when it comes before a consonant.

### 8b

- ▶ 11.3 Students are now going to listen to some more examples of the two different ways of saying *the* and practise saying them. Play the recording so they can listen and repeat.

## SPEAKING  Talking about nature

### 9

- ▶ 11.4 Ask students to read the conversation through once before they listen to it. Tell students to ignore the word choices on the right for the moment as they will focus on those in Exercise 10.
- Check answers and elicit that, according to the two speakers, the Evans National Forest is very pretty, has a mountain, some deer and other wildlife.
- **Optional step.** Ask students to discuss, either in pairs or in class, whether the Evans National Forest sounds like the kind of place they would like to visit and, if it is, they can say:
  - what they would do there
  - how long they would stay there for
  - who they would go there with

> **Answer**
> Evans National Forest

## 10

- Model the conversation that students have just listened to aloud with a student. Then, have students work in pairs to practise the conversation together. Make sure they alternate between A and B roles.
- Have students practise the conversation again using the words on the right instead of the words in bold in the conversation.

## 11

- Direct students to the model questions and elicit or explain that you use the structure *How about* verb + *-ing ... ?* to make a suggestion.
- Put students into pairs to think of some ideas for things they could do together outside and reach an agreement about what they're going to do.
- Circulate and monitor students while they're talking to each other and give them feedback when they've finished.

> **TEACHING TIP**
>
> **Adding detail**
>
> In order to progress from A2 to B1 level, students will need to be able to give more detail when they're describing or discussing something. With this in mind, stronger students could make more detailed plans about what they're going to do together outside during Exercise 11. Some details they could give include: when they're going to do the activity, where exactly they're going to go, what they'll need to take with them, etc. They could even re-use the first conditionals they learned in Unit 9 by thinking about what could go wrong on their trip and making backup plans that would help them deal with these problems.

▶ Set Workbook pages 84 and 85 for homework.

▶ Photocopiable communicative activity 11.1. Go to page 183 for further practice of nature vocabulary. The teaching notes are on page 197.

## 11.2 Have you ever seen a bear?

### GRAMMAR  Present perfect

### 1

- ▶ 11.5 Direct students to the infographic. Ask them to read the statistics about British children and then decide how similar they think children in their home country are. Ask: *What do they have in common with British children and what is different?* Put students into pairs to discuss this.

11  Nature    119

- **Optional step**. Remind students to use language for comparisons as they do this – you may want to review this in class before students start the activity, e.g. *more ... than ...*, *less ... than ...*, *not as ... as*, *the same as ...*

- Conduct whole-class feedback on students' opinions and ask them to give reasons or supporting evidence for them.

## 2

- ▶ 11.6 Tell students they're now going to listen to a health expert giving some advice on how to help children connect with nature. Ask students to read the sentences and then play the recording so they can listen and complete them with the words they hear.

- Ask students to compare answers in pairs before checking answers in class.

### Transcript

*Many children around the world are having less contact with nature. They spend more time indoors than ever before. They lack basic knowledge of nature. What can we do about this? First, we as adults need to set an example for our children. Adults need to connect with nature as well. Take your kids camping. Go for a walk. Play games together in the park. When you do fun things with your kids outside, they will want to spend more time there.*

*And second, I'd suggest we need to look at why children are staying indoors more. They watch TV. They play on computers and other electronic devices. My advice for parents is to set aside a few hours a week as 'Turn off time'. For these few hours, don't allow children to use electronic devices, and instead, encourage them to do something outside.*

> **Answers**
>
> 1 set an example   2 staying indoors
> 3 use electronic devices

## 3

- Ask students to read the example sentences. The most important thing they need to take away from these examples is the fact that we use the past simple with a definite time in the past, but we don't use a definite time in the past with the present perfect.

- Students can check their answers and overall understanding of the present perfect by turning to the Grammar summary on pages 152.

- If you feel that students need more controlled practice before continuing, they could do the exercises in the Grammar summary. Otherwise, you could continue on to Exercise 4 in the unit and set the Grammar summary exercises for homework.

> **Answers**
>
> a 1
> b 2
> c We use the auxiliary *have* + past participle of the verb to form the present perfect and we add *not* between the auxiliary *have/has* and the past participle of the verb to make it negative.
> d go

> **Answers to Grammar summary exercises**
>
> **1**
> 1 've eaten
> 2 haven't collected
> 3 's been/gone
> 4 've never grown
> 5 's slept
> 6 hasn't studied
>
> **2**
> a gave, planted         4
> b learned/learnt, read  6
> c were, loved           1
> d bought, could         3
> e fed, went             2
> f didn't get, came      5

## 4

- Tell students they're now going to practise forming the present perfect in the context of a text giving one pre-school teacher's perspective on the issue of how connected to nature children are today. Ask students to put the verbs in brackets into the present perfect form, paying attention to whether they need to use *has* (for a third person singular pronoun or noun) or *have*, and the fact that some of the verbs have irregular past participles.

- Have students compare their answers in pairs before checking answers in class.

> **Answers**
>
> 2 haven't heard   3 've taken   4 've been   5 's climbed
> 6 's seen   7 've learned/learnt   8 've enjoyed

## LANGUAGE FOCUS Talking about past experiences

### 5

• ▶ 11.7 Students are now going to look at some examples of how we use and react to present perfect questions in conversation. Ask students to read the Language focus box and notice how to form and answer *Have you ever ... ?* questions about past experiences and then how to react to statements people make about their experiences to say what you have in common or how your experiences have been different. Draw students' attention to how we can add words like *ever*, *never* and *always* to present perfect sentences, and how we can use *neither* or *not either* to say that we also haven't done something that someone else hasn't done.

• Students can check overall understanding of the language focus by turning to the Grammar summary on page 152.

• If you feel that students need more controlled practice before continuing, they could do the exercises in the Grammar summary. Otherwise, you could continue on to Exercise 6 in the unit and set the Grammar summary exercises for homework.

---

**Answers to Grammar summary exercises**

**1**

1 Have you ever seen elephants in the wild?
I have
2 Have you ever found eggs in a bird's nest?
I haven't
3 Has your sister ever ridden a horse?
she has
4 Have you and your family ever kept chickens?
we haven't
5 Have any of your friends ever heard an owl?
they have
6 Has he ever run on a beach with no shoes on?
he has

**2**

2 been, Me neither / I haven't, either / Neither have I
3 taught, Really? I haven't
4 had, Neither have we / Me neither / Neither have I / We haven't, either / I haven't, either
5 seen, Really? I have
6 caught, Me too / So have I

---

### 6

• ▶ 11.8 Students are now going to practise forming *Have you ever ... ?* questions and other present perfect sentences about past experiences in a text about Foster Huntington's tree houses. Ask them to complete the sentences and tell them to refer back to the examples in the Language focus box to help them choose the correct options if they need to.

• **Optional step**. Tell students to check that they've used the correct past participle of the verb *build* as learners often make mistakes with it.

• Have students compare their answers in pairs before checking answers in class.

---

**Answers**

2 wanted   3 made   4 loved   5 built   6 connected

---

### 7

• Students are now going to practise forming questions and answers about past experiences in the present perfect and past simple. Tell students to make sure the short answer is in the same tense as the question and also to use the presence or lack of an expression for a time in the past to choose the correct tense in the answers. They can refer back to the examples in the Language focus box to help them choose the correct options if they need to.

• Have students compare their answers in pairs before you check answers in class.

• **Optional step**. In pairs, ask students to read the three exchanges they completed out loud, thinking about what intonation they need to use and which words they should stress.

---

**Answers**

1 have, went   2 Have, swum, swam   3 Did you see, saw

---

## Pronunciation Weak forms (2): *have*

### 8

• ▶ 11.9 Tell students to read the sentences. Then, play the recording so they can listen to someone saying them while reading them again and notice how the word *have* is pronounced.

• Put students into pairs to tell each other what they noticed about how *have* was pronounced. Conduct whole-class feedback, and elicit that *have* is a weak form in present perfect questions and long answers, like the one in sentence 3, but a strong form in short answers. Pronouncing *have* or *haven't* strongly in short answers helps you to affirm whether your answer is positive or negative.

• Play the recording again so students can listen and repeat the sentences.

11 Nature   121

## SPEAKING Experiences in nature

### 9  21st CENTURY OUTCOMES

*Manage the flow of information from a wide variety of sources*

• Students are now going to take part in a 'Find someone who …' mingle activity where they ask each other questions about their experiences in nature to practise asking and answering *Have you ever … ?* questions. Tell students they're going to stand up, walk around the room and ask other students the *Have you ever … ?* questions, either until they've found people who can answer *yes* to every question or until the time that you give them for this activity (e.g. five or ten minutes) is up. Remind students that they also have to think of a follow-up question to ask when they get a *yes* answer, and follow-up questions that follow present perfect questions are usually in the past simple, as they can see in the model conversation.

• In order to fulfil the 21st CENTURY OUTCOMES, students should be able to manage the information they get from the people they ask by keeping a record of which questions they've had a positive answer to and who gave them these positive answers. Monitor students and give them feedback when they've finished.

### Extra activity

#### Sharing and comparing your survey results

Ask students to make a note of the names of the people they found for each question and of the extra information they got when they asked their follow-up question. When students have finished the activity, put them into pairs or small groups to tell each other who has done each of the activities and add the extra details these people gave them, using the third personal singular form of the present perfect. They can also tell each other whether they got *yes* answers from the same people and then compare the information they got from these people.

▶ Set Workbook pages 86 and 87 for homework.
▶ Photocopiable communicative activity 11.2. Go to page 184 for further practice of the present perfect and nature vocabulary. The teaching notes are on page 197.

## 11.3 Small is beautiful

### READING The miracle of pollen

### 1

• Direct students to the definition of *pollen* in the glossary on page 121 and ask them to only read that. Put students into pairs to discuss what animals they know that help to carry pollen.

• Conduct whole-class feedback on students' ideas. Bees are the most obvious example of an animal that carries pollen, but hopefully they will have thought of other animals too.

| Answers |
|---|
| Students' own answers. |

### 2

• ▶ 11.10 Ask students to scan read the article to identify the animals which carry pollen that it mentions. They can then compare these with the animals they thought of in Exercise 1.

• Check answers in class.

• **Optional step**. Ask students if they were surprised that animals other than bees, such as birds and monkeys, can also carry pollen.

| Answers |
|---|
| bees, flies, beetles, birds, butterflies, ants, monkeys |

### Understanding gist

### 3

• Check the meaning of *pollinator* (an animal that moves pollen from one place to another helping plants to reproduce) and *reproduction* (the creation of babies, young animals or new plants). Give students 20 or 30 seconds to scan the article with the aim of identifying the gist, or general message, and then have them choose the best alternative title.

• In pairs, ask students to compare the titles they chose and explain why they chose them. Then, check answers in class.

| Answer |
|---|
| b |

### Understanding a process

### 4

• Students are now going to look at the steps in the process of pollination in more detail. Ask them to check the meaning of any words in the box that they don't know and then use them to complete the sentences. They could either complete the steps from memory, use the context of the rest of the sentence to help them or re-read the article to identify the order the steps appear.

• Students can check their answers in pairs before you check answers in class.

| Answers |
|---|
| 1 petals   2 nectar   3 body   4 pollen   5 seed |

## Understanding details

### 5

- Tell students to read the sentences, and then read the whole article again to find what it says about the issues mentioned and check whether the detailed information given is correct. They can then decide whether the sentences are true or false.
- Point out the glossary at the bottom of the text and tell students to refer to it as they read or to look at the words and definitions before they start reading.
- Check answers in class.

> **Answers**
> 1 T   2 T   3 F   4 F   5 F

## Understanding vocabulary

### 6

- Ask students to read the definitions and circle the correct options. If students are unsure about the meaning of any of the words in bold, they could look them up in a dictionary or look at how the words are used in context in the article.
- Check answers in class, and model and drill the pronunciation of *tear* /teə(r)/ as students may find this challenging.
- **Optional step**. Draw students' attention to the fact that the verb *tear*, meaning to pull apart, can also be the noun for a hole or split in something caused by it being pulled apart, but the word *tear* can also be pronounced /tɪə(r)/ when it's used as a noun to describe the salty drops of water that come out of your eyes.

> **Answers**
> 1 closer to   2 pulling with your hands
> 3 need   4 big   5 see

### 7

- Put students into pairs to brainstorm ideas for how we could protect pollinating plants. Stop them after a few minutes and conduct whole-class feedback.

▶ Set Workbook pages 88 and 89 for homework.

## 11.4 The hidden beauty of pollination

### TEDTALKS

### 1

- Tell students they're now going to watch a TED Talk by Louie Schwartzberg. Before they read the summary of his talk, direct them to its title and ask them to speculate about what Schwartzberg's idea worth spreading could be, based on what they learned about him in the article from **11.3**.
- Have students read the summary of the talk and choose the correct options in the definitions of some words from it which may be unknown to them. If students are unsure about which words to match with which items, encourage them to use deduction or simply have a guess.
- Students can compare their answers in pairs before you check answers in class.

> **Answers**
> 1 slow action appear fast   2 together   3 important

### 2

- ▶ 11.11 Tell students they're now going to watch Part 1 of Schwartzberg's talk, in which he introduces himself, his work and his desire to take action against Colony Collapse Disorder, which they read about in the article in **11.3**. Have students read the summary of Part 1 and predict the correct options. Then, play the recording and ask students to concentrate on listening out for the specific pieces of information in the options.
- Have students compare their answers in pairs before checking answers in class.

### Transcript

*It's great being here at TED. You know, I think there might be some presentations that will go over my head, but the most amazing concepts are the ones that go right under my feet. The little things in life, sometimes that we forget about, like pollination, that we take for granted. And you can't tell the story about pollinators – bees, bats, hummingbirds, butterflies – without telling the story about the invention of flowers and how they co-evolved over 50 million years.*

*I've been filming time-lapse flowers 24 hours a day, seven days a week, for over 35 years. To watch them move is a dance I'm never going to get tired of. It fills me with wonder, and it opens my heart. Beauty and seduction, I believe, is nature's tool for survival, because we will protect what we fall in love with. Their relationship is a love story that feeds the Earth. It reminds us that we are a part of nature, and we're not separate from it.*

When I heard about the vanishing bees, Colony Collapse Disorder, it motivated me to take action. We depend on pollinators for over a third of the fruits and vegetables we eat. And many scientists believe it's the most serious issue facing mankind. It's like the canary in the coalmine. If they disappear, so do we. It reminds us that we are a part of nature and we need to take care of it.

> **Answers**
> 1 little things   2 50   3 dance   4 bees

### 3  21st CENTURY OUTCOMES

**Listen effectively to decipher meaning, including knowledge, values, attitudes and intentions**

- ▶ 11.12  Tell students they're now going to listen to Part 2 of Schwartzberg's talk, in which he talks about what he's learned from making time-lapse films. Students are going to infer what he really wants to say in some examples of descriptive language that he uses in this part of the talk. Ask students to read the quotes and the two possible interpretations of them before they watch and consider which one is correct. Then, play Part 2 of the talk and ask students to listen out for the quotes and the context in which they're used to help them decide what the correct options are. In order to fulfil the 21st CENTURY OUTCOMES, students should listen effectively to how Schwartzberg says the sentences so they can accurately decipher the correct interpretations of what he's saying.

- Put students into pairs to compare their answers and say why they think these are the correct answers, and then check answers in class.

### Transcript

Because I realized that nature had invented reproduction as a mechanism for life to move forward, as a life force that passes right through us and makes us a link in the evolution of life. Rarely seen by the naked eye, this intersection between the animal world and the plant world is truly a magic moment. It's the mystical moment where life regenerates itself, over and over again.

So here is some nectar from my film. I hope you'll drink, tweet and plant some seeds to pollinate a friendly garden. And always take time to smell the flowers, and let it fill you with beauty, and rediscover that sense of wonder. Here are some images from the film. [Music]

Thank you. Thank you very much. Thank you.

> **Answers**
> 1 b   2 a   3 a

### TEACHING TIP

**Deciphering and using descriptive language**

Native speakers of English often use descriptive language in presentations and in everyday conversation to make what they're saying more interesting to listen to. Students at this level aren't expected to be able to use descriptive language regularly themselves, but it's important for them to develop the ability to recognize it and understand that not everything they hear will be meant literally; it may be a metaphor for something else, like *nectar*: the juice that comes out of a plant and *nectar*: the good or best stuff. In order to give them more practice doing this, you could ask students to re-watch a TED Talk, or a part of a TED Talk from a previous unit, and focus on identifying any examples of descriptive language the speaker uses in it, making a note of them and deciding what the speaker really means by them, as they did in Exercise 3. In the TED Talk from Unit 2, for example, A. J. Jacobs says that he *dived into genealogy* meaning that he suddenly and energetically started to study genealogy.

## CREATIVE THINKING

### 4

- Tell students that in this activity the creative thinking skill they'll be using is the ability to think about other possible subjects for a creative activity, namely time-lapse photography.

- Students could draw on other examples of time-lapse photography they've seen or think about natural processes that happen gradually over a long period of time, e.g. the sun setting, or things that happen on a very small scale which are usually difficult to see.

- Conduct whole-class feedback on students' ideas.

### Extra activity

#### A time-lapse video of your own

Nowadays there are many free smartphone apps, such as *Hyperlapse from Instagram*, that you can download and use to make short time-lapse videos on your phone. As a self-study task, have students download one of these apps and use it to make a time-lapse video of one of the subjects for time-lapse photography they thought of in Exercise 4. Students could either do this task individually, in pairs or in groups. Once students have captured their videos, ask them to prepare an accompanying commentary, in which they describe what is happening and how what they're seeing makes them feel. They can then present their videos with the commentary in the next lesson. Encourage students to give each other feedback on their video presentations and then add your own feedback.

## VOCABULARY IN CONTEXT

### 5

• ▶ 11.13 Play the clips from the TED Talk. When each multiple-choice question appears, pause the clip so that students can choose the correct definition. Discourage the more confident students from always giving the answer by asking students to raise their hand if they think they know.

#### Transcript and subtitles

**1** *You know, I think there might be some presentations that will **go over my head**, but the most amazing concepts are the ones that go right under my feet.*
If something **goes over your head**, _____.
  **a** you don't understand it well
  **b** you completely agree with it
  **c** you disagree with it

**2** *The little things in life, sometimes that we forget about, like pollination, that we **take for granted**.*
If **we take something for granted**, we _____ it.
  **a** are excited by
  **b** understand
  **c** no longer appreciate

**3** *To watch them move is a dance I'm never going to **get tired of**.*
If you **get tired of** something, you don't want to do it anymore because _____.
  **a** you need to sleep
  **b** you're bored with it
  **c** it's very difficult

**4** *When I heard about the vanishing bees, Colony Collapse Disorder, it motivated me to **take action.***
You **take action** when you want to _____.
  **a** work out why something happened
  **b** forget about a problem
  **c** do something about a problem

**5** *It's the mystical moment where life regenerates itself, **over and over again**.*
If you do something **over and over again**, you do it _____.
  **a** a lot of times
  **b** quickly
  **c** carefully

> **Answers**
> 1 a  2 c  3 b  4 c  5 a

### 6

• Students are now going to use two of the terms they looked at in Exercise 5 – *take action* and *over and over again* – to talk about some of their interests and experiences.

• Put students into pairs and ask them to say their own answers to the questions, giving as much detail as they can.

• Circulate and monitor students' discussions and give them feedback when they've finished.

## PRESENTATION SKILLS Calling others to action

### 7

• ▶ 11.14 Direct students to the Presentation skills box and check the meaning of *act* (here: take action, do something).

• Play the clip and ask students to pay close attention to how Schwartzberg says 'we need'. They can think about how they feel when they hear him saying it and which word he emphasizes.

• Have students tell each other what they noticed and then conduct whole-class feedback.

> **Suggested answer**
> Schwartzberg thinks that taking care of nature is something we should all do together and it's something that's very important. He puts emphasis on the word 'care' in 'we need to take care of it'.

### 8

• ▶ 11.15 Ask students to read the names of the speakers and the calls to action, and use what they can remember about their TED Talks to match the speakers with the calls to action they used.

• Play the clips so students can watch the speakers and check their answers. Confirm the correct answers in class.

> **Answers**
> 1 c  2 a  3 d  4 b

#### Extra activity

#### Key language for calls to action

Put students into pairs. Ask them to re-read the calls to action in Exercise 8 and identify the words or phrases which show us that they are calls to action. Words, such as *we all*, tell people what the speaker thinks, motivate them to do something and work together, and tell them why it's important for them to do this. Other words students could choose include: *I hope ...*, *it is up to us*, *we want ...*, *you can ...*, *we need to ...*

Then, ask students to think of something they would like other people to do, e.g. give blood, recycle their rubbish, exercise more, etc. and use the key language they've identified to write a call to action which is one or two sentences long. Weaker students could do this in pairs. Monitor students as they're writing and give them feedback when they've finished.

**9** **21st CENTURY OUTCOMES**

*Investigate and analyse environmental issues, and make accurate conclusions about effective solutions*

- Put students into small groups (three to four students) and ask them to infer the things they think Schwartzberg would like to see people do to 'take care of nature', based on what they've learned about him and his opinions. They can then discuss their ideas together, giving their opinions and suggestions, saying whether they agree or disagree with each other, and commenting on each other's responses. In order to fulfil the 21st CENTURY OUTCOMES, students should be able to use what they've learned about the threat to bees and nature more generally to suggest effective solutions to the problem that people don't do as much as they should to protect the natural world.
- Conduct whole-class feedback on students' ideas.

▶ Set Workbook page 90 for homework.

## 11.5 Getting out into nature

### COMMUNICATE Planning a weekend in the countryside

**1**

- Put students into groups of four or five and ask them to read the information and instructions. Check the meaning of *suitable* (right for a particular situation or person).
- Ask students to think back to their own experiences of going on camping trips and think about possible places where they could go camping. They can then use these ideas to discuss possible destinations for a weekend camping trip and reach a consensus about which one to choose. Remind them to also explain why their suggestion for a place is a good one during their discussions.

**2**

- Ask students to work together in their groups to brainstorm possible activities they can do on a camping trip. Encourage them to bring in their own experiences by thinking about the activities they've done on previous camping trips, but also to include activities they've never done before and activities that would help them to learn more about the natural world. Direct students to the model conversation and encourage them to also use the present perfect to ask each other whether they've done an activity before, and give their answers.

- Once students have agreed on six activities, have them discuss when would be a good time to do them during the weekend and complete the activity plan.

**3**

- Put each group together with another group. Have them present their plans for the camping trip to each other and listen carefully to the other group's presentation, so they can use the question starters in the Asking for more details box to come up with a few questions about their plans.
- Monitor students and give them feedback on how clearly and accurately they presented information, and asked and answered questions.

### WRITING Writing a journal entry

**4**

- **Optional step**. Either in pairs or in class, ask students to discuss whether they've ever kept a journal and, if they have, why they did this and what they wrote in it. Encourage students who've kept journals to reflect on what the benefits of doing it have been for them and if there have been any disadvantages to it.
- Have students look back at their plan for the first day of their camping weekend in Exercise 2 and imagine what it would have been like if they'd really done it with the other people in the group they were in for Exercises 1 and 2. Ask students to read the start of the model journal entry and then write their own.
- Circulate and monitor while students are writing, offering assistance and feedback where appropriate.

| Answers |
|---|
| Students' own answers. |

▶ Set Workbook page 91 for homework.

# 12 Discovery

## UNIT AT A GLANCE

**THEME:** Discovery
**VOCABULARY:** Discoveries
**LISTENING:** An amazing find
**SPEAKING:** Talking about a discovery, Discovery quiz
**GRAMMAR:** The passive
**PRONUNCIATION:** Numbers and dates, Irregular past participles

**READING:** *The dinosaur hunter*
**TED TALK:** *How we unearthed the Spinosaurus*. In this talk, Nizar Ibrahim tells us how he re-discovered a dinosaur known as the Spinosaurus.
**PRESENTATION SKILLS:** Using descriptive language
**WRITING:** Reporting the news

## WARM UP

• Books open. Draw students' attention to the unit title, the photo and the caption on page 125. Put students into pairs or small groups (three to four students) to discuss the questions.

• **Question 1**. Direct students to the photo and check the meaning of *cave* (a hole in a mountain or cliff that you can go inside). Bring in students' own experiences of visiting and exploring caves, and ask them to say whether this is something they enjoy doing and what risks or possible dangers are involved in it. Draw students' attention to the fact that the question is an *if*-sentence, or conditional sentence, and elicit or explain that this type of conditional asks you about the possible consequences of an imagined present condition. Tell students to use *I'd* + verb in their answers.

• **Question 2**. Bring in students' own experiences of going out walking and ask them to tell each other about anything interesting or unusual that they've found. This could be everyday objects that they've found in places you wouldn't expect them to be, a written message scratched on a stone or carved on a tree, or perhaps money or something valuable.

• **Question 3**. Tell students to think about recent discoveries of historical objects, human bones or animal remains. You could use the discovery of the skeleton of the English King Richard III as an example. His bones were found underneath a car park in Leicester, England, in 2012, and when they were examined, archaeologists discovered that he did, in fact, have a hunchback, just as Shakespeare had portrayed him in his play *Richard III*.

## 12.1 Recent discoveries

### VOCABULARY Discoveries

**1**

• Review the meaning of *discovery* (finding something or going to a place for the first time) and then direct students to the photograph of an artefact from the recently discovered tomb of a Celtic prince in Lavau, France, at the top of page 126.

Then, ask them to read the text, noticing how the words in bold are used. Students can then match the words in bold with their synonyms.

• Check answers in class. Model and drill the pronunciation of *excavate* /ˈekskəveɪt/ as students may find this challenging.

**Answers**
1 excavating  2 discovered  3 inspecting

**2**

• Students are now going to check their understanding of some key vocabulary connected with archaeological and palaeontological discoveries. Ask students to read the words in the box and look up the meaning of any words they don't know in a dictionary. They can then use the key content words in the sentences to help them choose the correct words from the box to complete them.

• Look at an example in class. Elicit or explain that the correct word for sentence 1 must be *ruins* because this is the only item in the box that you could see from the air.

• Check answers in class and model and drill the pronunciation of *tomb* /tuːm/. Elicit that the word *tomb* has a silent *b* at the end of it.

**Answers**
1 ruins  2 tomb  3 fossil  4 pottery  5 artefacts

**3**

• Put students into pairs and ask them to think of a museum or historical site they have visited. All of them should have visited such a place at some point, for example on a school trip.

• Direct students to the model and ask them to say something similar about the museum or historical site they've chosen. Encourage them to use a time expression and the right tense to say when they visited it, and to describe what you can see and do there in as much detail as they can.

- **Optional step.** Conduct whole-class feedback and ask some students to tell the rest of the group about the museum or historical site they chose.

### Extra activity

#### Finding more vocabulary online

Put students into pairs or small groups and ask each pair or small group to choose either archaeology or palaeontology, and go online to collect a few more items of vocabulary related to that topic and their definitions. Tell students to also make sure they know how to pronounce the words, e.g. by using an online dictionary where you can click on the loudspeaker icon to hear the words. Then, have each pair or group present and teach the words they've found to the class, and model and drill their pronunciation.

Draw a Venn diagram on the board with one circle for archaeology, one for palaeontology and an area in the middle for words that can be used to talk about both topics. In class, elicit where in the diagram the words each group has presented should go at the end of each presentation.

## LISTENING  An amazing find

**4**

- ▶ 12.1 Direct students to the Listening for numbers and dates box and ask them how easy or hard they find it to understand numbers and dates when they're listening to English. Tell students to listen out for and try to understand the numbers and dates they'll hear in the recording.

- Tell students they're going to listen to archaeologist Fredrik Hiebert, who they can see in the photo, talking about a discovery that he made. Ask them to read the words in the box and check they know the meaning of all four of them.

- Play the recording and ask students to identify and circle the item Hiebert found. Check answers in class.

### Transcript

**Narrator:** *In February 1982, archaeologist Fredrik Hiebert made an exciting discovery.*

**Fredrik Hiebert:** *One of the great stories that I have is about a time that I was excavating a trade site on the coast of Egypt. The site's more than 800 years old, and we were excavating a merchant's house who had been there seasonally, who had lived there in the summers when ships came, and then he would leave. And I was brushing the doorway, and I noticed there was a doormat. And I lifted up that doormat, and what was underneath that but a wooden key! That key was over 800 years old! And I picked it up and noticed that it had the name of the merchant written on it. Can you imagine? That merchant had been there 800 years ago, left his key, hoping to come back, and we found it. It was such a close connection with the past. It was awesome!*

### Answer
a key

**5**

- ▶ 12.1 Tell students they're going to listen to the recording again and focus on some of the detailed information about the discovery that Hiebert gives, including one number.

- Play the recording and ask students to focus on listening out for the answers to the questions so they can write them in the table.

- Students then compare their answers in pairs before you check answers in class. Elicit or explain that a *merchant* is a person who buys and sells goods, often internationally, for profit. Nowadays the term *merchant* is most often used to talk about jobs people did in the past rather than jobs they do today.

### Answers
1 Egypt   2 800   3 the summer

**6**

- Put students into pairs to discuss the question. They may find it helpful to look at the transcript of the recording to remind themselves of the details of Hiebert's discovery and then bring these into their discussions.

- Conduct whole-class feedback on what students think Hiebert's discovery tells us about the past.

### Suggested answer
People in the past did the same things that we do today, such as leaving a key under the doormat.

### Extra activity

#### Everyday things from days past

Ask students to discuss, either in pairs or in class, whether they've ever seen a similar example of an ordinary thing, like putting a key under the doormat, that people in the past did and we still do today, while visiting a museum or historical site. If they have, they can describe what the item was and how it shows us the similarities between the lives of people in the past and people's lives today.

## Pronunciation  Numbers and dates

**7**

- ▶ 12.2 Put students into pairs and ask them to say the numbers and dates out loud to each other as they think they should be said. Then, play the recording, and tell students to listen and notice any differences between the way they said the numbers and dates, and the way they should be said. Have students tell their partner what these differences were, e.g. *I said ..., but it should be ...*

- Play the recording again so students can listen and repeat the numbers and dates.
- **Optional step**. Draw students' attention to the fact that in British English the day comes before the month, as in the example they just listened to, but in American English the month comes before the day. In British English, the number of the day can also be followed by -*st* (1, 21, 31), -*nd* (2, 22), -*rd* (3, 23) or -*th* (all the other numbers).

> **TEACHING TIP**
>
> **Saying numbers and dates**
>
> Students will frequently need to say and write numbers and dates while they're using English, so it's important that they practise this. Elicit or draw students' attention to any differences that exist between the way numbers are said in their first language and in English, and tell them to keep these in mind. Also, tell students that although numbers and dates can be said in different ways, e.g. 1,500 can either be fifteen hundred or one thousand five hundred, and there are differences between British and American English in terms of how dates are formed, they should choose one way of saying numbers and dates which works for them, and use that all the time.

## SPEAKING Talking about a discovery

**8**

- ▶ 12.3 Ask students to read the conversation through once before they listen to it. Tell students to ignore the word choices on the right for the moment as they will focus on those in Exercise 9.
- Check answers and elicit that *identified* is a synonym for *found* and *discovered*.

| Answer |
|---|
| from the air |

**9**

- Model the conversation that students have just listened to aloud with a student. Then have students work in pairs to practise the conversation together. Make sure they alternate between A and B roles.
- Have students practise the conversation again using the words on the right instead of the words in bold in the conversation.

**10** **21st CENTURY OUTCOMES**

*Know when it is appropriate to listen and when to speak*

- Put students into pairs or small groups and ask them to think of any famous discoveries they know of which haven't been mentioned in the unit so far. Then, direct them to the model conversation and ask them to use it to tell each other what discoveries they've heard of. In order to fulfil the 21st CENTURY OUTCOMES, students should actively listen to what their partner tells them and then respond with a comment or question.
- **Optional step**. Ask students to mention the following points in their descriptions of the discoveries they choose:
  - what was discovered
  - who discovered it
  - where it was discovered
  - why the discovery is important.

If students are unsure about any of these details, and they have access to the Internet, they could go online and check.

- Circulate and monitor students while they're talking to each other and give them feedback when they've finished.

▶ Set Workbook pages 92 and 93 for homework.

▶ Photocopiable communicative activity 12.1. Go to page 185 for further practice of discoveries vocabulary. The teaching notes are on page 198.

## 12.2 Amazing finds

### GRAMMAR The passive

**1**

- ▶ 12.4 Direct students to the infographic. Elicit or explain that *find*, used as a noun, is a synonym for *discovery*, and then ask students to read the information about the five famous finds. Have students look up any words they don't know, e.g. *bury*, *bone*, *warrior*.
- Put students into pairs to tell each other which discovery they think is the most interesting and why, re-using some of the language from the infographic as they do so.
- Conduct whole-class feedback and establish which discovery the majority of students think is the most interesting.

| Answers |
|---|
| Students' own answers. |

12 Discovery 129

## 2

- ▶ 12.5 Tell students they're now going to listen to an expert talking about the terracotta warriors, which they read about in the infographic.

- **Optional step**. In order to engage students with the topic and help make their listening more focused, ask them to work in pairs to make notes on any information they already know about the terracotta warriors: this can include the information from the infographic and anything else they already knew.

- Ask students to read the sentences and then play the recording so they can listen and complete them with the words they hear.

- Have students compare answers in pairs before you check answers in class.

- **Optional step**. Ask students whether they found any of the information they heard about the terracotta warriors interesting or surprising, e.g. the fact that they were originally painted in bright colours.

### Transcript

The terracotta warriors were discovered in 1974. Since then, millions of people have visited this incredible site in Xian, China. Scientists have learned a great deal about the terracotta warriors in the past few decades. The site is actually a tomb. It was built for the first emperor of China over 2,000 years ago.

The 8,000 or so sculptures are all different – no two are alike. When tourists look at them today, they see brown. But the soldiers were originally painted in bright colours. This was done to make them look more realistic. The colours have faded over time.

> **Answers**
> 1 tomb   2 2,000   3 bright

## 3

- Ask students to read the example sentences and focus on the form of these passive and active sentences, and how the form of the passive sentences is different to that of the active sentences. Elicit or explain that in passive sentences the process or action is seen as being more important than the agent, whereas in active sentences the agent is seen as being more important than the process or action he/she/it is doing.

- Students can check their answers and overall understanding of the passive by turning to the Grammar summary on page 153.

- If you feel that students need more controlled practice before continuing, they could do the exercises in the Grammar summary. Otherwise, you could continue on to Exercise 4 in the unit and set the Grammar summary exercises for homework

> **Answers**
> 1
> a active
> b passive
> c We make the passive form with *to be* + the past participle of the verb used in the active sentence.
> d by
> e We might not know who discovered the terracotta warriors, or the action (what happens) is more important than the person who made the discovery.

> **Answers to Grammar summary exercises**
> 1
> 2 The city was taken over by the Romans in the 4th century BC
> 3 After the volcano, Pompeii was lost for over 1,500 years
> 4 The lost city was first discovered in 1599
> 5 Then, it was rediscovered by Rocque Joaquín de Alcubierre in 1748
>
> 2
> 1 is chosen   2 is divided   3 is found   4 are dug
> 5 are put   6 are carefully labelled   7 is taken
> 8 aren't broken

## 4

- Tell students that they're now going to practise using the past simple passive in context by identifying the past participles of the verbs given. If you think that students will need some help with this, they can look at the Irregular verbs table on page 174.

- Ask students to compare their answers in pairs before checking answers in class.

> **Answers**
> 1 discovered   2 revealed   3 painted   4 believed
> 5 found   6 studied

### LANGUAGE FOCUS Talking about discoveries

## 5

- ▶ 12.6 Ask students to read the Language focus box and notice how we form questions and answers in the present simple and past simple passive.

- Students can check overall understanding of the language focus by turning to the Grammar summary on page 154.

- If you feel that students need more controlled practice before continuing, they could do the exercises in the Grammar summary. Otherwise, you could continue on to Exercise 6 in the unit and set the Grammar summary exercises for homework.

### Answers to Grammar summary exercises

**1**

2 What were the bowls and spoons made of?
3 Who was the treasure discovered by?
4 When was it acquired by the British Museum?
5 When was the Hoxne hoard found?
6 Where is the Hoxne hoard displayed?
7 Who is the treasure now seen by?

**2**

1 The archaeologist ~~has~~ **was** invited to give a talk about his discoveries.
2 Before they are ~~displaying~~ **displayed** in a museum, all the objects are cleaned.
3 Mosasaurus dinosaur bones were ~~dig~~ **dug** up in 1764.
4 The cave paintings in El Castillo ~~was~~ **were** discovered by Hermilio Alcalde del Río.
5 The Rosetta Stone was originally displayed without protection, but in 1847 it **was** put in a special case.
6 Lots of Roman treasure was ~~showed~~ **shown** for the first time in 2016 at the Museum of Liverpool.

## Pronunciation  Irregular past participles

**6**

- ▶ 12.7 Tell students that the difference between the base verb of an irregular verb and its past participle is usually the vowel sound, e.g. *sing* and *sung*, otherwise the two verb forms can sound quite similar. It is, therefore, important to pronounce past participles correctly to make it clear that you're using this form of the verb and not its base form.

- Ask students to write in all of the past participles of the verbs first and then try saying them out loud to see if they can hear similarities between the sounds. This should help them to match the past participles with the same vowel sounds.

- Play the recording again so students can listen and check their answers. Then, play it again so they can listen to the past participles and repeat them.

### Answers

2 built  e written
3 bought  d taught
4 heard  a hurt
5 read  c said

**7**

- ▶ 12.8 Students are now going to practise identifying whether a verb should be used in its passive or active form in the context of a text about the Voynich manuscript. Tell students to refer back to the examples in the Language focus box to help them choose the correct options.

- Have students compare their answers in pairs before playing the recording so that students can check them.

- **Optional step**. If students have access to the Internet, they can search for some more images of the Voynich manuscript online.

### Answers

1 is written   2 contains   3 are made   4 discovered
5 is named   6 was created   7 was needed
8 wasn't invented

**8**

- Students are now going to practise forming questions and answers about discoveries with the passive. They can refer back to the examples in the Language focus box to help them do this if they need to.

- Have students compare their answers in pairs before you check answers in class.

- **Optional step**. In pairs, ask students to read the three exchanges they completed out loud.

### Answers

1 discovered, was found   2 is/'s, located, is seen
3 Was, buried, was removed

## SPEAKING  Discovery quiz

**9**

- Put students into AB pairs and ask them to turn to their respective files. Have them read the questions and answers, and think about how they're going to pronounce any unknown words, numbers and dates. Offer students assistance with this if necessary.

- Students then take it in turns to ask and answer their questions. Remind them to pause after each answer option to make it easier for their partner to understand them.

- Monitor students and give them feedback on their pronunciation and fluency when they've finished.

▶ Set Workbook pages 94 and 95 for homework.

## 12.3 It's in his bones

**READING** The dinosaur hunter

**1**

- Check the meaning of *palaeontologist* (a scientist who studies fossils of animals and plants) and model and drill its pronunciation /ˌpeɪlɪɒnˈtɒlədʒɪst/ as students may find this challenging.

- Ask students to read the introduction to the article (the text in italics), look at the photo of Nizar Ibrahim and then think of three questions they would like to ask him, without looking at the rest of the article. They can do this either individually or in pairs. Encourage students to think of questions related to the work that Ibrahim does and the discoveries he's made, recycling the vocabulary for discoveries that they learned in 12.1, where appropriate.

> **Answers**
> Students' own answers.

**2**

- ▶ 12.9 Ask students to scan read the text and focus on identifying the questions Ibrahim is asked and compare these with the questions they thought of in Exercise 1.

> **Answers**
> Students' own answers.

### Understanding gist

**3**

- Check the meaning of *thrilling* (very exciting). Give students 20 or 30 seconds to scan the article with the aim of identifying the gist, or general message, and then have them choose the topics that are discussed in the interview.

- Check answers in class.

> **Answers**
> a, b, c

### Understanding details

**4**

- Students are now going to focus on some of the detailed information Ibrahim gave in the interview. Ask students to read the sentences and think about whether they're true, false or not given, based on what they can remember from the first time they read the interview. Then, ask students to read the whole text again more slowly and carefully, looking for the information mentioned in the sentences, so they can choose the correct option for each one.

- Point out the glossary at the bottom of the text and tell students to refer to it as they read or to look at the words and definitions before they start reading.

- Ask students to compare their answers in pairs before you check answers in class.

> **Answers**
> 1 T   2 NG   3 F   4 T   5 NG

### Understanding pronoun referencing

**5**

- Elicit or explain that a *pronoun* is a word used to stand for (or take the place of) a noun, and examples include words such as *it*, *them* and *which* that they can see in bold in this exercise. *Pronoun referencing* is, therefore, using pronouns to refer back to a thing, person or place you mentioned earlier. Tell students that they're now going to look at some examples of pronoun referencing and identify what the pronouns refer to.

- Students can either choose the options that the pronouns refer to from memory or find the excerpts in the article and look back at the first part of the sentence to identify what they refer to. The excerpts are presented in the order in which they appear in the article.

- Ask students to compare answers in pairs before checking answers in class. Draw students' attention to the fact that pronoun referencing is a useful strategy because it enables you to avoid repetition.

> **Answers**
> 1 a   2 b   3 b   4 b

### Understanding vocabulary

**6**

- Ask students to read the sentences. Tell them to look back at the words in bold in the article and use them to complete the definitions. If students are unsure about the meaning of any of the items in bold, they may find it helpful to look at how the words are used in context in the article.

- Check answers in class. Model and drill the pronunciation of *discouraged* /dɪsˈkʌrɪdʒd/ as students may find this challenging.

> **Answers**
> 1 discouraged   2 violent   3 diverse   4 Obstacles
> 5 build-up

**7**

- Students are now going to practise using the word *challenging*, which they read in the interview, and what they learned about palaeontologists to give their opinions on the most challenging aspect of being a palaeontologist. Put students into pairs to give their opinions and say whether they agree or disagree with each other and why.

- Conduct whole-class feedback.

▶ Set Workbook pages 96 and 97 for homework.

## 12.4 How we unearthed the Spinosaurus

**TEDTALKS**

**1**

- Tell students that they're now going to watch a TED Talk by palaeontologist Nizar Ibrahim. Before students read the summary of the talk, direct them to the title of the talk and ask them to speculate about what Ibrahim's idea worth spreading could be, based on what they already know about him from the interview in **12.3**.

- Have students read the summary of the talk and choose the correct options in the definitions of the words in bold. If students are unsure about which words to choose, encourage them to use deduction or simply have a guess.

- Students can compare their answers in pairs before you check answers in class. Draw students' attention to the pronunciation of *quest* /kwest/ as they may find this challenging.

| Answers |
|---|
| 1 a long search for something   2 bones |
| 3 strange or unusual |

**2**

- Direct students to the illustration of a dinosaur on page 133 and tell them it's a Spinosaurus, the dinosaur that Ibrahim talks about in this TED Talk. Ask students if they've ever seen this dinosaur or a dinosaur like it before. Then, put them into pairs to discuss what its physical features and what it's doing in the illustration tell you about it.

- Conduct whole-class feedback.

| Answers |
|---|
| Students' own answers. |

**TEACHING TIP**

**Giving speaking activities a specific focus**

Sometimes it's a good idea to 'just let students speak'. This doesn't put them under any pressure; they can get some fluency practice and just enjoy saying what they want to say. However, giving a speaking activity a specific focus and telling students to use target language examples or language with a specific function can also be very beneficial. It raises students' awareness of the relevance of this specific language to a given communicative situation, enables them to concentrate on using specific examples of language or one type of language, thus improving their ability to use it, and may also 'force' them to expand the range of words and expressions they use.

In the speaking activity in Exercise 2, for example, you could ask students to focus on speculative language (*this might/may/could/must be …*), language for abilities (*can, enable, allow, let*), vocabulary for body parts or descriptive adjectives (*long, short, narrow, ugly, spiky, scaly*). You could either decide what the focus will be or give students some options, such as the ones above, and ask them to choose one themselves.

**3**

- ▶ **12.10** Tell students they're now going to listen to Part 1 of Ibrahim's talk. Ask them to read the notes and predict what the missing words could be. Then, play Part 1 and ask students to focus on the specific pieces of information Ibrahim knew about the Spinosaurus before he started looking for it.

- Students can check their answers in pairs before you check answers in class.

### Transcript

*These dragons from deep time are incredible creatures. They're bizarre, they're beautiful, and there's very little we know about them. These thoughts were going through my head when I looked at the pages of my first dinosaur book. I was about five years old at the time, and I decided there and then that I would become a palaeontologist. Palaeontology allowed me to combine my love for animals with my desire to travel to far-flung corners of the world.*

*And now, a few years later, I've led several expeditions to the ultimate far-flung corner on this planet, the Sahara. I've worked in the Sahara because I've been on a quest to uncover new remains of a bizarre, giant predatory dinosaur called Spinosaurus.*

*A few bones of this animal have been found in the deserts of Egypt and were described about 100 years ago by a German palaeontologist. Unfortunately, all his Spinosaurus bones were destroyed in World War Two. So all we're left with are just a few drawings and notes.*

12  Discovery

*From these drawings, we know that this creature, which lived about 100 million years ago, was very big, it had tall spines on its back, forming a magnificent sail, and it had long, slender jaws, a bit like a crocodile, with conical teeth, that may have been used to catch slippery prey, like fish. But that was pretty much all we knew about this animal for the next 100 years.*

| Answers |
| --- |
| 1 bones   2 100 million   3 back   4 crocodile   5 fish |

**4**

- ▶12.11 Students are now going to watch Part 2 of the talk, in which Ibrahim talks about how he collected the bones of a Spinosaurus and what he did with them. Ask students to read the sentences that summarize what Ibrahim discovered from the bones and then listen out for the pieces of information mentioned so they can circle the correct options.
- Check answers in class.

### Transcript

*Finally, very recently, we were able to track down a dig site where a local fossil hunter found several bones of Spinosaurus. We returned to the site, we collected more bones. And so after 100 years we finally had another partial skeleton of this bizarre creature. And we were able to reconstruct it.*

*We now know that Spinosaurus had a head a little bit like a crocodile, very different from other predatory dinosaurs, very different from the T. rex. But the really interesting information came from the rest of the skeleton. We had long spines, the spines forming the big sail. We had leg bones, we had skull bones, we had paddle-shaped feet, wide feet – again, very unusual, no other dinosaur has feet like this – and we think they may have been used to walk on soft sediment, or maybe for paddling in the water. We also looked at the fine microstructure of the bone, the inside structure of Spinosaurus bones, and it turns out that they're very dense and compact. Again, this is something we see in animals that spend a lot of time in the water, it's useful for buoyancy control in the water.*

*We CT-scanned all of our bones and built a digital Spinosaurus skeleton. And when we looked at the digital skeleton, we realized that yes, this was a dinosaur unlike any other. It's bigger than a T. rex, and yes, the head has 'fish-eating' written all over it, but really the entire skeleton has 'water-loving' written all over it – dense bone, paddle-like feet, and the hind limbs are reduced in size, and again, this is something we see in animals that spend a substantial amount of time in the water.*

| Answers |
| --- |
| 1 different from   2 water   3 in the water   4 bigger |

**5**

- ▶12.12 Students are now going to watch Part 3 of the talk, in which Ibrahim talks about why the discovery of the Spinosaurus was so incredible.
- Ask students to read the quote from Roy Chapman Andrews and think about what the dinosaur hunter meant when he said this. Then, play Part 3 and ask students to listen for the quote and notice the context in which Ibrahim uses it as this should help them to infer its meaning.
- Put students into pairs to discuss what they think Chapman Andrews meant. Tell them to try paraphrasing it. Then, conduct whole-class feedback on students' ideas.

### Transcript

*So, as we fleshed out our Spinosaurus – I'm looking at muscle attachments and wrapping our dinosaur in skin – we realize that we're dealing with a river monster, a predatory dinosaur, bigger than T. rex, the ruler of this ancient river of giants, feeding on the many aquatic animals I showed you earlier on.*

*So that's really what makes this an incredible discovery. It's a dinosaur like no other. And some people told me, 'Wow, this is a once-in-a-lifetime discovery. There are not many things left to discover in the world.' Well, I think nothing could be further from the truth. I think the Sahara's still full of treasures, and when people tell me there are no places left to explore, I like to quote a famous dinosaur hunter, Roy Chapman Andrews, and he said, 'Always, there has been an adventure just around the corner – and the world is still full of corners.' That was true many decades ago when Roy Chapman Andrews wrote these lines. And it is still true today. Thank you.*

| Suggested answer |
| --- |
| There are still lots of discoveries to be made. |

## CRITICAL THINKING

**6**

- Tell students that in this activity the critical thinking skill they'll be using is the ability to use what they do know about something to infer what may never be possible to know.
- Put students into pairs and have them brainstorm and discuss what they think we will never know about the Spinosaurus, based on what they've heard Ibrahim say about it.
- Conduct whole-class feedback on students' views.

### Extra activity

### Palaeontology processes

Palaeontologists are often described as dinosaur detectives. Put students into pairs and ask them to look at the transcript of Ibrahim's TED Talk so they can identify the steps in the process of bringing the Spinosaurus back to life.

He says that it started with contact from a local archaeologist who found some bones. Ask each pair to take this as their starting point and then take it in turns to say what the next step in the process was. Tell them to use the passive, where appropriate, as we usually use the passive to describe processes. Conduct whole-class feedback by going around the class and asking students to each say a step in the process from the beginning to the end. If you have a larger group, you can go through the process more than once.

## VOCABULARY IN CONTEXT

**7**

- ▶ 12.13 Play the clips from the TED Talk. When each multiple-choice question appears, pause the clip so that students can choose the correct definition. Discourage the more confident students from always giving the answer by asking students to raise their hand if they think they know.

### Transcript and subtitles

**1** But that was **pretty much** all we knew about this animal for the next 100 years.
**Pretty much** all you know means _____ you know.
   a  the most beautiful thing
   b  the most important thing
   c  almost everything

**2** But the really interesting information came from the rest of the **skeleton**.
What is your **skeleton**?
   a  all the bones in your head
   b  all the bones that support your body
   c  all the bones of your hand

**3** We returned to the site, we collected more bones. And so after 100 years we finally had another **partial** skeleton of this bizarre creature.
What does **partial** mean?
   a  beautiful
   b  upright
   c  incomplete

**4** And some people told me, 'Wow, this is a **once-in-a-lifetime** discovery.'
A **once-in-a-lifetime** event is something that happens _____.
   a  often
   b  very rarely
   c  never

**5** There **are not many** things **left** to discover in the world. If there **are not many** of something **left**, it means _____.
   a  they are all on the right
   b  they are not interesting
   c  most of them have gone

| Answers |
|---|
| 1 c   2 b   3 c   4 b   5 c |

**8**

- Students are now going to use two of the terms they looked at in Exercise 7 – *once-in-a-lifetime* and *be left* – to discuss an example they know and give their opinions.
- Put students into pairs and ask them to say their own answers to the questions, giving as much detail as they can. Circulate and monitor students' discussions and give them feedback when they've finished.

## PRESENTATION SKILLS Using descriptive language

**9**

- ▶ 12.14 Direct students to the Presentation skills box and check the meaning of *to paint a picture* (here: to help people imagine what something is like or looks like).
- Play the clip and ask students to notice the example of descriptive language Nizar Ibrahim uses to describe the Spinosaurus and the animal he compares it to.
- Check answers in class.
- **Optional step**. Elicit or explain that using the phrase *a bit like a …* is a simple but effective way of using descriptive language.

| Answer |
|---|
| a crocodile |

**10**

- ▶ 12.15 Tell students they're now going to look at some examples of other TED Talk speakers comparing the things they're talking about to other everyday objects. Ask students to read the sentences and then watch the clips and use what they hear to complete them.
- Ask students to compare their answers in pairs before you check answers in pairs.
- **Optional step**. Draw students' attention to the fact that the words *garbage* and *trash* are used in American English for things you throw away, whereas in British English the word *rubbish* is normally used.

| Answers |
|---|
| 1 tattoo   2 garbage   3 dance |

**11** **21st CENTURY OUTCOMES**

*Use information accurately and creatively for the issue or problem at hand*

- Put students into pairs. Ask them to turn back to page 123 and look carefully at the photo of a hummingbird feeding on the nectar of a flower. Tell them to think about something else from everyday life which they could compare what the hummingbird is doing to, and then use this to make a sentence. In order to fulfil the 21st CENTURY OUTCOMES, students should be able to show that they've responded to the input provided by the photo by creatively using language to describe it.

12   Discovery   135

- **Optional step.** Put each pair together with another two pairs and have them share the descriptive language each pair thought of. They then put their ideas together to come up with one sentence which contains their best idea or the best parts of all of their ideas.
- Conduct whole-class feedback on students' ideas.

> **TEACHING TIP**
>
> **Listening to English outside the classroom**
>
> If students are now coming to the end of their English course, draw their attention to the fact that continued exposure to listening material in English outside the classroom will help them to continue developing their listening skills and to make them more independent and autonomous learners. Students can also choose what they listen to themselves outside the classroom, rather than having to listen to the recordings which are a part of their course, and this should boost their motivation to listen. If students travel a lot or commute, they can also do some listening on their smartphones, mp3 or CD players. Encourage students to use what they've learned about listening techniques up to now to help them when they're listening alone. You can motivate students to do some listening in their own time by suggesting sources of podcasts and videos – www.ted.com is a good place to start!

▶ Set Workbook page 98 for homework.

## 12.5 What have you found?

### COMMUNICATE A newspaper interview

**1**

- Put students into AB pairs. Ask them to read the information and give them some time to prepare for the roleplay. Draw students' attention to the fact that they will need to use both active and passive forms in their questions and answers. They may want to refer back to the Language focus box in **12.2** to help them with this.
- Direct the Student As to the Explaining possibilities box and ask them to use these expressions when they're talking about the discovery. Also, tell the Student Bs to make notes on what their partner tells them about the discovery so they can use these in Exercise 3.
- Monitor students so you can give them feedback on their performance when they've completed Exercise 2.

**2**

- Have students switch roles and give them some time to prepare to do the roleplay again. Tell the Student As to make notes on what their partner tells them. Circulate and monitor the roleplays as you did before.
- When students have finished, ask them to reflect on their performance and tell their partner how they think they did in both parts of the roleplay. Then, give them the feedback you've collected in class.

### WRITING Reporting the news

**3**  **21st CENTURY OUTCOMES**

*Articulate thoughts and ideas effectively using oral, written and nonverbal communication skills in a variety of forms and contexts*

- Ask students to read the model news report and then use the notes they made in Exercises 1 or 2 to write one for the discovery their partner told them about. In order to fulfil the 21st CENTURY OUTCOMES, students should be able to clearly articulate the information they got from their partner in the form of a news report, using the style that the model text is written in.
- **Optional step.** Stronger students could extend the text and give more details, inventing some extra details about the discovery if they need to. Weaker students can write shorter and simpler news reports.
- Circulate and monitor while students are writing, offering assistance and feedback where appropriate.

| Answers |
| --- |
| Students' own answers. |

**4**

- Put students into different pairs and have them read the news reports they wrote in Exercise 3 out loud to each other. Remind them to stress the key content words to make sure their partner understands the most important parts of the news story and to use their voice to show enthusiasm about the story so their partner will want to listen to them talking about it.

▶ Set Workbook page 99 for homework.

▶ Photocopiable communicative activity 12.2. Go to page 186 for further practice the passive and discoveries vocabulary. The teaching notes are on page 198.

# Presentation 4 | UNITS 10–12

## MODEL PRESENTATION

**1**

• Tell students they're going to read the text of a presentation. The aim of the presentation is to tell people about a recent discovery.

• Ask students to read the text of the presentation all the way through and think about what the missing words could be as they do so. Then, ask them to look at the words in the box, read the text all the way through again and complete it with the correct words. Encourage students to look at what comes before and after the gaps to help them decide which words should go in them.

• Students can compare their answers in pairs, but don't confirm answers at this stage as they will find out what the correct answers are when they watch the presentation in Exercise 2.

> **Answers**
> 1 was made   2 was created   3 has eaten
> 4 discovered   5 amazingly   6 forests   7 fossils
> 8 have been   9 has been   10 Hopefully

**2**

• ▶ P.4 Play the recording of the presentation and ask students to listen closely for the words the presenter says in the gaps so they can check their answers from Exercise 1. Check answers in class.

• **Optional step.** Draw students' attention to the use of the past simple passive to describe processes that happened in the past (e.g. *was made, was created*) and the use of the present perfect to describe things that started in the past and continue up until now (e.g. *it has been open to the public since 2013*) in the presentation they've just watched.

**3**

• ▶ P.4 Ask students to read the list of presentation skills and think back to when they looked at using descriptive language (Unit 12), calling others to action (Unit 11) and dealing with the unexpected (Unit 10). Students can look back at the Presentation skills boxes from those units to refresh their memory of how presenters can do these things. Put students into pairs and ask them to discuss which of these skills they remember the speaker using in his presentation.

• Play the recording again so students can watch and check their answers. Elicit or explain that the example of descriptive language that the speaker uses is: *In some places the cave is big enough to fit a jumbo jet inside!*

• **Optional step.** Ask students to discuss, either in pairs or in class, whether they think the presentation would have been better if the speaker had done the things he didn't do: numbering key points and giving a call to action, or if these things wouldn't have made his presentation any better or actually would have made it worse.

> **Answers**
> The speaker uses questions to signpost, personalizes the presentation, closes the presentation effectively, provides background information, uses his voice effectively, tells an anecdote, uses supporting evidence, uses an effective slide and uses descriptive language. He doesn't number key points, give a call to action or deal with the unexpected (because nothing unexpected happens).

## YOUR TURN

**4**

• Ask students to think of an amazing discovery. This could be one of the discoveries they read and talked about in Unit 12 or another discovery they could do some online research to find out more about.

• Give students some time to prepare their presentations. Tell them to read the questions and make notes on their answers to all of them.

• Direct students to the list of presentation skills in Exercise 3 and tell them that the objective is to use all of them in their own presentations. They will, therefore, also need to think about how they can include the points in their presentations while they're preparing to speak.

• If time allows, and students are interested in working on their ability to create slides, they can also create a slide (or several slides) to accompany their presentations, and they can do this either as a self-study task or in class, either on the computer or on paper. Otherwise, you can ask students to omit the objective of using an effective slide from the list.

**5**

• Direct students to the Useful phrases box. Ask them to read its contents and note down the words and phrases they want to use in their presentations. Tell students to use at least one word or phrase from each of the four categories in the box.

**6**

• Put students into pairs and tell them they're now going to take it in turns to give their presentations.

• Have students give their presentations and tick the skills their partner uses while they're listening to them. Make sure students are aware that when they're giving their partner feedback they're going to say two things they liked about it and one thing that could be improved, so they will also need to be thinking about this while they're listening.

**7**

- Ask students to read the example feedback in the speech bubble and use it as a model for giving their own feedback to their partner. Encourage them to start with a positive comment, as in the example, and then mention the good things their partner did, using the ticks they made in their checklist, before saying something that their partner could improve.

- **Optional step.** When students have finished giving each other feedback, add your global feedback on students' presentations to their comments and highlight some areas for improvement for next time.

> **TEACHING TIP**
>
> **Recording students' presentations**
>
> Making video recordings of students' presentations can be very valuable when it comes to encouraging self-reflection on their performance and facilitating peer and teacher feedback – assuming that students are prepared to be recorded and to watch the recording back afterwards. Students may be reluctant at first, but if you explain the benefits to them, they'll most likely be willing to give it a try.
>
> Recording students' presentations will probably be more useful as a feedback tool if you ask them to choose something they want the person/people giving the feedback to focus on when they're watching the recording, and this also makes it easier for the person/people giving feedback. The focus they choose could be one of the presentation skills in the box in Exercise 6.

# TEST 1 | Units 1–3

Name: _____

Total score: _____

## VOCABULARY

**1** Read the conversation and tick (✓) the correct answer. The first one is done for you.

*Sarah:* I'm having lunch with my sister and her husband tomorrow.
*Ahmad:* Oh, great. What's your sister's name again? Emma, isn't it? And what's your **(0)** … name?
*Sarah:* His name's Steve.
*Ahmad:* OK. What does he do?
*Sarah:* He's a scientist. He studies frogs, toads and other **(1)** … .
*Ahmad:* Wow, that's **(2)** … . He must have a really interesting job.
*Sarah:* I don't know. I wouldn't want to cut up dead frogs like he does. Sounds **(3)** … !
*Ahmad:* Yeah, but I'm sure he **(4)** … how important it is to learn as much as you can about the animals that share the planet with us. There's still so much we don't know about them, but **(5)** … we're figuring it out.
*Sarah:* Hmm, yes, but have you heard the loud noises some of those frogs make? It's the kind of thing you have nightmares about. They're **(6)** … if you ask me.
*Ahmad:* I think you're over-reacting. It'd be a **(7)** … if we decided not to study or protect animals just because they do things we find a bit strange. Where's your sense of **(8)** … about the world around you?
*Sarah:* I *am* interested in learning more about the world around me. There are just some types of animals that I don't like. I prefer a cute monkey or a panda.
*Ahmad:* Yes, I suppose **(9)** … like those are cuter and cuddlier! I'm sure Steve will be very happy to tell you why frogs are so great over lunch though!
*Sarah:* Yes, he likes to **(10)** … about how he's the world's leading frog expert, so I'm sure he will.

| | | | | | | | |
|---|---|---|---|---|---|---|---|
| **0** | **A** | brother's ☐ | **B** | nephew's ☐ | **C** | brother-in-law's ✓ |
| **1** | **A** | amphibians ☐ | **B** | reptiles ☐ | **C** | insects ☐ |
| **2** | **A** | marvellous ☐ | **B** | revealing ☐ | **C** | complicated ☐ |
| **3** | **A** | moving ☐ | **B** | disgusting ☐ | **C** | mysterious ☐ |
| **4** | **A** | turns out ☐ | **B** | adopts ☐ | **C** | appreciates ☐ |
| **5** | **A** | little by little ☐ | **B** | practically ☐ | **C** | the sound of it ☐ |
| **6** | **A** | surprising ☐ | **B** | charming ☐ | **C** | terrifying ☐ |
| **7** | **A** | identity ☐ | **B** | real shame ☐ | **C** | glimpse ☐ |
| **8** | **A** | wealth ☐ | **B** | curiosity ☐ | **C** | sympathy ☐ |
| **9** | **A** | mammals ☐ | **B** | amphibians ☐ | **C** | reptiles ☐ |
| **10** | **A** | ban ☐ | **B** | insult ☐ | **C** | boast ☐ |

Marks (out of 10): _____

**2** Read the conversations and tick (✓) the correct answer. The first one is done for you.

**0** What did you think of the karate film we saw yesterday?
   **A** It was really disgusting. ☐
   **B** It was very dramatic. ✓
   **C** It was very charming. ☐

**11** Have you changed your mind about coming to the concert?
   **A** Yes, I'm going to come. ☐
   **B** Yes, I still don't want to come. ☐
   **C** No, I want to come now. ☐

12  Have you seen how some people treat their pets?
    A  I know. They're always playing with them. ☐
    B  I know. They should ban pets. ☐
    C  I know. It's disgusting. ☐

13  Have you noticed how ambitious Cathy is?
    A  Yes, she really wants to be successful. ☐
    B  Yes, she's always boasting. ☐
    C  Yes, she has my sympathy. ☐

14  Fingers crossed, Selma will pass her driving test.
    A  Oh, that's a real shame! ☐
    B  Yes, I hope she does. ☐
    C  Congratulations, Selma! ☐

15  Do you know what type of animal a butterfly is?
    A  Yes, it's an amphibian. ☐
    B  Yes, it's an insect. ☐
    C  Yes, it's a reptile. ☐

16  I cried when Juliet woke up and found Romeo's body.
    A  Yes, things turned out well. ☐
    B  Yes, that's very common. ☐
    C  Me too. It was very moving. ☐

17  My great-great grandfather was an actor.
    A  Oh, you have really interesting ancestors. ☐
    B  I love hearing about your mother- and father-in-law. ☐
    C  You have a big extended family. ☐

18  I like the sound of a free holiday in the Caribbean.
    A  Me too. I love that kind of music. ☐
    B  Yes, that would be marvellous. ☐
    C  That's practically a revolution. ☐

19  What are your favourite mammals?
    A  I love amphibians. ☐
    B  Flamingos are my favourite. ☐
    C  I'd say elephants and monkeys. ☐

20  Mark told me the text I wrote was really bad!
    A  Mark's so charming. ☐
    B  He's just boasting. ☐
    C  Don't listen to him. ☐

Marks (out of 10): _____

## GRAMMAR

**3** Read the sentences and tick (✓) the correct answer. The first one is done for you.

0  At the moment, twins Noelle and Jason … a family reunion.
   A  plan ☐    B  are going to plan ☐    C  are planning ✓

21  They … all of their extended family to the reunion next week.
    A  invite ☐    B  're inviting ☐    C  don't invite ☐

22  Noelle and Jason even invited their great-aunt … lives in Australia.
    A  which ☐    B  who ☐    C  where ☐

23  This afternoon, they … for a hotel where they can hold the reunion.
    A  're looking ☐    B  're going to look ☐    C  look ☐

24  Jason … to have the reunion in a really fancy hotel.
    A  is wanting ☐    B  wants ☐    C  is going to want ☐

25  But Noelle … it would be too expensive.
    A  thinks ☐    B  is thinking ☐    C  's going to think ☐

26  She's found a nice village hall … they could hold the party for just £150.
    A  which ☐    B  who ☐    C  where ☐

27  And she … them right now to see if the hall is available on 20th March.
    A  's going to call ☐    B  calls ☐    C  's calling ☐

**28** The hall is available, and Jason and Noelle ... the man who manages it this evening. His name is John.
  **A** are meeting ☐   **B** are going to meet ☐   **C** meet ☐

**29** While they were there, John showed them all of the furniture ... they could use.
  **A** who ☐   **B** which ☐   **C** where ☐

**30** Noelle and Jason decided to book the hall and they ... like they made a good choice.
  **A** 're going to feel ☐   **B** feel ☐   **C** 're feeling ☐

Marks (out of 10): _____

**4** Complete the conversation with the words in the box. The first one is done for you.

| ~~Do~~ | 'm | 'm going to ask | 'm going to do | where |
| who | that | aren't | 'm driving | 'm having | 'm doing |

*Claire:* **(0)** ___Do___ you want to come to the cinema with me on Thursday evening? I want to see the film **(31)** _____ won the Best Picture.

*Rebecca:* Oh, yes, that looks really good, but I **(32)** _____ dinner with Sabrina on Thursday.

*Claire:* Oh, OK. What about Friday then?

*Rebecca:* I can't do Friday either. I **(33)** _____ a friend **(34)** _____ has broken her leg to her parents' house in the afternoon.

*Claire:* Oh, no. Is that Phoebe – the one whose parents live in the house **(35)** _____ ghosts appear in the middle of the night?

*Rebecca:* Ha ha ha, yes, but that's just a story. There **(36)** _____ really any ghosts there. I **(37)** _____ free on Saturday though. How about going to the cinema then?

*Claire:* Hmm, I **(38)** _____ an exam then.

*Rebecca:* Oh, are you? Is that your French exam?

*Claire:* Yes, it is. I **(39)** _____ some more revision for it this afternoon actually.

*Rebecca:* We should go and celebrate when you come out.

*Claire:* Yes, that would be good. I **(40)** _____ a few friends to come over to mine. Do you want to come over too?

*Rebecca:* Yes, that would be great. Fingers crossed the exam goes well!

*Claire:* Thank you! I hope it's not too hard.

Marks (out of 10): _____

# READING

**5** Read the email and complete the notes. Write one or two words in each space. The first one is done for you.

---

TO: *Click here to add recipients*    CC:

SUBJECT:

Dear Uncle George,

I hope that you and Auntie Mavis are well. I'm writing because Sam says you didn't get the family reunion invitation that I sent. The date is 4th May and it's going to be a big get-together with about 50 people. I'm hiring a big room at the White Rose Hotel in Exeter for all of us. Do you know where that is? It's just at the bottom of the big hill when you walk east away from the town centre.

We're going to have dinner at the hotel and we have the room from 5 pm, so everyone's going to arrive just after 5. It'd be a real shame if we didn't get to see you and you didn't get to see everyone. I've even booked a band to play some live music in the evening, so I think it will be really fun. You also have a choice of three different meals from the menu so Auntie Mavis should find something she likes.

I'd really appreciate it if you could email me back and tell me if you can come. I really hope you can!

Best wishes,

Katrina

---

**Hodgkins family (0)** ___reunion___
**Date: (41)** _____
**Time:** From **(42)** _____
**Venue:** The **(43)** _____ Hotel in **(44)** _____
**Number of people coming: (45)** _____ 50
**Food: (46)** _____ at the hotel with a choice of **(47)** _____ different meals.
**Entertainment:** A **(48)** _____ playing **(49)** _____ music
**Contact person:** Email **(50)** _____ if you can come.

Marks (out of 10): _____

# LISTENING

**6**  🎧 **T.1** Listen and tick (✓) the correct answer. You will hear the conversation twice. The first one is done for you.

**0** The people in the photo are …
  **A** taking a photo of a quokka. ☐
  **B** taking a photo of an Australian island. ☐
  **C** taking a photo of themselves with a quokka. ✓

**51** Chia didn't know …
  **A** that quokkas live in Australia. ☐   **B** what a quokka was. ☐
  **C** how cute quokkas were. ☐

**52** Quokkas are …
  **A** small mammals. ☐   **B** large mammals. ☐   **C** exotic mammals. ☐

**53** Chia and Brendan think quokkas' smiles are …
  **A** completely different to a human's. ☐
  **B** a little bit like a human's. ☐
  **C** very similar to a human's. ☐

**54** When quokkas see humans, they usually …
   **A** run away from them. ☐   **B** cut them with their claws. ☐   **C** move closer to them. ☐

**55** Quokkas and kangaroos can both …
   **A** jump. ☐   **B** move quickly. ☐   **C** smile. ☐

**56** Brendan and Chia think that quokkas can be …
   **A** endangered. ☐   **B** dangerous. ☐   **C** ambitious. ☐

**57** What do quokkas usually eat?
   **A** fruit ☐   **B** bread ☐   **C** plants ☐

**58** What do Brendan and Chia think about tourists who give food to quokkas?
   **A** They do it so they can take a photo with them. ☐   **B** They're helping the quokkas. ☐
   **C** They're doing the wrong thing. ☐

**59** When does Chia want to go to Australia?
   **A** when she starts university ☐   **B** next summer ☐   **C** in two years' time ☐

**60** What does Chia forget?
   **A** how long it takes to get to Australia ☐   **B** how expensive it is to go to Australia ☐
   **C** when it's summer in Australia ☐

Marks (out of 10): _____

## SPEAKING

**7** Student A, read the information about a famous novel. Student B, ask Student A some questions to find out about it. Then swap roles.

**Student A**
**Name:** *The Great Gatsby*
**Genre:** American fiction
**Plot:** Nick Carraway moves to New York / His neighbour is the mysterious Gatsby / Nick slowly learns more about Gatsby, his past and his relationships with the beautiful Daisy.
**Setting:** Long Island and New York in the 1920s
**Theme:** The death of the American Dream
**Opinion:** A charming and surprising classic American novel

**Student B**
What / called?
Why / type?
What / about?
What / setting?
What / theme?
What / you / think?

Marks (out of 10): _____

## WRITING

**8** A friend of yours thinks spending time with family isn't important. Write an email to your friend to tell him/her why it is.
   • Give two reasons why some people, like your friend, don't think spending time with family is important.
   • Give two reasons why spending time with family is important.
   • Encourage your friend to get in touch with his/her family.

Write 35–50 words.

Marks (out of 10): _____

# TEST 2 | Units 4–6

Name: _____
Total score: _____

## VOCABULARY

**1** Read the definitions and complete the words. The first one is done for you.

| 0 | very small | t <u>i n y</u> |
|---|---|---|
| 1 | the opposite of curved | s _ _ _ _ _ _ _ |
| 2 | music that sounds cheerful and positive | u _ _ _ _ _ |
| 3 | you do this when you are happy, when you pass an exam, for example | c _ _ _ _ _ _ _ _ |
| 4 | the opposite of smooth | r _ _ _ _ |
| 5 | how you feel when you hear sad music | d _ _ _ _ _ _ _ |
| 6 | different in a way that is easy to see | d _ _ _ _ _ _ _ _ _ |
| 7 | music that sounds quiet and soft | g _ _ _ _ _ |
| 8 | describing the shape that a circle has | r _ _ _ _ |
| 9 | what you do when you help someone to be successful | s _ _ _ _ _ _ |
| 10 | very bright | v _ _ _ _ _ _ |

Marks (out of 10): _____

**2** Read the conversation and tick (✓) the correct answer. The first one is done for you.

**0** *Lizzie:* This is a great space for a concert. You must be really ... of yourself for finding it.
  **A** proud ✓  **B** obsessed ☐  **C** wondering ☐

**11** *Philip:* I know. I was almost going to ... up and then I saw this place online.
  **A** go ☐  **B** get ☐  **C** give ☐

**12** *Lizzie:* I think the stage has a very ... shape. I've never seen one like it before.
  **A** distinctive ☐  **B** triangular ☐  **C** dramatic ☐

**13** *Philip:* Yes, none of its edges are straight, they're all ...
  **A** smooth. ☐  **B** curved. ☐  **C** sharp. ☐

**14** *Lizzie:* I like the colours too. They're all so bright and ... .
  **A** vibrant. ☐  **B** silky. ☐  **C** pale. ☐

**15** *Philip:* Yes, I know some people ... about how bright it is, but I really like it.
  **A** registered ☐  **B** complained ☐  **C** brought up ☐

**16** *Lizzie:* I like the ... between the light and dark areas.
  **A** trouble ☐  **B** symbolism ☐  **C** contrast ☐

**17** *Philip:* Me too. What type of music is the band playing tonight anyway? I hope it's something ... and lively.
  **A** relaxed ☐  **B** loud ☐  **C** gentle ☐

**18** *Lizzie:* The keyboard player told me it's a combination of ... and electronic music.
  **A** classical ☐  **B** classic ☐  **C** class ☐

**19** *Philip:* Sounds interesting! I'm ... with that. Can't really imagine what it sounds like.
  **A** encouraged ☐  **B** obsessed ☐  **C** unfamiliar ☐

**20** *Lizzie:* Well, I was ... that myself because I've never heard it either. I'm sure it'll be a good night though.
  **A** analysing ☐  **B** wondering ☐  **C** paying attention to ☐

Marks (out of 10): _____

# GRAMMAR

**3** Match the conversation halves. The first one is done for you.

| | |
|---|---|
| Amol: | How many tins of paint did you buy? |
| Stefanie: | **0** _J_ |
| Amol: | That's far too many. We only need about ten! |
| Stefanie: | **21** _E_ |
| Amol: | But twenty's definitely too many! |
| Stefanie: | **22** _C_ |
| Amol: | He's the reason why we have too much paint then. |
| Stefanie: | **23** _G_ |
| Amol: | No, but I haven't got much more to do. |
| Stefanie: | **24** _I_ |
| Amol: | Do you mean that part above the window? |
| Stefanie: | **25** _A_ |
| Amol: | I don't know. It's strange. |
| Stefanie: | **26** _K_ |
| Amol: | I don't think I did. Peter said it looked fine. |
| Stefanie: | **27** _H_ |
| Amol: | Don't worry. I can paint the wall again. |
| Stefanie: | **28** _D_ |
| Amol: | But I can do it. Just give me one more chance. |
| Stefanie: | **29** _B_ |
| Amol: | Of course! I just left the darker part in the shape of a heart as a sign of how much I love you. |
| Stefanie: | **30** _F_ |
| Amol: | With pleasure. I told you it was too much paint! |

**A** Let's have a look ... Do you see the area in the shape of heart up there? What's that?
**B** Can you paint so that the whole wall is the same shade of blue?
**C** The man in the shop said it was better to have too much paint than too little.
**D** No. Don't make any more changes. Let's find a proper painter instead.
**E** I thought that would be too few.
**F** Hmm, really? Take these tins of paint and put them in the car so we can take them back to the shop.
**G** He was just doing his job and, speaking of jobs, have you finished painting Joe's room?
**H** Well, he doesn't live here!
**I** It looks like you used a lot more paint at the top of the wall than at the bottom.
**J** Twenty.
**K** Yes, it looks darker than the rest of the wall. How did that happen?

Marks (out of 10): _____

**4** Complete the conversation with the words in the box. The first one is done for you.

| ~~on~~ | said | told | few | many | know | knew | at | lot of | any | a |

*Richard:* Who was the woman **(0)** ___on___ the right of your parents at our graduation ceremony?
*Finn:* Oh, that's my old English teacher, Mrs Paxton.
*Richard:* Wow! That's great. I don't stay in touch with **(31)** _____ of my old teachers.
*Finn:* I still talk to a **(32)** _____ of them, but Mrs Paxton is special to me.
*Richard:* How come?
*Finn:* Well, I found English very difficult at school and she spent a **(33)** _____ time supporting me.
*Richard:* What did she do exactly?
*Finn:* She **(34)** _____ me to believe in myself and not to listen to anyone that **(35)** _____ I couldn't do it.
*Richard:* That's great! I don't think I ever had **(36)** _____ teacher like that.
*Finn:* I don't think there are **(37)** _____ of them around!
*Richard:* My mum told me she had a teacher who inspired her at school. One year she was **(38)** _____ the bottom of the class and the next year she got the second-best exam results.
*Finn:* That's amazing! What did the teacher do to help her improve that much?
*Richard:* I don't know. My mum said she **(39)** _____ how to make people feel confident about themselves.
*Finn:* I suppose that's the same thing that Mrs Paxton did for me. She told me to always **(40)** _____ what you want and then you can go and get it.

Marks (out of 10): _____

## READING

**5** Read the article. Circle T for true, F for false or NG for not given. The first one is done for you.

Many people are unfamiliar with so-called alternative concert venues, but they can be great places to listen to live music. Unusual examples of architecture, like old steel works, churches and Roman amphitheatres, are now venues for concerts by musicians playing everything from hip hop to classical music. The organizers who set up these concerts think it's the acoustics that count. If a venue has the right acoustics, i.e. the sound in the room is good, they'll use it.

The Cumberland Caverns in McMinnville, Tennessee in the USA, are some of the longest caves in the world. The curved and rough walls of the cave look beautiful with lights on them during a concert. People in this part of the world are obsessed with bluegrass music and that's why these bands usually play here. Then, there's the beautiful Forest Stage near to Berlin in Germany. The white roof over the stage contrasts with the dark green colour of the trees all around it. Concert halls can also be something special too. Look at the Aragon Ballroom in Chicago in the USA, for example. It has a dramatic painting of the night sky on its ceiling, so when the fans look up above them, they see stars.

| | |  |  |  |
|---|---|---|---|---|
| 0 | Most people know that unusual places for concerts exist. | T | (F) | NG |
| 41 | Unusual concert venues are different to the buildings you usually see around you. | T | F | NG |
| 42 | Musicians only play hip hop and classical music at unusual concert venues. | T | F | NG |
| 43 | The concert organizers try to encourage as many people as possible to come to their concerts. | T | F | NG |
| 44 | The organizers of concerts in alternative venues think the music itself is more important than the acoustics of the venue. | T | F | NG |

| | | | |
|---|---|---|---|
| 45 The Cumberland Caverns in McMinnville, Tennessee are 51 km long. | T | F | NG |
| 46 The walls of the Cumberland Caverns are curved and smooth. | T | F | NG |
| 47 People in Tennessee absolutely love bluegrass music. | T | F | NG |
| 48 The colour of the roof over the stage at the Forest stage is the same as the colour of the trees around it. | T | F | NG |
| 49 Concert halls can't be as special as alternative concert venues. | T | F | NG |
| 50 Fans can look down and see stars on the floor at the Aragon Ballroom in Chicago. | T | F | NG |

Marks (out of 10): _____

## LISTENING

**6** 🎧 **T.2** Listen and tick (✓) the correct answer. The first one is done for you.

**0** Lukas and Mandy are meeting each other …
 **A** for the first time. ✓  **B** for the second time. ☐  **C** for the first time today. ☐

**51** Mandy is a …
 **A** music therapist. ☐  **B** music teacher. ☐  **C** musician. ☐

**52** Lukas thinks it isn't a problem that Mandy doesn't have …
 **A** any experience of music therapy. ☐  **B** a lot of experience as a musician. ☐
 **C** much experience of teaching music. ☐

**53** If Mandy gets the job, she'll help patients to …
 **A** feel bright and lively. ☐  **B** develop their talent for music. ☐  **C** feel comfortable and relaxed. ☐

**54** Mandy says being a music therapist is a job she …
 **A** wouldn't like to do. ☐  **B** would love to do. ☐  **C** wouldn't be able to do. ☐

**55** Mandy plays the …
 **A** violin. ☐  **B** viola. ☐  **C** cello. ☐

**56** Which type of music **hasn't** Mandy played?
 **A** classical ☐  **B** country ☐  **C** electronic ☐

**57** Mandy asks Lukas what type of … they work with.
 **A** music ☐  **B** patients ☐  **C** hospitals ☐

**58** Some of the people the music therapists work with have problems with …
 **A** co-operation. ☐  **B** communication. ☐  **C** complaining. ☐

**59** Lukas says music therapists want to inspire their patients to …
 **A** make big changes. ☐  **B** become musicians. ☐  **C** forget about their problems. ☐

**60** Is Mandy still interested in the job?
 **A** No, she isn't. ☐  **B** She isn't sure. ☐  **C** Yes, she is. ☐

Marks (out of 10): _____

## SPEAKING

**7** Student A, ask Student B some questions to find out about the rooms in Buckingham Palace. Student B, read the information and answer Student A's questions. Then swap roles

**Student A**
What / colour / staircases?
Why / throne room / so special?
What / the Queen's gallery / like?
What / Queen's bedroom / like?
What / design / the ballroom carpet / have?
Why / music room / curved ceiling?

**Student B**
**Staircases:** Dramatic contrast between white walls and red floors.

**The throne room:** Red and gold design symbolizes power and wealth of the royal family

**The Queen's gallery:** Long room with smooth orange walls

**The Queen's bedroom:** A lot of subtle small golden flowers on the walls and bed

**The ballroom:** Red carpet has distinctive design with black circles inside black squares

**The music room:** Curved ceiling improves the acoustics when people play music.

Marks (out of 10): _____

## WRITING

**8** A website is having a competition. To enter the competition, you have to write a short article about a musician or band that has had a big effect on you. Write an article so you can enter the competition. Include the following:

- what type of music the musician or band plays and why you like it
- what effect this musician or band has had on you and why
- the name of a song or album by this musician or band that other people should listen to.

Write 35–50 words.

Marks (out of 10): _____

# TEST 3 | Units 7–9

Name: _____
Total score: _____

## VOCABULARY

**1** Read the definitions and complete the words. The first one is done for you.

| | | |
|---|---|---|
| 0 | A green space where children play and people walk their dogs | p <u>a r k</u> |
| 1 | describing animals that can move around freely on a farm | f _ _ _ - r _ _ _ _ |
| 2 | give money to charity | d _ _ _ _ _ |
| 3 | An area in a city where there are factories and warehouses. | i _ _ _ _ _ _ _ _ _  e _ _ _ _ _ |
| 4 | describing a city with a lot of people where a lot is happening. | b _ _ _ _ _ _ _ |
| 5 | objects produced for sale | g _ _ _ _ |
| 6 | A part of a city where people live. | r _ _ _ _ _ _ _ _ _ area |
| 7 | A place where people sell second-hand objects outdoors. | f _ _ _   m _ _ _ _ _ |
| 8 | An earthquake is an example of this. | n _ _ _ _ _ _   d _ _ _ _ _ _ _ |
| 9 | The central part of the city which is also the oldest part of it. | h _ _ _ _ _ _ _   c _ _ _ _ _ |
| 10 | someone who is not paid for what they do | v _ _ _ _ _ _ _ _ |

Marks (out of 10): _____

**2** Complete the email with the words in the box. The first one has been done for you.

| | | | | | |
|---|---|---|---|---|---|
| ~~organic~~ | 24/7 | bustling | care about | dozens of | hang |
| impact | peaceful | range | required | training programme | |

TO: *Click here to add recipients*
CC:
SUBJECT:

Dear Mum and Dad,

I found a job! I'm working on an **(0)** _organic_ fruit farm in Currumbin Valley at the moment. The farm is 30 miles from the city. It's very calm and **(11)** _____ here. I like being in the countryside and not in the **(12)** _____ city. The working conditions are good. We aren't **(13)** _____ to start work until 7am (that's late for a farm) and then we work until 2pm with a lunch break in between. Jen and Carl, who own the farm, are great. They really **(14)** _____ the work they're doing and they want to have a positive **(15)** _____ on the land they own. They're really well-organized too – when I first arrived, I did a **(16)** _____ that they prepared so I would know exactly what to do.

When I'm not working, I'll go into the city where there are **(17)** _____ parks and lakes where you can **(18)** _____ out with friends and relax. There is also a supermarket that is open **(19)** _____ where they have a **(20)** _____ of products. It should be easy for me to find everything I need.

I'll write to you again soon.

Lots of love,

Martha

Marks (out of 10): _____

## GRAMMAR

**3** Read the conversations and tick (✓) the correct answer. The first one is done for you.

**0** Can you pick me up from the airport?
    **A** Yes, if you called me when you land. ☐
    **B** Yes, if you call me when you land. ✓
    **C** Yes, if you're calling me when you land. ☐

**21** Can you babysit for me this evening?
    **A** I hope so. ☐    **B** I will if you pay me! ☐    **C** If you'd like to. ☐

**22** Do you like eating out?
    **A** No, I like eating in restaurants. ☐    **B** Yes, I like taking in the view. ☐    **C** No, I prefer to cook. ☐

**23** I think Ben and Judith will get married next year.
    **A** Yes, I think they will too. ☐    **B** Yes, they do. ☐    **C** Yes, they won't. ☐

**24** Joe needs a lift home today because his car's broken down.
    **A** He'll give me a lift. ☐    **B** I'll give him a lift. ☐    **C** I'll give a lift him. ☐

**25** Did you check out any interesting bars in Majorca?
    **A** I found a couple of good ones. ☐    **B** I chilled out. ☐    **C** No, we didn't eat out. ☐

**26** Don't go out like that! What will you do if it rains?
    **A** It didn't rain! ☐    **B** It isn't raining! ☐    **C** It won't rain! ☐

**27** What do you look for in a hotel?
    **A** It must have free wifi! ☐    **B** I'm looking forward to it. ☐    **C** It always looks good. ☐

**28** I'll pick you up from the airport.
    **A** If you tell me when you'll arrive. ☐    **B** It's OK. We can take the train. ☐
    **C** Will you pick us up? ☐

**29** I think we'll all have driverless cars in ten years' time.
    **A** Yes, they will. ☐    **B** No, it won't. ☐    **C** I don't think we will. ☐

**30** We won't have any time to stop there on the way home.
    **A** I'm sure we will. ☐    **B** If we drive very fast. ☐    **C** I think so. ☐

**4** Read the sentences and tick (✓) the correct answer. The first one is done for you.

**0** Do you think … raise more than £1,000?
    **A** we ☐    **B** we're ☐    **C** we'll ✓

**31** If anyone … £50 or more, we'll give them a free t-shirt.
    **A** will donate ☐    **B** donates ☐    **C** won't donate ☐

**32** Jasper says he'll sponsor me, if I … as a fluffy rabbit.
    **A** dress up ☐    **B** dressed up ☐    **C** will dress up ☐

**33** Our charity provides a safe space where young people can just … out together.
    **A** hang ☐    **B** get ☐    **C** head ☐

**34** … the fundraising event next week be the first one you've held?
    **A** If ☐    **B** Do ☐    **C** Will ☐

**35** If I … a bad day, I just think about how much money the charity raises every day.
    **A** 'll have ☐    **B** have ☐    **C** had ☐

**36** We're holding an event in that hall tomorrow, so they need to …
    **A** up it clean. ☐    **B** clean up it. ☐    **C** clean it up. ☐

**37** He wants to make a difference to people in the town where …
    **A** he grew up. ☐    **B** he up grew. ☐    **C** grew he up. ☐

**38** James will help you prepare the food for the event … you need more help.
    **A** unless ☐    **B** if ☐    **C** will ☐

**39** I think we … enough sponsorship forms for everyone who's coming. We'll have to get some more.
   **A** have ☐   **B** 'll have ☐   **C** won't have ☐

**40** Jack and Rose are really happy with the holiday they won. They said they were looking forward to … the museums and restaurants in Paris.
   **A** hanging out ☐   **B** taking in ☐   **C** heading off ☐

Marks (out of 10): _____

## READING

**5** Read the article. Are the sentences true (T) or false (F)? The first one is done for you.

In November 2016, Kevin Newton's Bus Shelter opened its doors for the first time on the Isle of Wight in the UK. It's actually an old double-decker bus that Kevin changed to be a place where people can live, sleep and cook. The bus is located in the peaceful suburbs of the island's main town and is open 24/7. Anyone who doesn't have anywhere to sleep can head to the bus and expect a warm welcome.

Kevin's goal was to make it unnecessary for people on the Isle of Wight to sleep outside. Anyone without a place to sleep can live in the shelter for as long as they want if they're willing to follow the Bus Shelter's rules. Residents are required to get help from local agencies who help homeless people find housing and jobs. They also have to do paid or voluntary work to keep the bus running. So far, the Bus Shelter project really seems to be having a positive impact on the Isle of Wight. Kevin hopes that people in other parts of the UK will start using old buses to house the homeless soon, too.

**Example:**

**0** Kevin Newton is the first person the Bus Shelter helped. _____F_____

**41** The Bus Shelter on the Isle of Wight closed in November 2016. _____

**42** The Bus Shelter is a type of restaurant. _____

**43** Kevin made changes to the bus so homeless people could stay there. _____

**44** The people staying at the Bus Shelter can cook there. _____

**45** The Bus Shelter is in the centre of the Isle of Wight's main town. _____

**46** The Bus Shelter is always open. _____

**47** The people who stay on the bus can work there if they want to. _____

**48** Kevin wants there to be no need for people on the Isle of Wight to be homeless. _____

**49** The Bus Shelter is having a positive effect on the lives of people on the Isle of Wight. _____

**50** People in other parts of the UK are now using old buses as homes for the homeless. _____

Marks (out of 10): _____

## LISTENING

**6** 🎧 T.3 Listen and tick (✓) the correct answer. The first one is done for you.

**0** Frank thinks that Greenwood …
   **A** will definitely win the election. ☐   **B** might win the election. ☐   **C** won't win the election. ✓

**51** Jemma thinks Greenwood is interested in helping …
   **A** the people who work for her. ☐   **B** normal working people. ☐   **C** the people who vote for her. ☐

**52** Jemma is surprised that Greenwood …
   **A** is doing well. ☐   **B** is the favourite at the moment. ☐   **C** isn't doing well. ☐

**53** Satari has more … than Greenwood does.
   **A** family members ☐   **B** money ☐   **C** TV interviews ☐

**54** Satari's advertisements are …
  A hardly ever on television. ☐
  B on television a lot. ☐
  C always on television. ☐

**55** When Jill went to one of Greenwood's events, she noticed there weren't …
  A any people there. ☐
  B many people there. ☐
  C any drinks there. ☐

**56** How does Frank feel about the possibility of Satari winning the election?
  A He's very happy about it. ☐
  B He's happy about it. ☐
  C He isn't happy about it. ☐

**57** Jemma is sure journalists will find something out about Satari that …
  A will help him to win. ☐
  B women will like. ☐
  C will make him look bad. ☐

**58** Frank doesn't understand why …
  A Satari has so much money. ☐
  B people like Satari so much. ☐
  C Satari hasn't done anything illegal. ☐

**59** Jemma thinks Satari needs more support from …
  A working families. ☐
  B Greenwood's supporters. ☐
  C women. ☐

**60** When will the election take place?
  A in two months' time ☐
  B in two weeks' time ☐
  C in two days' time ☐

Marks (out of 10): _____

## SPEAKING

**7** Student A, read some predictions about the future of fair-trade products for the next five years. Student B, ask Student A some questions to find out about them. Then swap roles.

**Student A**

**Fair-trade sales:** Biggest increase in North America

**Most popular products:** Tea, vanilla and sugar

**Companies making fair-trade products:** Increase by about 20 per cent.

**Fair-trade companies' top priority:** Reducing waste

**Main waste-reduction strategy:** Using things we usually throw away as raw materials

**Price of fair-trade products:** Decrease by 10 per cent

**Student B**

Where / biggest increase / fair-trade sales?

What / most popular products?

How much / companies making fair-trade products / increase?

What / fair-trade companies' top priority?

How / companies / reduce waste?

Price of fair-trade products / decrease?

Marks (out of 10): _____

## WRITING

**8** A friend is thinking about visiting the town or city where you live. Write an email to your friend, telling him/her about your town or city and why he/she should visit it.
Say:

- how you would describe the town or city
- what parts of the town or city there are
- what you can do there.

Write 35–50 words.

Marks (out of 10): _____

# TEST 4 | Units 10–12

Name: _____

Total score: _____

## VOCABULARY

**1** Read the conversation and tick (✓) the correct answer. The first one is done for you.

*Lauren:* Hi, Jake. How was your weekend?

*Jake:* Oh, good thanks, I **(0)** … camping with my brother and a couple of friends.

*Lauren:* Great! Did you camp **(1)** … Javeson Forest?

*Jake:* Yes, we did. We went on a **(2)** … there on the Saturday and saw that area where the archaeologists **(3)** … those old coins.

*Lauren:* Oh, yes. I know the place you mean. There are **(4)** … of an old house are there too, I think.

*Jake:* Yes, you're right. We walked around **(5)** … the whole forest and saw some really **(6)** … views through the trees. Then we **(7)** … of walking so we sat down in that area with the ancient stuff and chilled out.

*Lauren:* How did you make your camp?

*Jake:* Well, we used a tent and made a campfire. I used the same tent last summer and thought I could remember how to put it up but, apparently, my **(8)** … isn't very good! My brother helped in the end, but it still required a lot of **(9)** … . We found the instructions to build the tent, but they were very difficult to follow! Oh, did I tell you what happened later that night?

*Lauren:* No. Tell me! What happened?

*Jake:* It's quite a funny story.

*Lauren:* What happened? Nothing too serious, I hope.

*Jake:* No, no. We were asleep in our tents and then this 'animal' came along and started to **(10)** … our tent open.

*Lauren:* Oh, no! That sounds terrible. Was anybody hurt?

*Jake:* No. The funny thing was that the 'animal' was just a big dog out for a walk in the evening. The owner was really sorry for letting him go into our camp. He said there usually isn't anybody camping in the forest at night!

| 0 | A | went on ☐ | B | went for ☐ | C | went ✓ |
|---|---|---|---|---|---|---|
| 1 | A | in ☐ | B | on ☐ | C | under ☐ |
| 2 | A | walking ☐ | B | walked ☐ | C | walk ☐ |
| 3 | A | inspected ☐ | B | dug ☐ | C | discovered ☐ |
| 4 | A | tombs ☐ | B | ruins ☐ | C | fossils ☐ |
| 5 | A | over and over again ☐ | B | partially ☐ | C | pretty much ☐ |
| 6 | A | breathtaking ☐ | B | flat ☐ | C | wild ☐ |
| 7 | A | took for tired ☐ | B | got tired ☐ | C | went tired ☐ |
| 8 | A | balance ☐ | B | memory ☐ | C | sensation ☐ |
| 9 | A | dreams ☐ | B | emotions ☐ | C | concentration ☐ |
| 10 | A | scratch ☐ | B | attract ☐ | C | tear ☐ |

Marks (out of 10): _____

**2** Match the conversation halves. The first one is done for you.

Annette: Apparently, a significant collection of Roman writing tablets was found in London in 2016.
Mark: **0** ___B___
Annette: It says here these artefacts are nearly 2,000 years old.
Mark: **11** _____
Annette: They're the oldest examples of writing ever found in London.
Mark: **12** _____
Annette: Archaeologists were called in to excavate the site where a new bank was being built.
Mark: **13** _____
Annette: It seems that every time people want to build something, they find a skeleton or some pottery!
Mark: **14** _____
Annette: Definitely. It says here the writing tells us a lot about life in London in its first few years as a city.
Mark: **15** _____
Annette: True. I'm sure we're just scratching the surface of their lives here.
Mark: **16** _____
Annette: Luckily for us, they're at the Museum of London now.
Mark: **17** _____
Annette: Yes, some of them have been translated.
Mark: **18** _____
Annette: Yeah, that would pretty much be my dream job.
Mark: **19** _____
Annette: Yes, a series of lectures will be given by the archaeologists next month ...
Mark: **20** _____
Annette: Yes, I do. They obviously know a lot about archaeology.

**A** Translating ancient writing must be a really interesting job.
**B** Oh, OK. Why is it so important?
**C** I see. That's how a lot of these things are discovered.
**D** Great! I love listening to archaeologists talk about the discoveries they've made, don't you?
**E** Those people's words are all that's left of them now.
**F** Yes, but, on the other hand, it's a good thing they can save what's underneath.
**G** How were they discovered?
**H** Can the tablets be read and understood?
**I** But, in the meantime, do you know if we can talk to the people who found them?
**J** Probably, yeah. So what's happened to the tablets?
**K** Wow! That's extremely old!

Marks (out of 10): _____

# GRAMMAR

**3** Read the conversations and tick (✓) the correct answer. The first one is done for you.

**0** How often do you brush your teeth?
- **A** twice a day ✓
- **B** easily ☐
- **C** after a while ☐

**21** Have you ever been to Egypt?
- **A** Yes, I did. ☐
- **B** No, I haven't. ☐
- **C** Yes, I went. ☐

**22** How did they make this bone necklace?
- **A** Tools were used to cut the bone. ☐
- **B** Bones cut the tools. ☐
- **C** Tools were cut with the bone. ☐

**23** Did Jason get to school in time for the exam?
- **A** Unfortunately, he got there in time. ☐
- **B** Luckily, he got there two minutes before it started. ☐
- **C** He walked to school as quickly as he could. ☐

**24** Who was this picture painted by?
- **A** Picasso was painted it. ☐
- **B** By painting Picasso. ☐
- **C** Picasso painted it. ☐

**25** Have you ever lived abroad?
- **A** I spent six months in France three years ago. ☐
- **B** Yes, I've lived. ☐
- **C** Unfortunately, I didn't live abroad. ☐

**26** How long did you study to become a doctor?
- **A** slowly and carefully ☐
- **B** for a long time ☐
- **C** for a while ☐

**27** When was The Great Wall of China built?
- **A** It's built for 2,000 years. ☐
- **B** It finished in the sixteenth century. ☐
- **C** It was finished in the sixteenth century. ☐

**28** Have you ever been diving?
- **A** Yes, I've been. ☐
- **B** I went in Mexico last year. ☐
- **C** No, I didn't go diving. ☐

**29** Is this archaeological site protected?
- **A** Yes, it is. ☐
- **B** Yes, it was. ☐
- **C** Yes, they are. ☐

**30** When are you making dinner?
- **A** in a couple of hours ☐
- **B** until I go to bed ☐
- **C** all day ☐

Marks (out of 10): _____

**4** Complete the conversation with the words in the box. The first one is done for you.

| ~~in~~ | I've | every | I | was | in |
| constantly | hard | fortunately | definitely | | hopefully |

*Angela:* So what did you do **(0)** ___in___ the summer holidays?

*Roberto:* Well, **(31)** _____, I didn't have to work! My dad **(32)** _____ invited to teach at a summer school in California, so we all went over there and stayed with him.

*Angela:* Wow! That sounds amazing! **(33)** _____ always wanted to go there.

*Roberto:* Oh, **(34)** _____, you'll be able to go when you're older. Anyway, when we were in California in the summer, we went to a different theme park **(35)** _____ week.

*Angela:* So you went to eight theme parks **(36)** _____ eight weeks?

*Roberto:* Yes, we were **(37)** _____ going online to find out which theme park we should go to next!

*Angela:* **(38)** _____ went to Thorpe Park a few years ago. That was really fun!

*Roberto:* Yes, but Thorpe Park is **(39)** _____ not the same as the parks in California. You can't compare them.

*Angela:* I know, Roberto, but some people have to work! I was working really **(40)** _____ to save up to buy a car.

*Roberto:* Well, I can just ask my dad to buy me a car, so I don't have to worry about that!

Marks (out of 10): _____

## READING

**5** Read the blog post and complete the notes. Write one or two words in each space. The first one is done for you.

> Have you ever dreamed of being an archaeologist? If your answer is yes, why not take up this once-in-a-lifetime opportunity to work on an archaeological dig in the breathtaking hills of Peru. We usually take it for granted that people will take action to protect our heritage, but this will only happen if people like you volunteer.
>
> You'll work on amazing Incan ruins that were discovered a few years ago. Your main task will be to photograph, draw and register the structures and artefacts we've found there, three days a week. You'll also help us to clear plants and other objects from the site, and keep the site clean so we can work more efficiently. On the other two days, you'll work with the artefacts at a local museum.
>
> We'll organize a place for you to stay with a host family, who will provide you with breakfast and dinner every day. We require you to spend at least two weeks with us, but we're flexible about start dates.

**Work experience opportunity**

**Location: (0)** _Peru_

**Type of work experience:** Working as a volunteer **(41)** _____

**Type of work:** Assisting with an archaeological **(42)** _____ of Incan **(43)** _____

**Tasks:** Photographing, drawing and **(44)** _____ structures and **(45)** _____

**Working times: (46)** _____ days a week. You'll work at the dig site and at a local **(47)** _____ .

**Accommodation: (48)** _____ family

**Length:** At least **(49)** _____

**Dates: (50)** _____ start dates

Marks (out of 10): _____

## LISTENING

**6** 🎧 **T.4** Listen and tick (✓) the correct answer. The first one is done for you.

**0** Why can't Rachel remember what she dreams about?
   **A** She doesn't sleep very much. ☐    **B** She sleeps deeply. ✓    **C** She always forgets her dreams. ☐

**51** Why does Jonathan need to interpret a dream?
   **A** He's interested in dreams. ☐    **B** He's writing a book about dreams. ☐
   **C** It's his psychology homework. ☐

**52** What did Rachel dream about a few months ago?
   **A** falling from a mountain ☐    **B** a car accident ☐    **C** a plane crash ☐

**53** Jonathan thinks Rachel had this dream because she …
   **A** made a mistake. ☐    **B** watches too much television. ☐    **C** had a serious problem. ☐

**54** Rachel was the one who made …
   **A** something bad happen in her dream. ☐    **B** the problems before the dream happen. ☐
   **C** it difficult for her to remember the dream. ☐

**55** Rachel can't remember anything about …
  **A** how she felt on the day after she had this dream. ☐   **B** the day she had this dream. ☐
  **C** the car she was driving in this dream. ☐

**56** Rachel says her dream about walking in the Alps was …
  **A** really gorgeous. ☐   **B** really nice. ☐   **C** really frightening. ☐

**57** What did Rachel do in this dream?
  **A** balance on a piece of rock ☐   **B** fall from the top of a mountain ☐   **C** climb over rocks ☐

**58** Jonathan thinks this dream means that Rachel …
  **A** has been successful when she experienced difficulties. ☐   **B** likes going to the Alps. ☐
  **C** can't keep her balance in life and could fall down. ☐

**59** Rachel doesn't believe you can …
  **A** overcome obstacles in your life. ☐   **B** write about dreams in a psychology course. ☐
  **C** learn things about people from their dreams. ☐

**60** Jonathan thinks he can convince Rachel to …
  **A** try to remember her dreams. ☐   **B** believe in dream interpretation. ☐
  **C** do his psychology homework for him. ☐

Marks (out of 10): _____

# SPEAKING

**7** Student A, ask Student B some questions to find out about the Saxon Switzerland National Park in Germany. Student B, read the information and answer Student A's questions. Then swap roles.

**Student A**
Where / located?
When / opened?
How / big?
What / known for?
What / people / like / do there?
How many / castles?

**Student B**
**Location:** 19 miles, or 30 kilometres, south-east of Dresden in the east of Germany
**A national park since:** 1990
**Size:** 36 square miles or 93 square kilometres
**Distinctive feature:** Rough and wild stone peaks
**Popular activities:** Walking, free climbing, visiting castles and castle ruins
**Castles in the park:** Nine

Marks (out of 10): _____

# WRITING

**8** A psychologist wants to analyse people's earliest memories. Think about what your earliest memory is and write a text about it for the psychologist's study.
Say:

- what your earliest memory is
- why you think you can remember this and why it's important to you
- what you think people's earliest memories tell you about them.

Write 35–50 words.

Marks (out of 10): _____

# Answer key

To score each test as a percentage, take the total mark (e.g. 60), divide by 80 (e.g. 0.75) and multiply by 100 = 75%.

## Test 1 (Units 1–3)

### VOCABULARY

**1**
1 A  2 A  3 B  4 C  5 A  6 C  7 B  8 B  9 A  10 C

**2**
11 A  12 C  13 A  14 B  15 B  16 C  17 A  18 B  19 C  20 C

### GRAMMAR

**3**
21 B  22 B  23 B  24 B  25 A  26 C  27 C  28 A  29 B  30 B

**4**
31 that  32 'm having  33 'm driving  34 who  35 where  36 aren't  37 'm  38 'm doing  39 'm going to do  40 'm going to ask

### READING

**5**
41 4th May  42 5 pm  43 White Rose  44 Exeter  45 About  46 Dinner  47 three/3  48 band  49 live  50 Katrina

### LISTENING

**6**
51 B  52 A  53 C  54 C  55 A  56 B  57 C  58 C  59 B  60 C

### Transcript T.1

**Chia:** What are the people doing in that photo?
**Brendan:** They're taking a selfie with a quokka in Australia.
**Chia:** With a what?
**Brendan:** A quokka. Quokkas are small mammals that mainly live on Rottnest Island in Australia and they're really cute.
**Chia:** That's true. That smile on the quokka – it's practically human!
**Brendan:** I know. They're not afraid of humans, so they hop over to see what they're doing.
**Chia:** That's marvellous. My cousin went to Australia last year, but she didn't go to that island. She saw a lot of kangaroos though.
**Brendan:** Quokkas are similar to kangaroos, I think. They're the same type of mammal and they can both jump. Quokkas can be dangerous though; their claws are quite sharp and they could really hurt you with them.
**Chia:** Yeah, I can imagine. What do they eat?
**Brendan:** They're plant-eaters, but nowadays the tourists give them all kinds of things to eat: bread, French fries – you name it.
**Chia:** Oh, that can't be very good for them.
**Brendan:** No, it isn't. It can really harm them.
**Chia:** That's a shame.
**Brendan:** I know, but they still look happy, so I suppose it's not too bad.
**Chia:** I'm going to travel to Australia one day. It'd be great to go next summer when I finish my course.
**Brendan:** Yeah. Just remember though that when it's summer here, it's winter there.
**Chia:** Oh, yes. I forgot about that.

### SPEAKING

**7**
Put students in pairs to ask and answer questions about a novel. Give them one minute to read the information and prepare their questions and answers. Then have them ask and answer the questions. As they are speaking, monitor their English and award marks up to ten according to the criteria in the table below. Give two marks if the student meets each criterion well, one mark if their performance is satisfactory, and no marks if they do not meet the criterion at all.

| Did the student ...? | Marks |
| --- | --- |
| complete the task, i.e. ask or answer all of the questions? | |
| say the questions and answers intelligibly? | |
| use correct grammar and vocabulary most of the time? | |
| know when to listen to their partner and when to speak? | |
| use language presented in the units for talking about books? | |
| Total marks out of 10 | |

## WRITING

**8**

Use the following table to award ten marks. Give two marks if the student's writing meets each criterion well, one mark if their writing is satisfactory, and no marks if they do not meet the criterion at all.

| Did the text include ...? | Marks |
|---|---|
| two reasons why some people think spending time with family isn't important? | |
| two reasons why spending time with family is important? | |
| encouragement to their friend to get in touch with his/her family? | |
| accurate use of language for presenting arguments? | |
| accurate use of vocabulary for family and relationships? | |
| Total marks out of 10 | |

# Test 2 (Units 4–6)

## VOCABULARY

**1**

1 straight  2 upbeat  3 celebrate  4 rough
5 depressed  6 distinctive  7 gentle  8 round  9 support
10 vibrant

**2**

11 C  12 A  13 B  14 A  15 B  16 C  17 B  18 A
19 C  20 B

## GRAMMAR

**3**

21 E  22 C  23 G  24 A  25 K  26 I  27 H  28 D
29 B  30 F

**4**

31 any  32 few  33 lot of  34 told  35 said  36 a
37 many  38 at  39 knew  40 know

## READING

**5**

41 T  42 F  43 NG  44 F  45 NG  46 F  47 T
48 F  49 F  50 F

## LISTENING

**6**

51 C  52 A  53 C  54 B  55 A  56 C  57 B
58 B  59 A  60 C

### Transcript T.2

**Lukas:** Hello, you must be Mandy. I'm Lukas. Please take a seat.
**Mandy:** Nice to meet you.
**Lukas:** Good to meet you too. So, you said in your email that this was the first music therapist job you've applied for – is that right?
**Mandy:** Yes. I just wanted to bring that up so you'd know that I have a lot of experience as a musician, but I'm new to music therapy.
**Lukas:** OK. Well, that's not necessarily a problem. What we're looking for is bright, lively people who can use their talent for music to help our patients feel comfortable, relaxed and just let go of their problems while they're with us.
**Mandy:** Yes. That's the kind of thing I'd love to do.
**Lukas:** Great! So it says here that you play the violin – is that right?
**Mandy:** Yes, I mainly play classical violin, but I was also in a band that played country music a few years ago.
**Lukas:** Wow! That sounds like fun! Now, do you have any questions for me about the role before we go on?
**Mandy:** Yes, I wanted to know what types of patients you actually work with?
**Lukas:** Good question. We have a few main types of patients and they're people who have problems with communication, people who have emotional difficulties and people who've experienced some kind of trauma in their lives, like the sudden death of a close family member.
**Mandy:** I see. So we need to support them.
**Lukas:** Erm, it's not really supporting them exactly, it's more about giving them space to come back to themselves, if that makes sense. We help them to relax and not think about their problems for a little while. That might then inspire them to make some positive changes to their lives – that's what we want to happen, anyway.
**Mandy:** OK, I'm definitely still interested. It would be marvellous to help people with my music, even if it's just a little bit.
**Lukas:** Great. Let's go on with the interview then.

## SPEAKING

**7**

Put students in pairs to ask and answer questions about the rooms in Buckingham Palace. Give them one minute to read the information and prepare their questions and answers. Then have them ask and answer the questions. As they are speaking, monitor their English and award marks up to ten according to the criteria in the table below. Give two marks if the student meets each criterion well, one mark if their performance is satisfactory, and no marks if they do not meet the criterion at all.

| Did the student ...? | Marks |
|---|---|
| complete the task, i.e. ask or answer all of the questions? | |
| say the questions and answers intelligibly? | |
| use correct grammar and vocabulary most of the time? | |
| know when to listen to their partner and when to speak? | |
| use language presented in the units for talking about design? | |
| Total marks out of 10 | |

## WRITING

**8**

Use the following table to award ten marks. Give two marks if the student's writing meets each criterion well, one mark if their writing is satisfactory, and no marks if they do not meet the criterion at all.

| Did the text include ...? | Marks |
|---|---|
| information about the music the musician or band plays and why the student likes it? | |
| an explanation of the effect the musician or band has had on the student? | |
| a recommendation of a song or album by this musician or band? | |
| accurate use of language for explanations and recommendations? | |
| accurate use of vocabulary for music and inspiration? | |
| Total marks out of 10 | |

# Test 3 (Units 7–9)

## VOCABULARY

**1**

1 free-range  2 donate  3 industrial estate  4 bustling
5 goods  6 residential  7 flea market  8 natural disaster
9 historic centre  10 volunteer

**2**

11 peaceful  12 bustling  13 required
14 care about  15 impact  16 training programme
17 dozens of  18 hang  19 24/7  20 range

## GRAMMAR

**3**

21 B  22 C  23 A  24 B  25 A  26 C  27 A  28 B
29 C  30 A

**4**

31 B  32 A  33 A  34 C  35 B  36 C  37 A
38 B  39 C  40 B

## READING

**5**

41 F  42 F  43 T  44 T  45 F  46 T  47 F
48 T  49 T  50 F

## LISTENING

**6**

51 B  52 C  53 B  54 C  55 B  56 C  57 C
58 B  59 C  60 A

**Transcript T.3**

**Jemma:** So, do you know who you're going to vote for yet, Frank?

**Frank:** I don't know. I wanted to vote for Greenwood, but I don't think she'll win.

**Jemma:** Yeah, Greenwood seems to really care about ordinary working families. I don't know why she isn't doing very well.

**Frank:** It's probably because she isn't raising as much money as the others. She doesn't have as much money to spend on events and advertisements, and all that kind of thing, as Satari does. His adverts are on TV 24/7.

**Jemma:** Yes, you're probably right. Jill said she went to one of Greenwood's fundraising events at a hotel near the riverfront and there was hardly anyone there. Just a few people hanging out at the bar.

**Frank:** That doesn't sound very good.

**Jemma:** She doesn't really seem to be making an impact on people around here.

**Frank:** Well, I'm not very happy about it, but it looks like Satari will win.

**Jemma:** I don't know. I'm convinced the newspapers will find something bad or illegal that he did in the past, and then he'll be finished.

**Frank:** That'd definitely be good news for Greenwood. We'll have to wait and see. I don't understand why some people like Satari so much.

**Jemma:** Me neither. It's strange. A lot of women don't like Satari though. If he can get more women to vote for him, he'll definitely win.

**Frank:** Yeah, I think the way women vote will be really important this time.

**Jemma:** I can't believe there's still another two months to go until the election.

**Frank:** I know what you mean. I've already had enough of hearing about it all the time.

***Jemma:*** Maybe you can try turning your television off and going offline this weekend. It might help you take a break from it all!

***Frank:*** That's a good idea. I think I'll try that.

## SPEAKING

**7**

Put students in pairs to ask and answer questions about the future of fair-trade products. Give them one minute to read the information and prepare their questions and answers. Then have them ask and answer the questions. As they are speaking, monitor their English and award marks up to ten according to the criteria in the table below. Give two marks if the student meets each criterion well, one mark if their performance is satisfactory, and no marks if they do not meet the criterion at all.

| Did the student …? | Marks |
|---|---|
| complete the task, i.e. ask or answer all of the questions? | |
| say the questions and answers intelligibly? | |
| use correct grammar and vocabulary most of the time? | |
| know when to listen to their partner and when to speak? | |
| use language presented in the units for talking about ethics? | |
| Total marks out of 10 | |

## WRITING

**8**

Use the following table to award ten marks. Give two marks if the student's writing meets each criterion well, one mark if their writing is satisfactory, and no marks if they do not meet the criterion at all.

| Did the text include …? | Marks |
|---|---|
| a description of the town or city the student has chosen? | |
| a description of the parts of the town or city? | |
| a description of what you can do in the town or city? | |
| accurate use of language for descriptions? | |
| accurate use of vocabulary for cities? | |
| Total marks out of 10 | |

# Test 4 (Units 10–12)

## VOCABULARY

**1**

1 A   2 C   3 C   4 B   5 C   6 A   7 B   8 B   9 C   10 C

**2**

11 K   12 G   13 C   14 F   15 E   16 J   17 H   18 A   19 I   20 D

## GRAMMAR

**3**

21 B   22 A   23 B   24 C   25 A   26 B   27 C   28 B   29 A   30 A

**4**

31 fortunately   32 was   33 I've   34 hopefully   35 every   36 in   37 constantly   38 I   39 definitely   40 hard

## READING

**5**

41 archaeologist   42 dig   43 ruins   44 registering   45 artefacts   46 5/Five   47 museum   48 Host   49 2/two weeks   50 Flexible

## LISTENING

**6**

51 C   52 B   53 A   54 A   55 B   56 B   57 C   58 A   59 C   60 B

### Transcript T.4

***Jonathan:*** Can you remember what you dreamed about last night?

***Rachel:*** I don't know. I sleep really deeply, so I can't remember my dreams.

***Jonathan:*** Oh, come on. Haven't you ever had an interesting dream that you can remember? I need one to interpret for my psychology homework.

***Rachel:*** Let me think. A few months ago, I remember dreaming that I was in a car accident.

***Jonathan:*** A car accident? OK, that's good.

***Rachel:*** Is it?

***Jonathan:*** Yes. Wait a minute. That means you made some kind of mistake and you were worrying about it. Were you driving or watching?

***Rachel:*** Driving, and the accident was my fault.

***Jonathan:*** I see. You definitely made a mistake. Hopefully, nothing serious.

| | |
|---|---|
| Rachel: | I don't think it was anything serious because I can't remember anything about what happened on the day I had that dream now! |
| Jonathan: | OK. Have you got any other dreams for me? |
| Rachel: | Erm, well, I remember having a really nice dream about going walking in a gorgeous, mountainous place. I think it was in the Alps. |
| Jonathan: | OK, and you didn't fall or anything like that? |
| Rachel: | No, I didn't. Fortunately, I kept my balance and climbed over the rocks like a professional climber. |
| Jonathan: | Right. I'll see if I can find what that means. |
| Rachel: | It means I like going to the Alps, that's all! |
| Jonathan: | I don't know. It sounds like you were overcoming an obstacle in your life. |
| Rachel: | There aren't any obstacles in my life. I'm really not sure I believe in all of this dream stuff, Jonathan. I don't understand why your psychology teacher is making you learn it. |
| Jonathan: | It's a science, Rachel. It helps us to get inside the human brain and understand what's going on in there. Just give me one more dream to interpret and I'll show you what I mean. |

## SPEAKING

**7**

Put students in pairs to ask and answer questions about the Saxon Switzerland National Park. Give them one minute to read the information and prepare their questions and answers. Then have them ask and answer the questions. As they are speaking, monitor their English and award marks up to ten according to the criteria in the table below. Give two marks if the student meets each criterion well, one mark if their performance is satisfactory, and no marks if they do not meet the criterion at all.

| Did the student …? | Marks |
|---|---|
| complete the task, i.e. ask or answer all of the questions? | |
| say the questions and answers intelligibly? | |
| use correct grammar and vocabulary most of the time? | |
| know when to listen to their partner and when to speak? | |
| use language presented in the units for talking about nature? | |
| Total marks out of 10 | |

## WRITING

**8**

Use the following table to award ten marks. Give two marks if the student's writing meets each criterion well, one mark if their writing is satisfactory, and no marks if they do not meet the criterion at all.

| Did the text include …? | Marks |
|---|---|
| a description of the student's earliest memory? | |
| an explanation of why the student can remember this and why it's important to him/her? | |
| a suggestion for what people's earliest memories tell us about them? | |
| accurate use of language for explanation and interpretation? | |
| accurate use of vocabulary for the brain? | |
| Total marks out of 10 | |

# Communicative activities

## 1.1 What am I?

| | |
|---|---|
| 1<br><br>ant | 2<br><br>bird |
| 3 | 4<br><br>crocodile |
| 5<br><br>fish | 6<br><br>flamingo |
| 7 | 8<br><br>insects |
| 9<br><br>mammals | 10 |
| 11 | 12<br><br>amphibians |
| 13<br><br>reptiles | 14 |
| 15 | 16<br><br>elephant |
| 17<br><br>tuna | 18 |

## 1.2 Spot the differences

### Student A

Look at your picture. Don't show it to your partner! Write as many sentences as possible describing what you see. You must use the present continuous. Then compare your sentences with your partner's. Are there any differences? What are they?

### Student B

Look at your picture. Don't show it to your partner! Write as many sentences as possible describing what you see. You must use the present continuous. Then compare your sentences with your partner's. Are there any differences? What are they?

## 2.1 Family trees

**Student A**

**The Silva family**

Ana Silva is 24 years old. She isn't married. Ana lives with her sister, Marta, her brother-in-law, Luis, her niece, Paula, and her nephew, Nadir. Ana and Marta also have a brother called Fabio. Fabio is married to Aisha and they have no children. Aisha loves being an aunt to Paula and Nadir! Ana, Marta and Fabio's parents are Jessica and André Silva. Jessica's parents, Mark and Michela, are still alive. Paula and Nadir love their great-grandparents!

------------------------------------------------------------

**Student B**

**The Miller family**

Luis Miller is 10 years old. His father is Nadir and his mother is Katia. Katia has two brothers, Peter and Harry, and one sister, Michela. Peter isn't married. Harry's wife is called Marta and they have a son called Mark. Michela's husband is David, and they don't have any children yet. Luis's grandfather is Erik and his grandmother is Jessica. They are his mother's parents. Luis and his cousin, Mark, often stay with their grandparents at weekends.

------------------------------------------------------------

**Student C**

**The Novak family**

Dana Novak is 68 years old. Her husband is Fabio and they have two children: a daughter called Michela and a son called Mark. Mark is married to Jessica. Michela and her sister-in-law, Jessica, always meet for coffee on Wednesdays. Mark and Jessica have a baby called Marta. Little Marta has two cousins: Ana and Nadir. These are Michela's children with her husband, Harry. Harry's mother is called Aisha and his father is Erik.

| Erik | Ana | Fabio | SILVA | David |
|---|---|---|---|---|
| Marta | Nadir | Michela | André | Aisha |
| Harry | Katia | Mark | Dana | Luis |
| MILLER | NOVAK | Jessica | Peter | Paula |

## 2.2 A date for your diary

**Student A**

1 You want to arrange a dinner party next month. Invite Student B and suggest the following dates: 3rd, 5th, 8th, 11th, 13th, 16th, 25th and 28th.

 - - - - - - - - - - - - - - - - - - - - - - - - - - - - - - - - - - - - - - - - - - - - - - - - - - - - - - - - - - - - - - - -

**Student B**

| Mon | Tues | Weds | Thurs | Fri | Sat | Sun |
|---|---|---|---|---|---|---|
|  |  | 1 | 2 | 3<br>concert with nephew | 4 | 5<br>dinner with parents |
| 6 | 7 | 8<br>theatre with aunt | 9 | 10 | 11<br>golf with cousins | 12 |
| 13<br>shopping with niece | 14 | 15 | 16<br>cinema with grandfather | 17 | 18 | 19 |
| 20 | 21 | 22 | 23 | 24 | 25<br>bike ride with sister | 26 |
| 27 | 28 | 29 | 30 |  |  |  |

 - - - - - - - - - - - - - - - - - - - - - - - - - - - - - - - - - - - - - - - - - - - - - - - - - - - - - - - - - - - - - - - -

**Student B**

2 You want to arrange an outing to the beach next month. Invite Student A and suggest the following dates: 4th, 6th, 10th, 12th, 14th, 18th, 23rd and 29th.

 - - - - - - - - - - - - - - - - - - - - - - - - - - - - - - - - - - - - - - - - - - - - - - - - - - - - - - - - - - - - - - - -

**Student A**

| Mon | Tues | Weds | Thurs | Fri | Sat | Sun |
|---|---|---|---|---|---|---|
|  |  | 1 | 2 | 3 | 4<br>tennis with Dad | 5 |
| 6<br>Mum's birthday | 7 | 8 | 9 | 10<br>barbecue at parents' house | 11 | 12<br>gardening with aunt |
| 13 | 14<br>nephew's piano lesson | 15 | 16 | 17 | 18<br>beach with cousins | 19 |
| 20 | 21 | 22 | 23<br>library with niece | 24 | 25 | 26 |
| 27 | 28 | 29 | 30 |  |  |  |

## 3.1 A scary story

**1** Sally and Ben lived in a charming house in the countryside. It had _____

------------------------------------------------

**2** One day, Sally went into the garden and saw something surprising. An old man was _____

------------------------------------------------

**3** The old man told Sally a very moving story. He said _____

------------------------------------------------

**4** When Ben heard the old man's story, he didn't feel it was realistic. He thought _____

------------------------------------------------

**5** But Sally had a powerful feeling that she knew the old man. She wanted to help him and _____

------------------------------------------------

**6** The old man gave Sally some very complicated instructions. He wanted her to _____

------------------------------------------------

**7** There was something strange and mysterious about the old man. Ben was worried and _____

------------------------------------------------

**8** Then a really dramatic thing happened! The old man _____

------------------------------------------------

**9** It was terrifying for Sally and Ben. They _____

## 3.2 Facts from fiction

**Numbers 1–12 are people, places or things from famous books. Using the words in the box, write sentences explaining what each person, place or thing is. The first one has been done for you.**

| that | which | where | who |

**1** Tom Sawyer
In the novel, The Adventures of Huckleberry Finn, by Mark Twain, Tom Sawyer is the character who is Huck's best friend.

**2** Neverland

**3** Mr Darcy

**4** Finch's Landing

**5** Moby Dick

**6** District 12

**7** Manderley

**8** Bilbo Baggins

**9** Rocinante

**10** Hogwarts

**11** 221B Baker Street

**12** William Golding

## 4.1 My music

### Student A

**Read the blog post and talk about it with your partner. How many differences can you find between your text and Student B's? Do they have anything in common? Make a list of similarities and differences.**

I don't listen to the same type of music as most people I know. I don't especially like pop or rock, and all my friends think it's really funny that I like country music. A lot of people say that country music isn't very cheerful, but it never makes me feel depressed. To me, it's gentle and lovely, and it's also interesting. I mean, the songs always tell a story, which is something I enjoy. I'm a fan of easy listening music, too.

Last year, my brothers asked me to go to a classical concert. I didn't want to go because I find classical music very boring. But I didn't have any other plans that night so I decided to go along and now I'm so glad I did. It was amazing! Firstly, the concert hall was huge. I couldn't believe how many people were there. It was totally full and people of all different ages were there. As soon as the musicians started to play, I absolutely loved it. It was very romantic and soft, but not the kind of music that makes you feel sleepy. In fact, I was listening more carefully than I ever have to any music before. I didn't want it to stop! I felt so peaceful sitting there listening to beautiful music that somebody wrote hundreds of years ago. It was a very special feeling.

The next day I downloaded the same piece of music and I play it often. I feel relaxed whenever I listen to it and I always remember the first night I heard it at that concert hall with my brothers. If you think that classical music is boring, maybe you just haven't heard the right composers.

### Student B

**Read the blog post and talk about it with your partner. How many differences can you find between your text and Student A's? Do they have anything in common? Make a list of similarities and differences.**

My favourite type of music is heavy metal. I really like loud music! It's hard to explain, but it makes me feel more awake, you know? It's exciting! My wife thinks heavy metal is just angry music. I understand why she says that, but I don't agree. Actually, the songs are about important things and the guitars are always brilliant. The drums are usually amazing as well.

I also like other kinds of music, for example, hip-hop and electronic music. Actually, I like a lot of different styles, but, for me, music has to be really lively. I don't enjoy quiet, gentle music. It's boring! Anyway, for my birthday last week, my best friend, Jack, got me a ticket to a hip-hop gig and we went together. It was incredible! It was in a huge park in London and, luckily, the weather was good. I prefer concerts that are outside. I hate sitting inside a building when my favourite music is playing. I want to stand up and dance and really enjoy myself!

When we arrived at the park, thousands of people our age were already there. Everyone was wearing cool jeans and trainers … fashion is very important in hip-hop, you know. When the singer arrived on the stage, the crowd went crazy. He played his new songs first, and we all sang with him. It was so much fun! The lighting was fantastic, too. Everybody felt so upbeat.

Hip-hop is great because it's very rhythmic. The show continued for over two hours and, when it finished, we shouted and shouted for more. The singer came back twice. It's the best gig I've ever been to. I'll never forget it.

## 4.2 Countable or uncountable

| 1 START ⬇ | 14 album | 15 hip-hop music | 28 dance | 29 ⬆ go back five spaces |
|---|---|---|---|---|
| 2 music | 13 ⬆ go forward three squares | 16 applause | 27 classical music | 30 band |
| 3 concert hall | 12 country music | 17 | 26 keyboard | 31 radio |
| 4 | 11 emotion | 18 musician | 25 skip a turn | 32 heavy metal music |
| 5 electronic music | 10 singer | 19 ★ have an extra turn | 24 gig | 33 |
| 6 ⬆ go back to the start | 9 concert | 20 easy listening music | 23 rhythm | 34 genre |
| 7 song | 8 | 21 noise | 22 ★ have an extra turn | 35 ⬇ FINISH |

170  Communicative activities     © 2018 National Geographic Learning, a Cengage Learning company, ALL RIGHTS RESERVED.

## 5.1 Design memory game

### RULES

**Members of the team**
1. Imagine an object and describe its design. Listen to each other. Don't write anything.
2. When it's your turn, repeat what every student before you has said.
3. Then add a new design detail of your own.
4. Your new sentence can't have the same information that someone has already used.
5. The game continues until somebody forgets a detail or can't think of a new one.

**The score-keeper**
1. One student in the group is the score-keeper.
2. The score-keeper says the first sentence in each game.
3. The score-keeper also writes down every design detail that each student adds.
4. He or she should call out *Stop*! if anyone forgets a detail or makes a mistake.
5. Then the score-keeper adds up the total number of design details for that game.

### GAMES
*first sentences*

1. I bought a nice jacket.
2. We have a big sofa.
3. This painting has many shapes.
4. Those shoes are amazing!
5. He drives a red car.
6. That's my favourite shirt.
7. The new library is huge!
8. Your bag is so vibrant.

### USEFUL TIPS

What colour is the object?
Does it have more than one colour?
What size is it?
What shape is it?

Does it have more than one shape?
What does it feel like?
What other design details does it have?

**Example**

Student 1: I love this shirt.

Student 2: I love this shirt. It feels very silky.

Student 3: I love this shirt. It feels very silky. It has curved lines in the middle.

Student 4: I love this shirt. It feels very silky. It has curved lines in the middle. It's large.

Student 5: I love this shirt. It feels very silky. It has curved lines in the middle. It's large. The colours are vibrant …

## 5.2 Listen and draw

**Student A**

1. Look at the coat of arms, but don't show it to your partner. Describe the coat of arms, explaining clearly where each item is.

2. Listen and draw what Student B describes.

 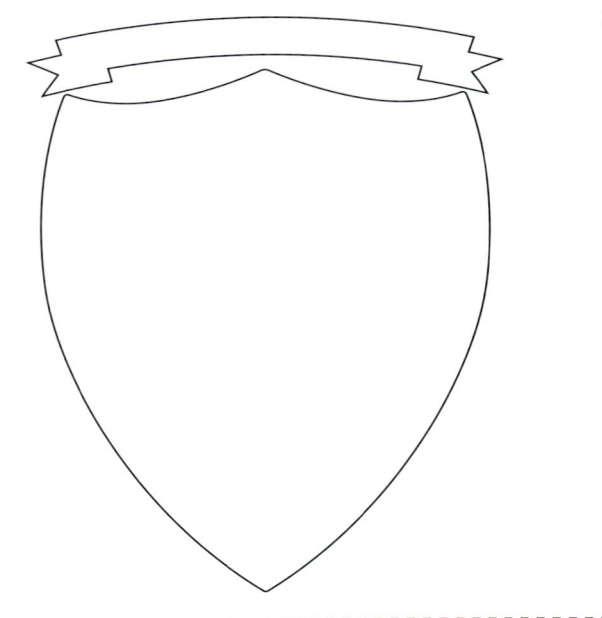

**Student B**

1. Listen and draw what Student A describes.

2. Look at the coat of arms, but don't show it to your partner. Describe the coat of arms, explaining clearly where each item is.

 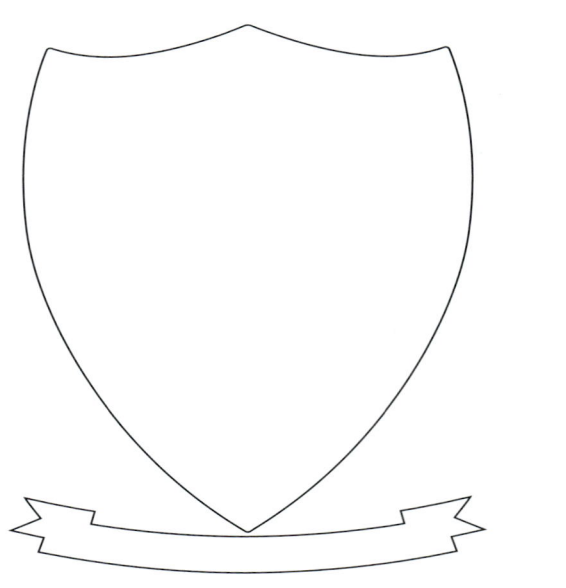

## 6.1 A thank-you speech

1 Read the situation.

2 Then read the questions and make notes. Use the phrases in the box to help you.

3 Use the notes to write a thank-you speech in your notebook.

4 Practise your speech. Then deliver it to a partner.

> **The situation**
> You are going to receive a special award. At the ceremony, you have to give a speech thanking all the inspirational people in your life and everyone who has helped you to succeed. Remember, the information in your speech doesn't have to be true!

| … was a great role model for me | … gave me excellent advice | … changed my life |
| … always supported me by … | … showed me that it's possible to … | … inspired me to … |

**My notes**

1 Who is your role model? Explain how this person is a great role model.

___

2 Who gave you the best advice? What was it?

___

3 Who changed your life? In what way?

___

4 Who has always supported you and what you do? How?

___

5 Who showed you that something was possible? What was it?

___

6 Who inspired you the most? How?

___

Communicative activities

## 6.2 Excuse me, you said …

**1A: Speaker**
A person I really admire is Carlos Acosta. He was born in Cuba on 22nd June, 1979. There were thirteen people in his family and their father was a very rich man. When Carlos was a child, he loved playing baseball, but when he was ten years old, his father sent him to classical ballet classes. He immediately loved ballet and his teachers could see that he was an excellent dancer. Today he is one of the most famous ballet dancers in the world.

**1B: Interrupter**
Name: Carlos Acosta
Born: 2nd June, 1973
Country of birth: Cuba
Family: poor
Family members: eleven
Early interests: football
Started ballet: aged nine
At first: he hated ballet
Famous for: ballet dancing

**2B: Speaker**
For me, Sheryl Sandberg is an important role model because she's an amazing business person who has a really cool job! Sheryl was born in the United Kingdom in 1979. She wasn't interested in studying, but she was popular. She went to university at Harvard, and her first job was at Google. Then, she worked for the UK government. Next, she got a big job at Facebook and today she has one of the most important jobs at the World Bank.

**2A: Interrupter**
Name: Sheryl Sandberg
Country of birth: United States
Year of birth: 1969
At school: worked hard; got excellent marks
University: Harvard
First place of work: the World Bank
Second place of work: the US government
Third place of work: Google
Fourth place of work: Facebook

**3A: Speaker**
I find Bill Cox very inspiring. He's a British artist and celebrity. Bill Cox was born in Ireland in May, 1958. When he was 20, he played in a band that had some hits! He studied biology at university and now he makes lots of television and radio programmes about nature. People like him because he's really funny. I like him because he can explain difficult ideas in a way that makes them easy to understand.

**3B: Interrupter**
Name: Brian Cox
Occupation: scientist
Country of birth: England
Born: March, 1968
As a teenager: played in a popular band
At university: studied physics
Today: makes programmes about science and space
Qualities: interesting; cool

**4B: Speaker**
Someone who inspires me a lot is Mary Robinson, who was born in the north of Ireland in 1945. She studied maths at Trinity College in Cambridge and later taught there. She also worked in politics, and, in 1991, she became the first female president of Ireland. She left in 1997 to accept a high-level job at the European Parliament. I admire her because she works hard to protect Irish people and others in difficult situations.

**4A: Interrupter**
Name: Mary Robinson
Born: in the west of Ireland
Year of birth: 1944
Studied: law
University: Trinity College, Dublin
Became president: 1990
1997: began working at the United Nations
Admired for: protecting poor people and others in difficult situations

## 7.1 Ask the expert

### Student A

**Situation**
1. You are a journalist and Student B is an expert on ethical food choices.
2. Ask Student B the questions below. Get as much information as you can.
3. Take brief notes as you listen to Student B's answers. Don't write full sentences.
4. Use your notes to write a short newspaper article based on Student B's opinions.

**Interview questions and notes:**

1. Do you think that **locally-produced food** is a good idea? Why or why not?

   _____

   _____

2. How does **sustainable farming** work?

   _____

   _____

3. What kind of **free-range foods** can people buy? Why do some people prefer to buy foods that are free-range?

   _____

   _____

✂ - - - - - - - - - - - - - - - - - - - - - - - - - - - - - - - - - - - - - - - - - - - - - - - - - - - - - - - - - - - - - - - - - - - -

### Student B

**Situation**
1. You are a journalist and Student A is an expert on ethical food choices.
2. Ask Student A the questions below. Get as much information as you can.
3. Take brief notes as you listen to Student A's answers. Don't write full sentences.
4. Use your notes to write a short newspaper article based on Student A's opinions.

**Interview questions and notes:**

1. Do you think that **genetically modified foods** are a good idea or a bad idea? Explain why.

   _____

   _____

2. Why do **organic foods** cost more money?

   _____

   _____

3. Where do **fair-trade foods** come from? Why do some people think it's important to buy fair-trade foods?

   _____

   _____

## 7.2 I predict …

**Instructions**
Pick a piece of paper and read out what it says.
In fifteen seconds, give your predictions on this topic.
You must use *will* or *won't* in your predictions.
You may not repeat any predictions you, or anyone else, has already said.
You get one point for every prediction you make.

| cars | climate change | diseases | endangered species |
|---|---|---|---|
| fair-trade foods | free-range foods | fresh water | genetically modified foods |
| leather | locally-produced foods | meat | nature |
| organic foods | public transport | sustainable farming | technology |
| the environment | the oceans and seas | vegetarians | world population |

## 8.1 Design your ideal city

Complete the worksheet to design your ideal city. Then use your notes to describe your city to your partner. Your partner will draw a map of your city.

---

**Your ideal city will be called _____.**

---

**What features will your city have? Choose at least eight.**

| ☐ amusement park | ☐ concert hall | ☐ flea market | ☐ galleries |
| ☐ historic centre | ☐ industrial estate | ☐ residential area | ☐ riverfront |
| ☐ suburbs | ☐ shops | ☐ restaurants | ☐ public transport |

☐ other features / your ideas:

---

**Decide where the features in your city will be and make notes. For example:**

- Is the amusement park outside town?
- Where is the riverfront?
- What's in the city centre?
- Are there any shops at the riverfront?
- Are there cafés in the historic centre?

Your ideas:

---

**Which adjectives would you use to describe your city and its features?**

| ☐ ancient | ☐ bustling | ☐ lively | ☐ multicultural | ☐ peaceful |

☐ other adjectives / your ideas:

## 8.2 City sentences

| 1 check out | 2 chill out | 3 clean up |
|---|---|---|
| 4 eat out | 5 end up | 6 get around |
| 7 go out | 8 grow up | 9 hang out with |
| 10 head to | 11 look at | 12 look for |
| 13 look forward to | 14 meet up with | 15 take in |

| a amusement park | b café | c concert hall |
|---|---|---|
| d flea market | e gallery | f historic centre |
| g industrial estate | h museum | i park |
| j public transport | k residential area | l restaurant |
| m riverfront | n shop | o suburb |

## 9.1 Fundraising for charity

### Situation
You and your team members work for a charity. You are having a meeting to plan a new fundraising campaign for your charity.

### Instructions
1 Choose a charity from the ones below or choose a different charity that you like.
2 Do some research to learn more about where the charity works and what kind of projects it does.
3 With your team, decide on a fundraising idea for your chosen charity.
4 Make notes first. Then write a paragraph describing your fundraising campaign.
5 Present your fundraising campaign to the class. Make sure you use the vocabulary in the box.

| The World Wildlife Fund |
| --- |
| The World Wildlife Fund (or WWF) is a global charity that works to protect endangered species. It does other important work, too, including conservation projects to help improve the environment. Worldwide, over a million people support WWF. |

| The Library Project |
| --- |
| In poor parts of the countryside in Asia, The Library Project sets up libraries and donates books to schools and orphanages. The goal of the project is to bring the joy of reading to children. The Library Project also trains teachers. |

| Doctors Without Borders |
| --- |
| In dangerous parts of the world where there is war or serious fighting, doctors, nurses and other professionals volunteer with this charity to help the people who have been hurt. In 1999, Doctors Without Borders received the Nobel Peace Prize. |

**Your idea**

_____
_____
_____

### Notes
- What is the name of your charity? _____
- What type of work does it do? _____
- Why have you chosen this charity? _____
- What is your fundraising idea? _____
- Where and when will your fundraiser take place? _____
- How will you organize your fundraising campaign? _____
- Any other points? _____

### Vocabulary

| | | | | |
| --- | --- | --- | --- | --- |
| raise money | donate time | make a donation | hold a fundraiser | volunteer |
| support a cause | sponsor an event | donate money | raise awareness | |
| hold an event | make a difference | support a charity | sponsor somebody | |

## 9.2 Negotiation

1  Practise the model dialogue with a partner.

> **Model dialogue, total number of points: _4_**
> A: If I volunteer at the soup kitchen on Saturday, will you volunteer too?
> B: No, sorry. The bus timetable is terrible on Saturdays!
> A: OK. If I pick you up at your house, will you do it?
> B: Well, will you take me food shopping if I volunteer with you?
> A: Yes. If you volunteer for at least three hours, I'll drive you to the supermarket afterwards.

2  Complete dialogues 1–5 with your partner. Each time, Student A tries to persuade Student B to do something.

3  Take turns being Student A. Both speakers should use the first conditional. You get one point every time you use the first conditional correctly.

**Dialogue 1, total number of points: ____**
A: If I run a marathon for charity, will _____
B: No, _____
A: _____
B: _____
A: _____

**Dialogue 2, total number of points: ____**
A: If I hold a fundraiser, will _____
B: No, _____
A: _____
B: _____
A: _____

**Dialogue 3, total number of points: ____**
A: If I donate money to this charity, will _____
B: No, _____
A: _____
B: _____
A: _____

**Dialogue 4, total number of points: ____**
A: If I organize an event, will _____
B: No, _____
A: _____
B: _____
A: _____

**Dialogue 5 (your own idea), total number of points: ____**
A: If I _____
B: No, _____
A: _____
B: _____
A: _____

# 10.1 Information-gap crossword

**Student A**

**Student B**

Communicative activities 181

## 10.2 Connect four

| | | | |
|---|---|---|---|
| all morning | quickly | interestingly | tomorrow |
| hopefully | every day | seriously | fortunately |
| frequently | obviously | during the winter | amazingly |
| extremely well | next year | never | at night |
| until I stopped | usually | carefully | honestly |
| soon | badly | correctly | the day after |
| luckily | happily | after a while | finally |
| times a day | softly | clearly | in the evening |
| finally | constantly | at the age of seventeen | calmly |
| sometimes | often | surprisingly | later |
| kindly | exactly | always | suddenly |

## 11.1 Postcards

| | | | |
|---|---|---|---|
| a bike ride | breathtaking | go for a walk | the coast |
| a cave | camping | gorgeous | the desert |
| a forest | climbing | mountainous | the mountains |
| a park | countryside | nature | the woods |
| a river | cycling | pretty | top of a mountain |
| a walking holiday | diving | safari | wild |
| an island | flat | the beach | wildlife |

## 11.2 Have you ever …?

| | |
|---|---|
| Have you ever slept in a cave? | Have you ever been hiking in the Himalayas? |
| I've never swum in the Indian Ocean. | Have you ever _____ ? |
| Have you ever been to a desert? | Have you ever been camping with your family? |
| I've never been on a cycling holiday. | Have you ever seen a tiger? |
| Have you ever played football on the beach? | Have you ever _____ ? |
| I've never been on safari in Africa. | I've never been bitten by a horse. |
| Have you ever climbed a tree? | Have you ever been ill on holiday? |
| Have you ever been sailing? | Have you ever stood at the top of a mountain? |
| I've never _____ . | I've never slept in a treehouse. |
| Have you ever been diving in Asia? | I've been stung by a bee. |
| Have you ever had a picnic on an island? | Have you ever seen a turtle? |
| Have you ever fallen asleep in the forest? | Have you ever _____ ? |
| Have you ever lived in the countryside? | Have you ever read about the Arctic? |
| I've never driven along the Californian coast. | I've never _____ . |
| Have you ever eaten an insect? | Have you ever picked wild flowers in the woods? |

## 12.1 An archaeological dig

1. Imagine that you took part in an archaeological dig.
2. Use the words in the chart to write a paragraph describing the dig. You must use every word in the chart.
3. When you have finished writing, your partner will interview you about the dig.

**Student A**

- discover
- valuable
- fossil
- tomb
- contain
- identify
- gold

**Student B**

- ancient
- pottery
- excavate
- ruins
- inspect
- site
- artefacts

**Student A interviews Student B**

1. Why are these ruins important?
   _____
   _____
2. Were the ruins part of an ancient city?
   _____
   _____
3. When were they excavated?
   _____
   _____
4. Where is the site?
   _____
   _____
5. What kind of artefacts were found?
   _____
   _____
6. Who inspected the artefacts?
   _____
   _____
7. What kind of pottery did they find?
   _____
   _____

**Student B interviews Student A**

1. How old is the tomb?
   _____
   _____
2. How was it discovered?
   _____
   _____
3. Did they identify the body?
   _____
   _____
4. What kind of fossils were found?
   _____
   _____
5. Was there any gold in the tomb?
   _____
   _____
6. What else did the tomb contain?
   _____
   _____
7. Did they find other valuable things?
   _____
   _____

## 12.2 Newsflash … dinosaur discovery!

### Situation
An exciting discovery has been made! A dinosaur fossil has been found and scientists believe it belongs to a species that no one has ever seen before.

### Instructions
In teams of four, create a five-minute news report about this discovery. Decide which role each person will have. Then plan your news report together. You must use the passive. Spend a little time practising, then deliver your news report to the class.

### Preparation

| Roles | Names |
|---|---|
| Studio newscaster: | |
| On-site reporter: | |
| Palaeontologist: | |
| Researcher/Expert: | |

### Process
**Suggested format of news report**

1. In the TV studio, the newscaster introduces the news story.
2. Newscaster asks on-site reporter one or two questions.
3. On-site reporter answers questions and gives more information.
4. On-site reporter asks on-site palaeontologist a question.
5. Palaeontologist answers the question and reporter signs off.
6. Back in the studio, newscaster thanks reporter and palaeontologist.
7. Newscaster now asks the expert in the studio a question.
8. Dinosaur expert in the studio answers the question.
9. Newscaster ends the report.

# Communicative activities | Teacher's notes

## 1.1 What am I?

A group activity guessing game.

**Language**

Types of animals vocabulary

**Preparation**

Make one copy of the worksheet for each group. Cut out one set of cards for each group.

**In class**

1 Divide students into groups of six.
2 Give everyone a few minutes to review the vocabulary on page 10. Make sure all books are closed for the rest of the lesson.
3 Tell students they are going to play a game. Explain that each card has a picture or a type of animal or species written on it. Groups have to guess what's on the card by asking a maximum of five questions. Emphasize that they may **only** ask questions that can be answered with a *yes* or *no* (or *I don't know*) answer.
4 Model a round with a student. Have him or her come to the front of the classroom. On a piece of paper, write any well-known animal featured in Unit 1, but don't use any that are already on the worksheet. For example, you could use *elephant*, *vulture*, *polar bear* or *snake*. Fold the piece of paper and hand it to the volunteer student.
5 Encourage the class to start asking questions. Reiterate that the answer could be a species or a particular animal. Remind everyone that the volunteer may only answer *yes* or *no* (or *I don't know*).
6 If the class is slow to think of questions at first, help them along. For example, say, *Are you a species? / Are you a very large animal? / Are you an endangered species? / Do you live in the sea? / Do you have feathers? / Can you swim?*
7 Draw students' attention to the structure of *yes/no* questions. Encourage them to begin their questions with *Are you … / Have you … / Do you … / Can you …*, etc.
8 Now give each group a set of cards placed face down or folded and in a bag or box. The first student draws a card and the team begins asking questions.
9 Check that groups are not simply guessing random animals; ensure that they are asking questions.
10 The winning group is the one that gets the most correct answers in the allotted time; 20–25 minutes should be enough. You could have an optional extension where students think up their own animals and get their team to guess them.

## 1.2 Spot the differences

A pair-work activity in which students practise using the present continuous to describe differences.

**Language**

Present continuous
Vocabulary from Unit 1

**Preparation**

Make a copy of the worksheet for each pair and cut it along the dotted line.

**In class**

1 Put students into pairs.
2 Spend a little time reviewing the present continuous on page 12. Make sure students are confident with this tense. Then have them close their books for the rest of the lesson.
3 Explain that you are going to give them a picture and they must write as many sentences as possible describing what they see. Emphasize that they **must** use the present continuous in every sentence.
4 Give the top half of the worksheet to all the Student As and the bottom half to all the Student Bs. Instruct them not to show their papers to each other.
5 Have students work separately to write their sentences first and make sure there is no talking. Allow about fifteen minutes for this part of the activity.
6 At this point, pairs work together to compare their work. Have them discuss their respective sentences, asking each other questions to find as many differences as possible. For example, *Does your picture have any monkeys? / What are they doing? / Is the panda sleeping in your picture? / Is anyone taking a photo?* etc.
7 Check answers as a class. Divide the board into Side A and Side B. Have students read out their sentences. Write them on the board as they are given, confirming or correcting any vocabulary or grammatical errors.
8 **Optional:** Introduce a points system of four points for every correct sentence, with a point deducted for incorrect grammar, the wrong animal identified or a spelling mistake.

***Suggested answers***

In Picture A, there are two monkeys. They're eating bananas. In Picture B, the two monkeys aren't eating bananas.
In Picture A, there is a rhino. In Picture B, there are two rhinos.
In Picture A, there are two elephants drinking water from the river. In Picture B, there is one elephant drinking from the river.
In Picture A, there is a gorilla climbing a tree. In Picture B, there isn't a gorilla.

In Picture A, there is a vulture flying above the river. In Picture B, there are two vultures.
In Picture A, a panda is lying down / sleeping on the grass. In Picture B, a panda is walking.
In Picture A, there is a man who is taking photos. In Picture B, there is a woman taking photos.
In Picture A, there are three crocodiles sitting next to the river. In Picture B, the crocodiles are sleeping.
In Picture A, there are four frogs sitting on the rocks in the river. In Picture B, there aren't any frogs on the rocks.
In Picture A, there are two turtles swimming. In Picture B, there are three turtles swimming.
In Picture A, there is a butterfly sitting on a flower. In Picture B, there isn't a butterfly. In Picture A, there are two tigers running. In Picture B, there is one tiger running.

## 2.1 Family trees

A group activity in which students create family trees.

### Language
Extended family vocabulary

### Preparation
Make a copy of one worksheet for each group. Cut along the dotted lines to make individual squares.

### In class
1. Divide the class into groups of three.
2. Spend a little time reviewing the vocabulary on page 20 of the Student's Book. Then ensure that all books remain closed for the rest of the lesson.
3. Tell students that they will work in groups of three: Student A, Student B and Student C, and create three different family trees (A, B and C) using the names supplied.
4. Explain that each student in the group will receive a short text that describes a family. Students should not show their texts to each other. They should first read the text quietly to themselves and then draw a picture of the family tree. They shouldn't show each other the family tree they have drawn.
5. Next, each student reads their text aloud to the other two students, who must use the names they are given to create a family tree based on the information they hear.
6. The student reading aloud should read clearly and not too quickly.
7. When the other two students have completed the family tree, one of them should describe it aloud. The student with the written text should compare the family tree with the one they have already drawn and with the text. Together, the group should confirm or correct all details.
8. **Note:** Let students know that they may not need to use all of the names supplied. Point out that the names are recycled throughout the activity.

Explain that the three families being described are not related in any way.

9. Check answers as a class by inviting volunteers to the board to draw the family trees.

### Answers
**The Silva family**

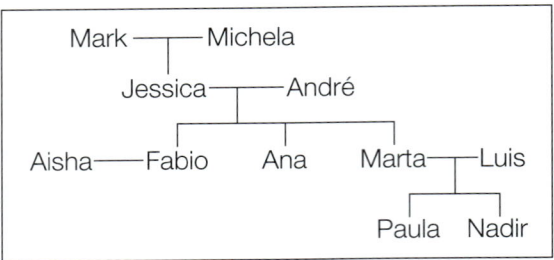

**The Miller family**

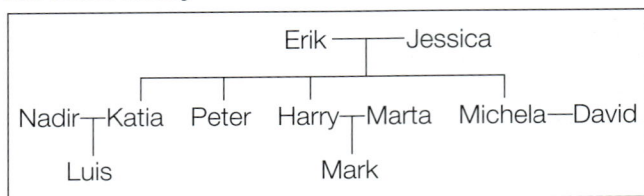

**The Novak family**

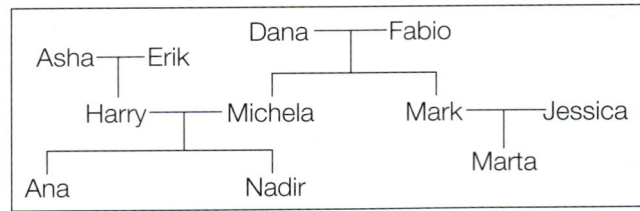

## 2.2 A date for your diary

A pair-work activity in which students practise making an arrangement.

### Language
Talking about future plans and arrangements
Family vocabulary

### Preparation
Make a copy of the worksheet for each pair. Cut along the dotted lines where shown.

### In class
1. Put students into pairs.
2. Give them a little time to review the grammar on page 22.
3. While they are doing that, write the following on the board:
   **A:** *I'm planning a night out next month. What are you doing on the 2nd?*
   **B:** *Let me see … on the 2nd, I'm _____.*
   **A:** *Oh, OK. Are you free on the 7th?*
   **B:** *No, sorry. On the 7th, I'm _____.*

4 Invite a volunteer to role-play the example with you. Use the present continuous for your first line, for example, *I'm driving my niece to the airport.* For your second line, use *be + going to + infinitive*, for example, *I'm going to paint my cousin's house.*
5 Explain to students that they are now going to do a similar role-play where Student A is arranging a dinner party and Student B must say what plans he/she has, using the information in the calendar.
6 Now, give Student A the instruction and Student B the calendar. Remind Student A to suggest the dates shown in the instruction and remind Student B to use the correct grammar.
7 Allow about ten minutes (or more, if your students need it) for Part 1 of the activity. When the time is up, have students switch roles and start Part 2 of the activity. Give Student B the second instruction and Student A the second calendar.
8 At the end, invite volunteers to role-play in front of the class.
9 **Optional:** You could set a follow-up task where students continue the activity using the blank dates in their calendars. They should come up with excuses of their own for not being free on those days.

## 3.1 A scary story

A group activity in which students write an original story.

### Language
Describing stories vocabulary

### Preparation
Make a copy of the worksheet for each group. Fold along the dotted lines so that only one section is visible at a time. Bring a stopwatch or other timer to class.

### In class
1 Divide the class into groups of three.
2 Review the vocabulary from page 30 by writing the nine adjectives on the board. Spend a little time checking students' understanding of each word. For example, say, *Which word means 'full of secrets'*? Or, with their books closed, have students call out their own definition of a word you point to. You could also invite volunteers to use each word in a sentence of their own.
3 Tell students that they are going to work in groups and write a story on a worksheet that you will give them. Tell them that the worksheet is folded into nine sections, numbered 1–9. The first student completes the first section, then folds it over so their writing can't be seen and only the second section is visible for the second student and so on. You could hold up a sample worksheet to demonstrate this.
4 Hold up one of the worksheets, folded like a fan so that only the first section is visible and point out the two blank lines. Explain that each student must try to write just enough to fill those two lines. Tell them they will only have three minutes to write their sentences.

5 Explain that it's a scary story in which a couple called Sally and Ben meet a strange old man. Point out that no more information is available and they need to make up the rest of the story themselves.
6 Each student will have three different turns to write. Again, emphasize that they should not look at the next part of the story or any of the previous parts, only the section that is in front of them.
7 Remind students not to take too long thinking about what to write and that it's important to work as quickly as possible. When their three minutes are up, they must stop writing even if they haven't finished their sentences.
8 Hand out the worksheets and tell groups to decide which student will write first, second and third. Tell the class you are starting the clock. Say, *Begin Part 1.* When three minutes are up, say, *Time is up for Part 1!* Then begin Part 2 and so on until all parts are done.
9 When they have finished, invite one volunteer from each group to read their completed story to the class.
10 **Optional:** Take a class vote on the best story in different categories, for example, the scariest story, the funniest story, the most interesting story, etc.

## 3.2 Facts from fiction

A pair-work activity in which students carry out research and use defining relative clauses to write sentences about characters, places or things from famous novels.

### Language
Defining relative clauses

### Preparation
Make a copy of the worksheet for each pair.
Give each pair access to the Internet.

### In class
1 Put students into pairs.
2 Write *that*, *which*, *where* and *who* on the board. Spend some time reviewing the defining relative clauses on page 32.
3 Tell students they are going to do a web research activity. Explain that they will be given a list of twelve subjects, which are either characters, objects or places from famous novels.
4 Explain that their task is to research each subject and use a defining relative clause to write an accurate sentence about it. They should also say what novel it's from and who the author of the novel is.
5 On the board, write *Tom Sawyer*. Ask if anyone has heard of Tom Sawyer before. If no one has, ask the class whether they think Tom Sawyer is an object, a place or the name of a character. When there is consensus that it's a character's name, elicit which defining relative clause they should use (*who* or *that*).
6 Practise the activity by giving the class several minutes to research Tom Sawyer online. Then check what they found out. Ask what novel he's from and who wrote the novel.

**Communicative activities | Teacher's notes**

As the information is given, write *The Adventures of Huckleberry Finn* and *Mark Twain* on the board.

7  Invite volunteers to come up with a sentence explaining who Tom Sawyer is, confirming or correcting as necessary. Remind them that they must use a defining relative clause.

8  On the board, write: *In the novel,* The Adventures of Huckleberry Finn, *by Mark Twain, Tom Sawyer is the character* **who** *is Huck's best friend*. Tell students they should follow this model when they write their own sentences.

9  Give each pair a worksheet. Tell the class they will get two points for every accurate sentence they write. They will lose a point if the information is not completely accurate or if they do not use a defining relative clause.

10  Start the activity. The winner is the pair that finishes first. At the end, check answers as a class.

### Suggested answers

2  *Neverland is where Peter Pan is from.*
3  *Mr Darcy is a character in Jane Austen's* Pride and Prejudice *who is in love with one of the main characters, Elizabeth Bennet.*
4  *Finch's Landing is the farm where the Finch family lived in* To Kill a Mocking Bird.
5  *Moby Dick is the whale who bites off Captain Ahab's leg.*
6  *District 12 is where Katniss Everdeen lives in* The Hunger Games.
7  *Manderley is the fictional place where Maxim de Winter lived in the novel* Rebecca.
8  *Bilbo Baggins is the main character who appears in* The Hobbit.
9  *Rocinante is the name of the horse that Don Quixote rides.*
10  *Hogwarts is the school that Harry Potter went to.*
11  *221B Baker Street is where Sherlock Holmes lives.*
12  *William Golding is the author who wrote* The Lord of the Flies.

## 4.1  My music

A pair-work activity to spot the differences between two blog posts about musical tastes and a concert attended.

### Language
Music vocabulary

### Preparation
Make one copy of the worksheet for each pair of students and cut the page along the dotted line.

### In class

1  Divide the class into pairs: Student A and Student B.
2  Spend about five minutes reviewing the vocabulary in 4.1 and checking students' understanding of the genres and adjectives.
3  Tell students they are each going to read a young person's blog post about the music they like and a concert that they went to.
4  Give each Student A a copy of the first text and give each Student B a copy of the second text. Ask them not to show their texts to their partner at any point in the lesson. Have all students read through their texts quietly.
5  Explain to the class that they are going to talk with their partner about what they read in their text by retelling the information to each other. Tell them that, for ten points, they need to find at least ten differences between the texts and explain that they will get extra points for any additional differences they can find. Make sure they don't simply read the text, word for word, back to their partner.
6  As the first student relays the information, the second student should take notes. When they have finished, the second student should relay the information from his/her text, while the first student takes notes.
7  Using their notes, the pair should work together to compile a list of all the differences between the two blog posts.
8  To guide students, encourage them to ask key questions as they work on the differences. For example, *What type(s) of music does your blogger usually listen to? Why? How does it make them feel? What kind of concert did they go to? When did they go? Why did they go? Who did they go with? Where was it held? What was it like? What other kinds of people were there? Did they enjoy the music at the concert? How did it make them feel?* etc. You may want to write these questions on the board. Each student can refer back to their own text if they feel the list of differences is missing any important points.

### Answers

| Blogger A | Blogger B |
| --- | --- |
| likes country and easy listening music | likes heavy metal, electronic, hip-hop |
| likes gentle music | doesn't like gentle music; likes loud music |
| went to a classical concert | went to a hip-hop concert |
| went with parents | went with best friend |
| concert was in a concert hall | concert was in a public park |
| people of different ages were there | people at the gig were the blogger's age |
| was sitting down for the concert | was standing up for the concert |
| music was romantic and soft | music was upbeat and rhythmic |
| it was peaceful | it was lively |
| the music was old | the music was new |

## 4.2 Countable and uncountable nouns

A group activity in which students make sentences using countable/uncountable nouns and quantifiers.

**Language**

Countable and uncountable nouns
Talking about quantity
Vocabulary from Unit 4

**Preparation**

You will need:
- Copies of the board game (one for each group)
- Dice (one die for each group) or write numbers 1 to 6 on pieces of paper and put them in a bag which students can draw from when it's their turn
- Place-markers (one for each student). For the place-markers, you could use small, coloured discs or pennies painted different colours. Students in the same group should not have identical place-markers

**In class**

1 Divide the class into groups of five or six.
2 Review the grammar on page 44 and check students' understanding of countable and uncountable nouns.
3 Tell the class that they are going to play a music-related game. On the board, write the seven quantifiers: *a little, a lot of, any, a few, many, much, some*.
4 Give each group a copy of the board game, plus their dice (or bag of six numbers) and markers. Allow a moment or two for them to look at the game.
5 Tell students that to play they should throw the dice, or draw a number from the bag, and move their place-marker the same number of squares. They must use the noun on that square, plus one quantifier from the board to make a correct sentence. Let students know that it's OK to use the plural form of any nouns on the board.
6 The game is played one student at a time. Students cannot use the same sentences. If a student repeats the same idea someone else in the group has already used, they must go back a space. And if a sentence is grammatically incorrect, the student must go back one space. The winner is the student who reaches FINISH first.

## 5.1 Design memory game

A group activity in which students describe an imaginary object.

**Language**

Design elements vocabulary
Talking about design

**Preparation**

Make one copy of the worksheet for each group.
Bring a prop to demonstrate the game, for example, an item of clothing, a vase, a piece of jewellery, etc. Try not to choose something too plain or students will not find much to say about it.

**In class**

1 Divide the class into groups of eight and give each student in the group a number, 1–8.
2 Give the class some time to review the vocabulary on page 52.
3 Have students close their books. Tell them they are going to practise describing an object using as many design elements as they can.
4 Show the prop you brought and invite a volunteer to say one thing about it. Emphasize that they must include a word from page 52, for example, *The colours in that vase are very vibrant.* Now ask another student to say something else about the item. They might say, *The lines are curved.* Repeat the two sentences and have the class chorus with you. Then ask a third and fourth student to add details and repeat each sentence in order, 1–4.
5 Tell students that this is how they will play the game.
6 Go through the rules of the game. Let students know that they must repeat all the details that have already been said by their team-mates and then add a design element of their own. One student in the group will be the score-keeper.
7 Explain the role of the score-keeper and tell students that they will each get a turn to be the score-keeper, starting with Student 1. The score-keeper is the only person allowed to make notes. He/She says the first sentence of each round and then writes each detail that is given by every other student, with one point for every new design element mentioned. The score-keeper stops the game if someone misses one of the design details or repeats something that has already been said. The idea of the game is to score as many points as possible.
8 Give a worksheet to each group. Allow some time for them to read through the rules and the useful tips. Invite them to ask questions if they aren't sure about anything.
9 Begin the first game with Student 1 as the score-keeper saying *I bought a nice jacket*.

## 5.2 Listen and draw

A pair-work activity to practise prepositions of place. Students draw a coat of arms based on a description their partner gives.

**Language**
Prepositions of place
Describing a coat of arms

**Preparation**
Make a copy of the worksheet for each pair of students. Cut along the dotted line in the centre as shown.

**In class**
1 Put students into pairs, Student A and Student B.
2 Give the class some time to review the prepositions of place on page 54. While they are doing that, write all the prepositions of place on the board and leave them there for the duration of the lesson.
3 Spend a few minutes reviewing the language. For example, draw various shapes in random positions on the board and invite volunteers to describe them, e.g. *The triangle is above the circle. The square is to the right of the triangle.*
4 Explain to students that they are going to draw a coat of arms, which their partner will describe to them. They should not look at their partner's worksheet. They must listen and draw.
5 Tell students that most of the design elements are very simple. Reassure them that they don't need to be good at drawing; the important point is to put the right things in the right places.
6 Hand out the worksheets. Read the instructions for part 1 aloud and make sure everyone understands what they need to do. When they have finished, move on to part 2.
7 At the end, invite volunteers to draw the final coats of arms on the board.

## 6.1 A thank-you speech

An individual writing and speaking activity in which each student produces a thank-you speech and delivers it to his/her partner.

**Language**
Sources of inspiration vocabulary
Talking about an inspirational person

**Preparation**
Make a copy of the worksheet for each student in the class.

**In class**
1 Divide the class into pairs.
2 Take a few minutes to review the vocabulary on page 62. Make sure that everyone knows how to use all of the key phrases in a sentence. Then have students close their books.
3 Tell students to pretend they are going to receive an award and they must give a thank-you speech at the ceremony. They should decide what the award is for and, in their speech, they must thank each person who inspired them. Emphasize that they should explain how they were inspired by these people.
4 Give a worksheet to every student and allow them a moment to read it quickly.
5 Then go through each part of the worksheet with the class. Read the instructions aloud and check that everyone understands what they need to do.
6 Invite a volunteer to read the situation aloud.
7 Draw students' attention to the notes section. Read through the questions with the class. Explain that this is where students should write their ideas, but they don't need to write full sentences here. You may want to set a time limit for the notes part of the activity.
8 Point out that the information they use doesn't need to be true. They can write about real people in their lives or make everything up.
9 Tell students to use their notes to write their thank-you speech in their notebooks. When they have finished, have them deliver their speech to a partner. Their partner should guess what the award is for.
10 **Optional:** Invite volunteers to deliver their speech to the class. Encourage the class to act like an audience, applauding the highlights, etc.

## 6.2 Excuse me, you said …

A pair-work game in which students talk to each other about people who have inspired others and practise reported speech to correct each other on certain points.

**Language**
Reported speech
Vocabulary from Unit 6

**Preparation**
Make a copy of the worksheet for each pair and cut along the dotted lines as shown.

**In class**
1 Divide the class into pairs.
2 Review reported speech on page 64. Spend a few minutes practising the language with the class. For example, ask one student a question: *What did you have for breakfast?* When the student answers, ask the class, *What did [student's name] say?* Go through a few examples of this to make sure all students are confident using reported speech.
3 Tell the class that they are going to play four games in AB pairs. Explain that, in each game, one student will be the speaker and the other will be the interrupter. In each subsequent game, they will swap roles. Check that students understand what *interrupt* means.

4 Do a short demonstration of the game using the following method. On a piece of paper, write a few simple sentences which are obviously untrue. For example, *Today is Sunday. / There are three teachers in the room. / The sun is shining.* Ask a volunteer to read the sentences aloud. Interrupt the volunteer each time saying, for example, *Excuse me, you said it was Sunday, but it's Monday. / Sorry, you said there were three teachers in the room, but there's only one. / Pardon me, you said the sun was shining, but it's raining outside.*

5 Tell students you are going to give each of them a piece of paper, which they must not show to their partner. Begin with the first game. Allow a few moments for each student to read the information on their paper.

6 Instruct the interrupter to listen carefully and to stop the speaker if anything he or she says is different from what's on the interrupter's paper. Emphasize that they **must** use reported speech whenever they interrupt.

7 The object of the game is for the interrupter to catch as many inaccuracies as possible. The interrupters should write down the number of inaccuracies they notice. At the end of each game, check answers as a class and hand out the papers for the next game.

## 7.1 Ask the expert

A pair-work activity in which students role-play being journalists and experts on ethical food choices and interview each other.

### Language

Ethical food choices vocabulary
Talking about ethical choices

### Preparation

Make one copy of the worksheet for each pair and cut in the centre as shown.
Give Student A the top half. Don't give Student B the bottom half of the worksheet until the first part of the activity has been completed.

### In class

1 Divide the class into pairs, Student A and Student B.
2 Write the six target vocabulary terms on the board: *fair-trade*, *free-range*, *genetically modified*, *locally-produced*, *organic* and *sustainable*.
3 Tell the class that they are going to do a role-play activity in which one student is a journalist and the other is an expert on ethical food choices and then they will switch roles. Point to the vocabulary on the board and explain that they will be asked questions about ethical food choices. Emphasize that the important thing is to demonstrate an understanding of the key terms.
4 Have students open their books to page 74 and give them some time to review the target language, making sure they fully understand each term. Remind them that, in the activity, they may be asked to explain some of the terms in their own words or they may be asked their opinion on these types of food. Encourage them to ask questions if they aren't sure about any of the words.

5 Finish the review period and get students ready to start the activity.
6 Explain the four steps of the activity. You could read this from the Situation section on the worksheet.
7 Tell students that they will have the questions they need to ask their partner.
8 Explain that they should take notes as they listen to their partner's answers. Remind them that note-taking means jotting down the main points, not writing full sentences.
9 When they have finished this part of the activity, tell them to switch roles and hand out the Student B sets of questions. It's best not to do this earlier in the lesson because it may distract students as they work on the first part of the activity.
10 Have the Student Bs interview the Student As and take notes.
11 When they have finished, tell all students to use the notes they took to write a short newspaper article in their notebooks summarizing what their partner said.

## 7.2 I predict …

A group activity in which students use *will* and *won't* to make future predictions.

### Language

*will* and *won't* for future predictions
Ethical food choices vocabulary

### Preparation

Make one copy of the worksheet for each group.
For each group, cut out the instructions and cut the topics into separate squares.
**Optional:** Containers for each group to put the topics into, e.g. a hat, a jar, a box.

### In class

1 Divide the class into groups (minimum: four students; maximum: eight students per group).
2 Do some class practice by asking questions such as, *What do you think the weather will be like tomorrow? / Who do you think will win the next World Cup? / When will you get married?* Tell students they can begin some of their answers with *I think …* or *I believe …* Remind them that they **must** include *will* or *won't*. Encourage them to use *probably* and *definitely* as well. Give your own answers to some of the questions, for example, *I think it will probably rain tomorrow. / I believe Brazil will win the next World Cup. / I definitely won't get married until I'm 30.*
3 Give students a little time to review the grammar on pages 76 and 77.
4 If possible, have groups sit in a circle. Begin the activity.

5 Explain that students will take turns being time-keepers and score-keepers. Assign the first time-keeper and score-keeper in each group. After the first turn, these roles should move on to the next two students in the group, and so on, throughout the activity.

6 Tell students they will be given 20 different topics either in a box or placed face-down on the desk. The important thing is that they don't see the topics in advance.

7 A student picks a topic and must make predictions about it using *will* or *won't*.

8 As soon as someone picks a topic, the time-keeper starts the time and, at the end of fifteen seconds, the time-keeper shouts *Stop!* They can use a watch or phone to keep the time.

9 As soon as the speaker starts to make predictions, it's the score-keeper's job to give one point for each prediction made using *will* or *won't*. The score-keeper gives no points if a prediction is made without *will* or *won't* and deducts one point if a prediction is repeated.

10 At the end of fifteen seconds, the next student picks a topic and begins making predictions.

11 Tell students that their predictions don't have to be realistic. If there is time at the end, you could have groups share their funniest predictions with the class.

## 8.1 Design your ideal city

A pair-work activity in which students design their ideal city.

### Language
Features of a city vocabulary

### Preparation
Make one copy of the worksheet for every student.

### In class

1 Divide the class into pairs, Student A and Student B, and give each student a worksheet.

2 Tell the class that they are going to design their ideal city and then describe it to their partner, who will draw a map of it.

3 Allow some time for everyone to review the vocabulary on page 84.

4 Go through each section of the worksheet with the class. Tell students they can make up a name for their fictional city.

5 Draw their attention to the list of features and explain that they can choose as many as they want, but no fewer than eight.

6 Explain that they need to think about what their city looks like and where the various features are.

7 Point out that they can include other features and adjectives that are not on the list. Encourage students to be creative and to make their city as interesting as possible.

8 Remind them that the worksheet is for making notes that will help them to describe their city later.

9 Give students enough time to fill in the worksheet; 20 minutes should be adequate, but you can adjust the timing to suit your own class's needs.

10 When the time is up, explain that Student A should describe his/her city to Student B, who will draw a map of it. Then they switch roles and Student A draws Student B's city. They should draw the maps in their notebooks. Emphasize that students should not give the worksheet to their partner; they must describe their city in clear detail.

11 Walk around the classroom giving support where needed. Mention that the student drawing the map can ask questions to clarify where the features are.

12 **Optional:** When all students have finished drawing their maps, invite volunteers to come to the front of the class and describe their partner's city to the class. You could also take a class vote on whose city most people would like to live in.

## 8.2 City sentences

A small-group activity in which students make sentences using the nouns and phrasal verbs provided.

### Language
Phrasal verbs
Features of a city vocabulary

### Preparation
Make one copy of the worksheet for each group.

### In class

1 Put students into groups of three or four and give each group a worksheet.

2 Tell students they are going to write as many sentences as possible about cities. Explain that they will be given a set of nouns and phrasal verbs that they must work with.

3 Spend some time reviewing the grammar on pages 86 and 87, with a particular focus on separable and inseparable phrasal verbs. Read out a few of the phrasal verbs from the worksheet and have students say whether they are separable or not. (Not separable: *chill out*, *eat out*, *end up*, *go out*, *get around*, *grow up*, *hang out with*, *head to*, *look at*, *look for*, *look forward to*, *meet up with*; Separable: *check out*, *clean up*, *take in*.) Make sure students understand where the pronoun goes in separable phrasal verbs.

4 Give them a few minutes to look over the examples, then have them close their books for the remainder of the lesson.

5 Explain that they must write sentences about cities and every sentence has to include a phrasal verb, 1–15, and a noun, a–o.

6 Draw students' attention to the grid of phrasal verbs. Let them know that they can use any verb tense they want; they don't have to write all sentences in the present tense. Now direct students' attention to the grid of nouns. Explain that they can use the singular or plural form of any noun.

7 Point out that groups may use the same phrasal verb more than once and the same noun more than once, but they

**may not** reuse the same combination of phrasal verb + noun in any other sentences.

8   Tell students that there must be variety in their sentences; they cannot repeat the same idea in multiple sentences. For example, if they have already written *I hang out with my friends at the riverfront*, they may not also write *I hang out with my friends in the suburbs*.
9   Let students start the activity and tell them how long they have, for example, 15–20 minutes.
10  When the time is up, have groups swap their list of sentences to be marked by another group: one point for every correct sentence. The winning group is the one with the most points.

## 9.1 Fundraising for charity

A group activity in which students choose a charity and design a fundraising campaign for it, which they then present to the class.

### Language
Fundraising vocabulary

### Preparation
Make one copy of the worksheet for each group.
Make sure that groups have access to the Internet for research.

### In class
1   Give students a little time to review the vocabulary on page 94. Tell them they will need to use these terms in the activity. Then have them close their books.
2   Put students into groups of four and give each group a copy of the worksheet.
3   Go through the worksheet with the class. Begin by reading the situation and the five steps at the top of the page aloud. Make sure everyone understands what they need to do and invite them to ask questions if they aren't sure.
4   Have a few volunteers read the overview of each charity aloud.
5   Explain that each group must choose one of these charities, or a charity of their own, and do some research on it.
6   Students should find out where the charity is based, what kind of work it does and who it helps.
7   Draw students' attention to the Notes section in the middle of the worksheet. Read the prompt questions aloud. Explain that they need to work together to complete this section.
8   Tell the groups how much time they have to research their charity and come up with their fundraising idea. Around 20 minutes to make their notes should be enough, but you can allocate more time if you feel your students will need it.
9   Point out that they have to develop their fundraising idea, that is, they have to be able to explain it and answer questions about it.
10  When the allocated time for research and making notes is up, give the groups a little time (five minutes or so) to practise presenting their fundraising idea. Their presentation should include all of the bullet points from the Notes section. Remind them that they must use as much vocabulary from the box as possible.
11  Have each group present their fundraising idea to the class. When all groups have finished presenting, take a class vote on which campaign most people would donate to.

## 9.2 Negotiation

A pair-work activity in which students use the first conditional to negotiate a situation related to charity or giving.

### Language
*will* for offers and first conditionals
Fundraising vocabulary

### Preparation
Make one copy of the worksheet for each pair.

### In class
1   Give students some time to review the grammar on pages 96 and 97, which they will need to use for this activity. Then have them close their books.
2   Put students into pairs and give each pair a copy of the worksheet. Give them a moment to read through the worksheet on their own.
3   On the board, write *negotiation*. Ask whether anyone knows what it means and, if not, explain that *negotiation* means trying to reach an agreement by discussing something.
4   Tell the class they are going to role-play a negotiation activity in which two students try to persuade each other to do something. Explain that *persuade* means making someone agree to do something.
5   Point out the sample dialogue at the top of the page. Tell the class they are going to practise the sample dialogue with you. You will be Speaker A and they will be Speaker B.
6   When you have finished, ask *Did Speaker A persuade Speaker B to do something?* (yes) Then ask, *Did Speaker B also negotiate?* (yes)
7   Using the dialogue, ask whether the speakers used the first conditional. Invite volunteers to read out each usage of the first conditional.
8   Have students practise the model dialogue in pairs.
9   Now explain that they need to complete the remaining dialogues using the first conditional to negotiate. Tell them they get one point every time they use the first conditional correctly and the winning pair is the one with the most points.
10  Encourage students to have fun with the activity. Point out that they don't have to be realistic when they negotiate with each other; the most important thing is to use the first conditional as much as possible.
11  At the end, invite some pairs to perform their best dialogue in front of the class.

## 10.1 Information-gap crossword

A pair-work activity in which students complete a crossword puzzle.

### Language
Brain functions vocabulary

### Preparation
Make one copy of the worksheet for each pair of students. Cut the page in half so that each student gets one half of the crossword.
Draw a section of a crossword on the board with numbers in some of the squares to demonstrate the terms students will need, such as *1 down*, *4 across*, etc.

### In class

1. Divide the class into pairs. Give Student A the partially-completed crossword from the top half of the worksheet and Student B the bottom half. Emphasize that they should not show their crosswords to each other at any time during the activity.
2. Tell the class they are going to do a crossword puzzle using the vocabulary for brain functions.
3. Point to the crossword sketched on the board and draw students' attention to the numbers and the across and down direction of the words
4. Give the class some time to review the target language on page 106 and in the transcript 10.1. Tell them they need to understand all of the vocabulary clearly enough to explain it to someone else. Encourage students to ask questions if there are any words they're not sure of.
5. Explain that Student A has half of the words that are needed to complete the crossword and Student B has the words to complete the other half.
6. Allow a few minutes for students to quietly read through the words in their half of the crossword. Tell them to make sure they fully understand each word. If necessary, give them one more opportunity to look at page 106.
7. In their pairs, students ask each other to give them clues for their missing words, e.g. *What is 1 down?* Their partner should offer an answer, e.g. *It's what we need to help us stand and walk without falling.* They should not just give the word needed!
8. As pairs are doing the activity, walk around the class and listen in, giving support and prompts where required.

### Answers

## 10.2 Connect four

A pair-work activity in which students make sentences using adverbs and adverbial phrases of time, manner and attitude.

### Language
Adverbs and adverbial phrases

### Preparation
Make one copy of the worksheet for each pair.

### In class

1. Tell the class they are going to play a game using adverbs and adverbial phrases. Give them a few minutes to review the grammar on page 108. Tell them to pay attention to the different types of adverbs, making sure they know the difference between them and where to place them in a sentence.
2. Have them close their books and do a little classroom practice. Call out some adverbs or sentences and have students say which type they are. For example, *The brain sends millions of messages* every minute. (time) / *I completed the application form very* carefully. (manner) / *Fortunately*, *we understand more about the brain these days.* (attitude)
3. Put students into pairs and give each pair a copy of the worksheet.
4. Tell them they will take turns choosing different adverbs and adverbial phrases, and making sentences with them. Explain that they must try to complete four adverbs in a row and the row can be in any direction – across, down, diagonal – as long as the four items are connected.
5. Students can either agree on who goes first or toss a coin to decide.
6. When a student uses an adverb or adverbial phrase correctly, they write their initials in that box on the worksheet. If they make a mistake, for example, if they use the adverb in the wrong place, they may not write their initials in the box.

7 Students get one point for every correct sentence they make. Be available to arbitrate if anyone thinks their partner's sentence is grammatically incorrect or doesn't make sense.
8 In order to win, partners would try to block each other from successfully linking four adverbs in a row.
9 Once a student manages to 'connect four', they draw a line through their four boxes.
10 The winning student is the one with the most boxes with their initials.

## 11.1 Postcards

A whole-class activity in which students write postcards and send them to each other.

### Language
Nature vocabulary

### Preparation
Make a copy of the worksheet for every student in the class. Cut along the dotted line at the top so that the list of words is separate and cut out the six postcard images. Make a few extra copies in case any students make a mistake and ask you for a new one.

### In class
1 Give students a little time to review the vocabulary on page 106 and to make sure they are familiar with all the terms.
2 Tell the class that they are going to write postcards to each other. Explain that you will give each student six pictures showing different nature scenes. They should choose one and imagine they are on holiday in that place.
3 On the back of their chosen picture, they should write a postcard describing their holiday and send it (give it) to someone in the class. No student can receive more than one postcard.
4 Explain that everyone will also be given a list of nature words and phrases, which they must use when they write their postcards. The idea is to include as much of this vocabulary as possible, but they must use it in a way that fits with the scene they have chosen. For example, they can't write, *I'm having a great holiday in the mountains. The scenery here is really flat.* or *It's lovely relaxing on this beach. We go on safari here every day.*
5 Before they begin, encourage them to think about what they should write on their postcard. Ask some questions to help them. For example, *Where are you on holiday? Who are you with? What's the landscape like? What kinds of things do you do every day?* etc.
6 Remind students that postcards are informal and they should use informal language. If necessary, go over some standard greetings and endings, for example, *Hi!*, *All the best*, *See you soon*, etc.
7 Hand out the worksheets. Tell students how long they will have to write their postcards. You could allocate ten or fifteen minutes for this part of the activity. When the time is up, have students 'send' their postcard to another student.

8 The student who receives the postcard should read it and give one point for every vocabulary item from the wordlist that has been used correctly (and no points where the vocabulary is repeated). The winning student is the one with the most points.
9 **Optional:** If you have more classroom time available, you could have students write more than one postcard and/or ask the recipients to write a reply thanking the sender for the postcard and asking more questions about the holiday.

## 11.2 Have you ever …?

A group activity in which students ask and answer questions or respond to statements, using the present perfect.

### Language
Present perfect
Nature vocabulary

### Preparation
Make one copy of the worksheet for each group. Cut each worksheet into strips along the dotted lines. Put the strips into a container, such as a box or a jar, for each group.

### In class
1 Put students into groups. Six is a good number for this game, but groups of four or eight will work well, too. If possible, have groups sit in a circle.
2 Give the class some time to review the grammar on pages 118 and 119, then have them close their books. Tell them they are going to use this language to play a game.
3 Spend a few minutes doing some classroom practice. For example, say *Have you ever met anyone famous? / I've never been to Australia. / I've had three coffees every day this week.* Check that students are using the correct language to respond, confirming or correcting as necessary.
4 Give each group their container. Tell students they should take turns taking a piece of paper from the container and reading what's on it. It will be a statement or question. They do not put the slip of paper back in the container.
5 Explain that the student on their left should respond to the question or statement. If this student's response is grammatically correct, he/she then takes a slip of paper from the container and reads what's on it. If the response is not grammatically correct, they skip a turn and the student on their left draws from the container instead.
6 Tell students that some slips of paper have unfinished questions or statements. When they pick one of these, they must think up a question or statement of their own. They can't use an idea that's already been used.
7 Emphasize that students don't have to give answers that are true. The important thing is to be grammatically correct.

**Communicative activities | Teacher's notes**

## 12.1 An archaeological dig

A pair-work activity in which students write about an imaginary archaeological dig, interview each other about it and summarize their partner's experience.

### Language
Discoveries vocabulary

### Preparation
Make one copy of the worksheet for every student. Cut out the sections along the dotted lines as shown. Each student gets the instruction, a matrix of vocabulary and a list of interview questions. At first, only give students the instructions and the vocabulary.

### In class

1 Give the class some time to review the vocabulary on page 126. Ensure that everyone understands all of the target words. Tell students they will need to use this vocabulary in the activity.
2 Put students into pairs and hand out the instructions and the respective vocabulary charts.
3 Read the instructions aloud. Make sure everyone understands the situation: They should pretend they were part of a team that made a new archaeological discovery.
4 Explain that they must write a paragraph describing the dig and the discovery. Emphasize that they must use all of the vocabulary items in their chart.
5 Allow about ten or fifteen minutes and tell students they should write eight or more sentences.
6 When the time is up, hand out the respective interview questions to the Student As and the Student Bs. Tell the pairs not to show their paragraphs or their list of interview questions to each other.
7 Allow ten minutes for Student A to interview Student B and ten minutes for Student B to interview Student A. Explain to students that they should take notes as they interview their partner. Remind them that note-taking just means jotting down the main points, not writing full sentences.
8 When the interview stage is over, have students use their notes to write a summary of their partner's experience. They should write the summaries in their notebooks.
9 If there is time, have some students read their summaries to the class.

## 12.2 Newsflash … dinosaur discovery!

A team-work activity in which students develop and deliver a news report using the passive.

### Language
The passive
Discoveries vocabulary

### Preparation
Make one copy of the worksheet for each group.

### In class

1 Put students into groups of four and give each group their copy of the worksheet. Give them a moment to read through the worksheet on their own.
2 Give the class some time to review the grammar on pages 128 and 129. Make sure that everyone understands how to form the passive and when it is used.
3 While they're reviewing the materials, write the following on the board:
- Use every opportunity to use the passive.
- Keep your news report to five minutes.
- Use your own names or make up names for each role.
- Consider giving the new dinosaur species a made-up name.
- As this dinosaur discovery is not real, make up as many facts about it as you want.
- Try to include the following details in your report:
  - where the fossil was found
  - why it is special
  - how old it is
  - what this species probably looked like; how big/heavy it was
  - how this particular dinosaur probably died
  - your own ideas.
4 Now, read each part of the worksheet aloud. Make sure everyone understands the instructions. Explain each of the roles. The *newscaster* is the person who reads the news in a radio or TV studio. The *on-site reporter* is the person who travels to the place where the news story actually happened and reports back to the studio. A *palaeontologist* is an expert on dinosaurs. And the *researcher* (or expert) is a person who has been doing scientific research in this area. Explain that each person on the team must choose a role and write their name next to it.
5 Go through the suggested format with the class. Advise the teams to divide their notebook into nine sections and to write their ideas under each section. The team should work together to agree on the questions and script for their news report, but it's a good idea to have only one student write the text.
6 Draw students' attention to the points you have written on the board and make sure they understand each one. Emphasize that they must use the passive in their news reports.
7 Allow about 30 minutes for the teams to write their news reports and about five minutes for them to practise delivering it.
8 Have teams deliver their news reports to the class.
9 **Optional:** If your school has other rooms you can use, you might consider getting each team to video their news report on their phones.